NEW ENGLAND PATRIOTS

The Complete Illustrated History

Christopher Price

MVP
BOOKS

For my family, which always provides the best home-field advantage.

First published in 2010 by MVP Books, an imprint of MBI Publishing Company and the Quayside Publishing Group, 400 First Avenue North, Suite 300, Minneapolis, MN 55401 USA

Text copyright © 2010 by Christopher Price

MVP Books titles are also available at discounts in bulk quantity for industrial or sales-promotional use. For details write to Special Sales Manager at MBI Publishing Company, 400 First Avenue North, Suite 300, Minneapolis, MN 55401 USA.

To find out more about our books, visit us online at www.mvpbooks.com.

Library of Congress Cataloging-in-Publication Data

Price, Christopher.
  New England Patriots : the complete illustrated history / Christopher Price.
      p. cm.
  Includes index.
  ISBN 978-0-7603-3851-3 (hb w/ jkt)
  1. New England Patriots (Football team)—History. 2. New England Patriots (Football team)—Pictorial works. I. Title.
  GV956.N36P75 2010
  796.332'640974461--dc22

                                           2010005434

Edited by Josh Leventhal
Designed by Greg Nettles
Design Manager: LeAnn Kuhlmann

Printed in China

On the frontispiece: The Patriots mascot leads the team onto the field before a game at Gillette Stadium, November 2007 (Hunter Martin/Getty Images).
On the title page: Tom Brady looks to pass in a game against the Miami Dolphins, December 2009 (Ronald C. Modra/Sports Imagery/Getty Images).
On this page: Mosi Tatupu runs the ball during the divisional play-offs against the Los Angeles Raiders, January 1986. (Rob Brown/NFL/Getty Images).
On the back cover: Tedy Bruschi, October 2004 (Jim Rogash/NFL/Getty Images); Asante Samuel, Rodney Harrison, and Mike Vrabel during Super Bowl XXXIX (Brian Bahr/Getty Images); Gino Cappelletti, 1962 (Walter Iooss Jr./*Sports Illustrated*/Getty Images); John Hannah, 1983 (Andrew D. Bernstein/Getty Images); Patriots fans during AFC Wild Card Game, January 2007 (Al Messerschmidt/Getty Images); Randy Moss, November 2008 (Jim Rogash/Getty Images); Steve Grogan, December 1987 (Mark Lennihan/AP Images); Stanley Morgan, 1986 (John Sandhaus/NFL/Getty Images); Andre Tippett, September 1992 (Allen Dean Steele/NFL/Getty Images).

CONTENTS

INTRODUCTION

Veteran quarterback Babe Parilli helped bring credibility to the young Patriots franchise, and he helped steer the team to the AFL Championship Game in just its fourth year of existence. *Tony Tomsic/NFL/Getty Images*

For most of the first 40 or so years of their incarnation, the Patriots were the fourth team in a four-team town. They were the Rodney Dangerfield of the Boston sports scene, an afterthought behind championship contenders like the Red Sox and Celtics, and a second cousin to Boston's beloved Bruins.

A stadium to call their own? Not for the first 11 years of their existence. Decades between plus-.500 appearances. Hall of Famers were mostly a rumor. Playoff games? That was something that took place in other NFL cities. Instead, the Patriots were consigned to second-class status.

There were occasional signs of life. The franchise enjoyed brief stretches of success in the middle of the 1970s, 1980s, and 1990s, even making it to a pair of Super Bowls along the way. They had a string of talented players, many of whom would go on to become consistent Pro Bowlers.

But each time it looked like the Patriots were about to break through and achieve real sustained success, they would go on to suffer one ignominious letdown after another. In just their fourth year of existence, they reached the 1963 AFL Championship Game, only to be humiliated on the national stage by the San Diego Chargers. The loss, and the discord within the organization in the years following, sent the franchise reeling. The Patriots wouldn't make the postseason for the next 12 years. They came within one game of making it to the AFC championship in

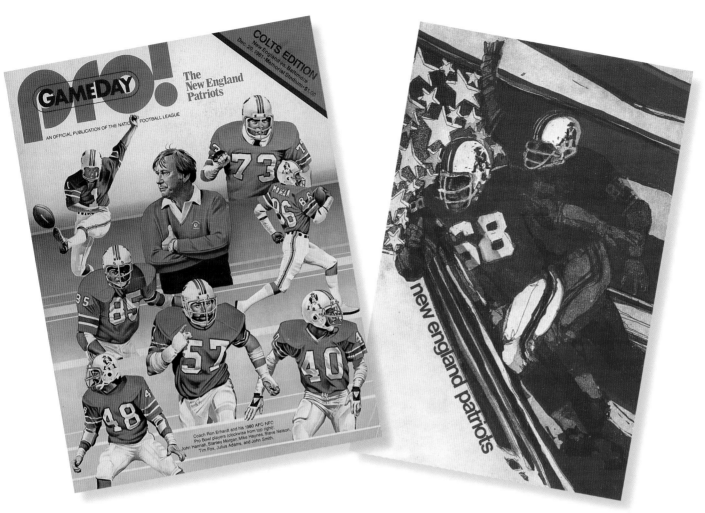

1976, only to miss out due to a lousy call in the game against the Oakland Raiders. The fallout from that game would come two years later, when the coach and owner suffered an acrimonious breakup.

When New England did finally break through for its first Super Bowl appearance in 1986, the Patriots suffered the worst defeat in Super Bowl history—and it was followed by a drug scandal that rocked the team to the core. When the Patriots got back to the Super Bowl 11 years later, the internal soap opera of a coach-versus-owner feud overshadowed any success the franchise achieved.

But the franchise that never seemed to get it right finally righted the ship in the early years of the twenty-first century. After a power struggle with Bill Parcells in the mid-1990s, owner Robert Kraft installed Bill Belichick as his head coach and then stepped back and gave his personnel department free reign to run the franchise as it saw fit. As a result, the Patriots—who had been dogged by horrible drafts, questionable coaching decisions, and flat-out bad luck—saw their fortunes start to turn in 2000.

One four-month stretch completely changed the franchise. First, Belichick was hired by Kraft. Second, Belichick brought Scott Pioli into the mix as general manager. A formidable tandem, the two overhauled the front office and rewrote the team's mission statement to read, in part, "We are building a big, strong, fast, smart, tough, and disciplined football team that consistently competes for championships."

Third, in the spring of 2000 the Patriots selected quarterback Tom Brady in the sixth round of the NFL Draft. A relatively quiet selection—not one reporter quizzed Belichick about the pick of the lanky signal-caller in his post-draft press conference—it soon became clear that New England might have a unique player on its hands, as evidenced by Kraft's first encounter with his new quarterback.

"I was leaving late one night," Kraft recalled, "and this tall, skinny kid approached me holding a pizza box. I said, 'I know who you are. You're Tom Brady, our sixth-round pick out of Michigan.' And he replied, 'And I'm the best decision this organization has ever made.'

"I was stunned," Kraft added. "He didn't say it to be cocky or arrogant. He was sincere."

In 2001, everything changed. Brady took over the starting job when Drew Bledsoe went down in Week 2 against the Jets, and with a collection of mostly bargain-basement free agents, mid-range draft picks, and other assorted diamonds in the rough, New England came together as a team. They stormed through the regular season and pulled off one of the most remarkable playoff runs in NFL history, beating the Raiders in a blizzard, the Steelers on the road in Pittsburgh, and the heavily favored Rams in Super Bowl XXXVI to shock the world.

And it wasn't a one-and-done situation with the Patriots, either. Despite stumbling in 2002 and missing the playoffs, Brady and Belichick were building a coach-quarterback bond that was every bit the equal of Montana and Walsh in San Francisco, Bradshaw and Noll in Pittsburgh, or Starr and Lombardi in Green Bay. And the franchise grew. On offense, complementary players like Troy Brown were transformed into stars, and kicker Adam Vinatieri continued to come through in the clutch time and again. New England also assembled a world-class defense, led by veterans Tedy Bruschi, Rodney Harrison, Richard Seymour, and Mike Vrabel.

The team that had suffered through 40 years of heartache and misery suddenly became the gold standard for how teams should operate in the pursuit of success. The team-building maxims espoused by Belichick and Pioli—"team above individual"; "the strength of the wolf is the pack"; "it's not about collecting talent, it's about assembling a team"— became words to live by throughout the National Football League. Teams watched as New England went on to win three Super Bowls in four years, an

Quarterback Tom Brady and the rest of the New England Patriots celebrate after defeating the Carolina Panthers in Super Bowl XXXVIII to capture their second championship in three years. They would add a third title the following year. *Jeff Gross/Getty Images*

During the 2000s, it sure seemed as if the Patriots were faster than a speeding bullet, more powerful than a locomotive, and able to leap over the rest of the National Football League in a single bound—and the New England faithful were certainly appreciative of their beloved team. *Al Messerschmidt/ Getty Images*

unprecedented feat in the age of the salary cap, free agency, and planned parity.

As for Kraft, he showed that timing was everything when he became the first NFL owner to move his team into a sparkling new stadium the year after his team won the Super Bowl.

According to a *Forbes* magazine article in September 2004, Kraft was proving wrong the conventional wisdom on two key fronts: "Dynasties are not possible in the NFL in this age of salary caps (the team will be going for its third Super Bowl in four seasons this year) and you cannot finance a new stadium without significant taxpayer money. (Gillette Stadium was financed by private debt backed by revenue from the new stadium.)"

Belichick, for his part, was celebrated for becoming the first coach in NFL history to win three Super Bowl titles in four years.

"Under the circumstances as they are now, we may never see another coach win three Super Bowls in our lifetime," said Bears GM Jerry Angelo.

The Patriots are no longer second-class citizens. Instead, they are power players on the NFL

landscape. The franchise is one of only a handful of American professional sports franchises valued at more than $1 billion. Kraft is considered one of the most powerful men in the league. And even though they haven't won a Super Bowl since 2005, the combination of Belichick and Brady remains one of the most dangerous in the league.

Here is the story of how it all came together over half a century of New England Patriots football.

CHAPTER 1

NOMADS

1960–1970

Billy Sullivan Jr. joined the "Foolish Club" of AFL owners after getting spurned by the NFL in his attempts to gain a franchise for Boston. *Pro Football Hall of Fame/Getty Images*

They called themselves "The Foolish Club," and there was every reason to think they were right on the money.

In the late 1950s, the idea of going up against the National Football League was considered equivalent to financial suicide. The NFL was one of the most well-established professional leagues on the map, with a sporting (and financial) foothold on the entire United States. By the end of the decade, it had 12 teams stretched coast to coast, including established franchises like the New York Giants, Baltimore Colts, Cleveland Browns, Detroit Lions, Los Angeles Rams, and Chicago Bears.

Small wonder that everyone who had some disposable income and a desire to be the next great American sportsman wanted in on the action, and Texas millionaires Bud Adams Jr. and Lamar Hunt were no exception. The drama of the 1958 NFL Championship Game between the Colts and Giants made pro football America's new pastime, and Adams and Hunt desperately wanted to be a part of it.

At one point, Hunt, Adams, and Bob Howsam of Denver all believed they had an opportunity to enter the league by purchasing the woeful Chicago Cardinals, the weaker of the two Chicago-area teams. (The Cardinals had suffered for many seasons having to go against the mighty Bears of George Halas.) But none of the three was able to secure controlling interest in the Cardinals, and when their attempts fell through, they approached NFL commissioner Bert Bell about possibly expanding the NFL, adding a handful of teams throughout the country.

Bell, worried about expanding too quickly, decided against it. On his way back to Texas from meeting with Bell, Hunt, a Dallas native, started drawing up plans for the American Football League, and he put together a list of investors he believed might be a good fit. Dallas, Houston, Denver, and Minneapolis-St. Paul were all part of the first wave of cities that jumped on board the AFL bandwagon. Soon, Los Angeles and New York were included. In August 1959, the first league meetings were held. Soon it was clear that the NFL was taking notice.

The established league decided to try to undermine the new circuit by offering would-be AFL owners partial stakes in existing NFL teams, as well as promises of new teams when expansion did take place. Contrary to Bell's initial response, the NFL decided to combat the new league with expansion into those same markets the AFL was eyeing. Still, "The Foolish Club" plunged ahead. Later in 1959, the group awarded a team to Buffalo and Ralph Wilson, bringing the total to seven.

That's when Billy Sullivan entered the picture. The New England businessman—a former PR chief of the Notre Dame football team and the Boston Braves—had also previously taken a shot at trying to lure the Chicago Cardinals to Boston. Similarly rebuffed, he decided to cast his lot with the AFL crew. For $25,000, professional football was coming to Boston, filling out the eight-team league. (Sullivan had to convince his wife to use part of the money he had saved to purchase a summer home on Cape Cod on the AFL entrance fee instead.)

In retrospect, Hunt said it might not have been the best idea in the world, but they were glad to have a team in a new market—even if it didn't have a stadium and had to borrow a sizable portion of the franchise fee. "It shows how desperate we were to take a man we'd never met and who had no money and no stadium," Hunt said in the book *The New England Patriots: Triumph and Tragedy.*

"Boston probably had the most unusual beginnings of any franchise in history; in fact, I'd call them very improbable, especially from the standpoint of how we do things today: all the research that goes into the people, the city, the Stanford Research Institute reports, all that kind of thing," Hunt added. "But I guess there never would have been an American Football League if we'd had enough sense to do those things."

There was some business that needed to be attended to before the league could get off the ground. Minneapolis-St. Paul had accepted the NFL's offer for an expansion team and pulled out of the AFL, which left a vacancy in the fledgling league and caused some acrimony between the Minnesota ownership group and the rest of the owners. (The Vikings began play in the NFL in 1961.) Oakland replaced Minneapolis-St. Paul early in 1960, and it was decided: the Buffalo Bills, Dallas Texans, Denver Broncos, Houston Oilers, Los Angeles Chargers, New York Titans, Oakland Raiders, and Boston Patriots were set to start playing in the fall of 1960.

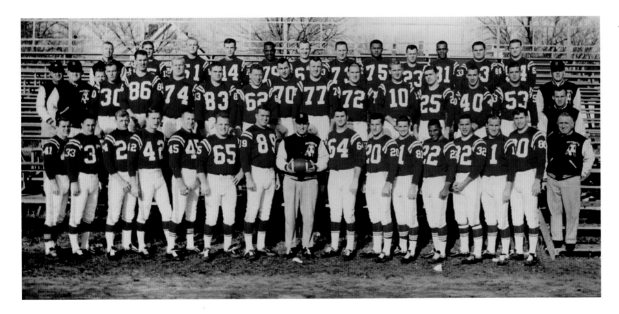

The 1960 Boston Patriots.

Cliff Battles runs the ball for the Boston Redskins of the National Football League in 1933. Battles led the NFL in rushing as a rookie in 1932 and, on October 8, 1933, became the first player to rush for more than 200 yards in a game. *Pro Football Hall of Fame/NFL/Getty Images*

NEW DAY DAWNS IN BOSTON

In Boston, it was a pleasant change—the city's sports fans had been treated to the successes of the Bruins and Celtics, while the Red Sox had not yet begun to take hold of the sporting public consciousness. Pro football in the Hub had a spotty history at best. Things started well enough. The city received an NFL franchise in 1932, and the team posted a 4–4–2 record in its debut campaign. The club played at Braves Field (home of baseball's Boston Braves) on Commonwealth Avenue, and the football team was also known as the Boston Braves in its first season of existence. Coached by Lud Wray, the Braves featured future Hall of Famers like running back Cliff

Battles and offensive tackle Turk Edwards. The following year, the team moved down Commonwealth Avenue to Fenway Park, rechristened itself the Redskins, and went 11–11–2 over the next two seasons. After a 2–8–1 showing in 1935, the Redskins caught fire in 1936 and made it all the way to the NFL Championship Game, but fewer than 5,000 fans showed up for the regular-season finale. Angered by the lack of interest, owner George Marshall moved the NFL Championship Game to the Polo Grounds in New York. (Turns out, Marshall never really enjoyed Boston—he wanted to place his team in New York but was blocked because of the NFL's territorial rule.) A year later, he pulled the plug

entirely on his time in Boston, and the Redskins have belonged to Washington, D.C., ever since.

Boston got another shot at pro football the next decade, when the Boston Yanks debuted in 1944. (Like Marshall, owner Ted Collins also wanted a team in New York—and he named his team the Yanks in the hopes of having his team operate out of Yankee Stadium—but ended up settling for Boston.) Collins and the Yanks played their games at Fenway Park, as well as the Manning Bowl, located north of the city in Lynn. After posting a 2–8 mark in their inaugural season, the Yanks merged with the Brooklyn Tigers for the 1945 season because World War II had drained the league's talent pool. The

combined team played four home games in Boston and one in New York. But fans from neither city cared, as the team finished with a 3–6–1 record. After three more losing seasons, Collins finally got his wish. He moved the team to New York for the 1949 season and renamed it the New York Bulldogs. (They became the New York Yanks in 1950 before folding in 1951.)

Following the Yanks' departure from Boston, the city was without professional football again for another 11 years, during which time most fans in New England allied themselves with the New York Giants—geographically, they were the closest team, and most every weekend, Giants games

The Boston Yanks take on the Detroit Lions at a snowy Fenway Park on November 4, 1945. The loss kicked off a five-game losing streak to end the Yanks' second season in the league. *AP Images*

Lou Saban had an impressive pedigree from his playing days in Cleveland when he joined the fledgling Patriots organization as its first head coach in 1960.

Butch Songin took most of the snaps for the Patriots in their debut season of 1960. He completed 187 passes and finished second in the league in passer rating. *Pro Football Hall of Fame/ Getty Images*

were broadcast throughout the New England area. (Despite the recent successes of the Patriots, many old New Englanders retain their loyalties to the Giants to this day.)

When Sullivan finally was able to pull together the cash for the entry fee, he got the official thumbs-up from the rest of the AFL to become the league's eighth and final franchise. And there was a new team in town.

"He had the vision. His vision was that he believed so strongly that football could be a dominant sport in New England," Sullivan's son Patrick told Sportsradio 850 WEEI in a 2009 interview. "He had worked for Boston College in the 1940s when they had won the national championship, and they regularly sold out Fenway Park, and there was a huge following for BC. So he knew there were football fans in the region. It was never a situation where it was, 'Oh my God, we're not gonna make payroll this week' or things like that." Patrick Sullivan acknowledged that it was a very small operation, with the offices housed in three rooms on Commonwealth Avenue before the team upgraded to a five-room office on Lansdowne Street. "It was not nearly the enterprise it has become today."

They didn't have a lot of space, but Billy Sullivan and his franchise quickly went to work. The official approval from the league came on November 16, 1959, and the first draft was held only a week later. As a result, Boston went through its first draft without a director of player personnel—Mike Holovak was hired for the job roughly a month later, becoming the first executive hired by the fledgling franchise. Northwestern running back Ron Burton was the first player selected by the Patriots, who also claimed Syracuse running back Gerhardt Schwedes as its first territorial draft choice.

The Patriots hired Lou Saban, who had played linebacker for the legendary Paul Brown in the 1940s, to be their first head coach in the winter of 1960, giving the 39-year-old Saban his first coaching job in pro football. Saban recalled in a 1994 interview with the *Boston Globe* that the Patriots' ownership had been impressed by the fact that Saban's pedigree included a stop with the great Cleveland teams coached by Brown.

"[They] wanted to get a guy to coach the Patriots who had played under the Paul Brown system, and I was one of those," Saban said. "Gosh, I remember Mr. Brown gave us playbooks, playbooks an inch thick . . . nobody ever had playbooks before . . . and you know the funny thing, Mr. Brown used to take the playbooks back at the end of the season. He must have put 'em all in the attic of his house, hundreds and hundreds of 'em."

Saban had coached at the collegiate level for Northwestern and Western Illinois and would go on to coach at the high school, college, and professional levels for nearly 50 years. Considered a forward-thinker, he instantly realized the uphill battle he was facing in taking the Patriots job.

"We had tryouts in the city of Boston from one end to the other," said Saban in that same *Boston Globe* interview. "We had bricklayers, we had carpenters, we had stoker men, and you name it, we had it. We had 125 helmets in one tryout camp and we put a head in every helmet. I remember our first real camp at the University of Massachusetts out there in Amherst. I couldn't tell you how many players we had out there. We must have had 350."

The sheer numbers made it tough to keep track of everyone who was there, according to Gino Cappelletti. "Saban would put up a list of cuts in the dorm," Cappelletti recalled later to *Sports Illustrated*. "He didn't have time to tell everybody personally, and after every practice we'd run like hell for the dorm to see if we got cut. A lot of guys who were cut stuck around a few days, eating three square meals and sleeping there."

Professional football had arrived in New England, but it wasn't exactly top of the line just yet. Saban told of a team practice held at a school in Lexington, which exemplifies the point.

"I swear this is true," Saban recalled in the 1994 interview. "We were out there in our pads and doing our drills when the kids got out on recess and we had to stop! The kids would be getting in the huddles. We tried to shoo them away. A teacher came over and said the school grounds belonged to the kids and not to us, and when it was recess time, it was the kids' time. So we had to get off the field every time there was a recess."

But Saban was able to whip things into shape, and hope was high as the inaugural season dawned.

RON BURTON

Ron Burton is remembered for many things. As a collegian in 1959, he was drafted as a No. 1 pick by three professional football teams, including the Boston Patriots of the newly created American Football League, the NFL's Philadelphia Eagles, and the Ottawa Rough Riders of the Canadian Football League. He ended up going with the Patriots and became the first draft pick in the history of the franchise.

The speedy Burton set numerous franchise records in his seven-year career with the Patriots, but it was what he did after his playing career that really distinguished him. Once his football career was done, he purchased 305 acres in Hubbardston, Massachusetts, and established the Ron Burton Training Village. A camp set up to serve young men between the ages of 11 and 18 years old, it remains Burton's legacy, a way to give back to some of New England's disadvantaged youth and touch the lives of so many people throughout the region.

"I used to think—Ron always said, 'Love you big guy'—that he only said that to me," Robert Kraft, the Patriots owner told the *Boston Globe* shortly after Burton died of bone cancer in 2003. "He really meant it when he said it. But going to the funeral, I realized that he said it to a lot of people, and . . . he really meant it."

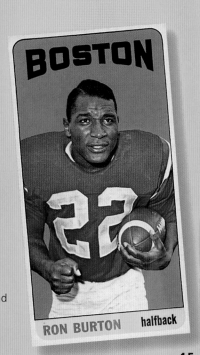

RON BURTON halfback

BOSTON PATRIOTS
1960
Pro Football Schedule

Away Games

Sept. 16—Boston at New York
Oct. 8—Boston at Los Angeles
Oct. 16—Boston at Oakland
Oct. 23—Boston at Denver
Dec. 4—Boston at Buffalo
Dec. 11—Boston at Dallas
Dec. 18—Boston at Houston

Season tickets available at
520 Commonwealth Ave., Boston

(OVER)

BOSTON PATRIOTS
1960
Pro Football Schedule

Home Games
All games played Friday
nights at 8 p.m. at Bos-
ton University Field
(Formerly Braves Field)

Sept. 9   Denver
Sept. 23   Buffalo
Oct. 28   Los Angeles
Nov. 4   Oakland
Nov. 11   New York
Nov. 18   Dallas
Nov. 25   Houston

(OVER)

The Patriots, while not expected to be among the new league's elite, were talented enough to be taken seriously at the start. In its league preview before the inaugural AFL season, *Sports Illustrated* said the Patriots could surprise. "Boston . . . has the two good quarterbacks, Tommy Greene and Butch Songin, and a fine pass-catching end from the Canadian League, Jim Colclough," wrote Roy Terrell. "Gerhardt Schwedes, the Syracuse star, was a disappointment and has been traded to New York. But Ron Burton, who was possibly the best back in the Big Ten last year, may turn out to be the most exciting runner in the AFL."

THE GAMES GET UNDERWAY

The Patriots played their first game at Boston University Field against the Denver Broncos on September 9, 1960. Denver came away with the victory, 13–10, thanks to a late punt return for a touchdown by Gene Mingo. Red Miller, who coached the Patriots offensive line that first year and later returned to the team as the offensive coordinator in the mid-1970s, talked about the game in a 2006 interview with the *Boston Globe*.

"I'll never forget, it was kind of like a college crowd; we didn't have an affiliation with the fans at the time," said Miller. "People came out, but it was more like they were asking, 'What is this new deal here?'

"I think we made a few fans that night, though. It was a terrific game."

The Patriots picked up their first win a week later, a 28–24 victory over the New York Titans. Following three straight losses in October, the team put together a three-game winning streak in November but closed the season with a four-game skid to finish at 5–9 and in last place in the AFL East.

The offensive stars of the debut season were Songin, who threw for 2,476 yards and 22 touchdowns, and fullback Alan Miller, who led the team in rushing with 416 yards and was second in receiving yards with 284 yards. Cappelletti had 4 interceptions as cornerback and led the team in scoring as a kicker with 60 points. Burton, the franchise's first-ever draft pick, became the first Patriot to rush for over 100 yards in a single game when he gained 127 yards in 16 carries against Denver on October 23—which until 1983 stood as the rookie single-game rushing record.

Things turned around dramatically for the Patriots the following season, as they kicked off a four-year run in which they went 35–17–4 and reached the AFL Championship Game in 1963. In large part, the turnaround could be credited to Mike Holovak, who was named coach midway through the 1961 season. Taking the reins from Saban, Holovak lifted the Patriots to seven wins in their last nine games on the way to a 9–4–1 mark. A former All-American running back and coach at Boston College, Holovak was known as a true players' coach, someone who could wring the most talent out of his team.

Babe Parilli came on board in 1961 and split the quarterbacking duties with Songin before taking over as the regular QB in 1962. Billy Lott and Larry Garron spearheaded the running game, while Cappelletti, making the shift to offense, pulled in 45 receptions and 8 receiving touchdowns to go along with his 99 points as placekicker.

The team also got a boost from the fans during that second season. On November 3 against the Dallas Texans, the Patriots enjoyed their first-ever home sellout. On the final play of the game, Dallas was going for what would be a game-tying score. The Texans' quarterback dropped back and lofted a pass for receiver Chris Burford—only to have it fall incomplete when a man stepped in front of the ball, knocking it down and preserving the victory. In the midst of the craziness, no one was completely sure what happened, but the call stood, and Boston came away with a 28–21 win.

Another 9–4–1 season, and another second-place finish to the Houston Oilers, came in 1962. Flanker Jim Colclough earned an all-star spot with 40 catches for 868 yards and 10 touchdowns.

In 1963, the combination of good young talent and Holovak's coaching helped the Patriots to a 7–5–1 record through the first 13 weeks of the season. All Boston had to do to guarantee itself a spot in the AFL Championship Game was beat the Chiefs in Kansas City the last week of the season. But the Chiefs, who were already out of the playoff picture, rose up and dominated the Patriots, crushing them 35–3. That, combined with Buffalo's 19–10 win over the New York Jets, left the Patriots and the Bills with identical 7–6–1 records. As a result, the Patriots traveled to Buffalo for a playoff game for the right to face San Diego in the title game, making it arguably the biggest game in the history of the young franchise. The Patriots responded. Parilli tossed for 300 yards and two touchdowns, and Cappelletti kicked four field goals to lead the Patriots to a 26–8 win over the Bills, vaulting Boston into the AFL Championship Game.

The Patriots would face San Diego, which had steamrolled over the Western Division that season, finishing with an 11–3 record. The Patriots and Chargers had met twice during the regular season, with San Diego winning both, first 17–13 at Balboa Stadium in Week 2 and then 7–6 at Fenway Park in Week 10. Both games were extremely competitive, largely due to the extraordinary efforts of the Patriots defense. Heading into the championship game, however, Holovak didn't sound optimistic that his defense could hold back the powerful Chargers a third time. "It's asking our defense a lot to keep San Diego as low as we did in the regular season," Holovak told reporters in the days leading up to the game. "For us to win, we have to score quite a bit, if that's possible."

On January 5, 1964, the two teams took the field at Balboa Stadium in front of a crowd of 30,127.

The Patriots hosted the Raiders at Boston University Field in November 1961 and walked away with a 20–17 victory.

By 1962, Babe Parilli (15) was the Patriots' full-time starter at quarterback, and in 1964 he was named All-Pro. Here he finds an open receiver in a game against San Diego at Fenway Park in the early 1960s.

Turns out, Holovak knew what he was talking about, as the Patriots trailed 7–0 three plays into the game. They cut San Diego's lead to 14–7 when Garron scored on a 7-yard touchdown run, but that was about it. By the end of the first quarter, the score was 21–7, and it was clear that the Patriots' ground attack, which had outgained the opposition by more than 500 yards during the season, was not up to the task this day. Garron went down with a concussion, and the Chargers ended up outgaining the Patriots on the ground 318 yards to just 75. At halftime, it was 31–10, and the Chargers kept pouring it on in the second half on the way to a 51–10 final.

What should have been the Patriots' finest hour turned into an embarrassment that still lingers today—the 610 yards of total offense allowed stands as an all-time franchise record in futility. San Diego running back Keith Lincoln accounted for 349 yards on his own; he rushed for 206 yards on 13 carries and added an additional 123 yards on 7 pass receptions. (He even had 20 yards passing.) The Chargers so thoroughly dominated the game that San Diego star receiver Lance Alworth was spotted nonchalantly taking home movies from the sidelines in the waning moments.

In the subsequent months, the loss fueled the Boston franchise, which now appeared to be heading in the right direction as one of the better teams in the AFL. The Patriots opened the 1964 season on a roll with four straight wins, including a 33–28 victory over the Chargers in San Diego. In a little piece of payback for the championship loss the year before, the Boston defense held Lincoln to 29

yards rushing and 22 yards receiving. The Patriots picked up wins in 10 of their first 13 games, and even when they didn't win, they managed to send people home entertained—a remarkable 43-all tie with the Oakland Raiders on October 16 included a near-scoreless first quarter, a 21-point outburst from the Raiders in the second quarter, an even more remarkable 22 points in the fourth quarter from the Patriots, and 422 passing yards from Parilli.

With that kind of scoring, it was no surprise that a Maryland teenager named Bill Belichick found the upstart new league exciting.

"It seemed like there was less defense," Belichick later recalled about the early years of the AFL, "a lot of high-scoring games. There were a lot of exciting players in that league—maybe it was because there wasn't much defense, I don't know. It seemed like there was a lot of 41–38 [games], some of those kinds of games. It was entertaining. It really was."

As had been the case the season before, the AFL East came down to two teams in 1964, Buffalo and Boston. The Bills looked like they had things all wrapped up when they started the year 9–0, but a small stumble late in the season opened the door for a late push by the Patriots. After a five-game win

A 15-yard field goal by Boston's Gino Cappelletti cut San Diego's lead to 24–10 in the second quarter of the 1963 AFL Championship Game, but the Chargers went on to score 27 more unanswered points to secure a blowout victory. *Hy Peskin/Sports Illustrated/Getty Images*

GINO CAPPELLETTI

In later years, players like Steve Grogan and then Troy Brown, Tedy Bruschi, and Tom Brady would come to be identified as the face of the franchise. But the first man to really become a spokesman for the Patriots was Gino Cappelletti.

A quarterback and kicker at the University of Minnesota, Cappelletti took a circuitous route to New England: He first tried out with the Detroit Lions after graduating in 1955, but he failed to make the team. He then played in the Canadian Football League in 1958 before joining the Boston Patriots of the newly organized American Football League in 1960.

With the Patriots, Cappelletti instantly clicked, playing 10 years for the franchise and becoming a dependable presence local football fans came to rely on. During his pro career, he also returned punts and kickoffs, played defensive back, and even had one pass completion, for a touchdown.

He retired in 1970 as the Patriots' all-time leading scorer with 1,130 points (with 42 touchdowns, 176 field goals, and 342 points after touchdowns). In addition, he led the AFL in scoring five times, and he holds records for two of the top five scoring seasons in NFL history—155 points in 1964 and 147 points in 1961. He's also the Patriots' third all-time leading receiver with 292 catches for 4,589 yards and holds the Patriots' records for extra points attempted (353), extra points made (342), field goals attempted (333), and field goals made (176) A five-time AFL all-star, he was one of only three players to play in every game in AFL history, and he finished as the AFL's all-time leader in points and field goals.

As of 2009, Cappelletti works alongside Gil Santos as a color commentator for the Patriots' radio broadcasts on the Patriots Rock Radio Network. There's a small band of New England football fans who believe Cappelletti deserves to be recognized for the amazing breadth of his career. It's a group that includes Patriots owner Bob Kraft, who, in 2009, called upon writers to make a place in the Pro Football Hall of Fame for Cappelletti, as well as for Santos, his longtime broadcast partner who believes the voters need to look past their AFL biases and put Cappelletti up for enshrinement.

Cappelletti did it all for the Patriots in the 1960s—kicking, receiving, defending. Here he plows ahead for extra yardage after making one of his seven catches against the Bills in November 1962. *Walter Iooss Jr./ Sports Illustrated/Getty Images*

John Cappelletti, 1963

Although the Patriots won 10 games in 1964, Coach Mike Holovak's team failed to make the playoffs. Holovak posted a 52–47–9 record in his eight years in Boston but earned only one postseason win.
AP Images

streak put them at 10–2–1, the Patriots hosted the 11–2 Bills for a winner-take-all regular-season finale at Fenway Park on December 20.

But unlike the previous season's clash, this one didn't go Boston's way. Buffalo jumped on top early and never trailed, using one touchdown pass from Jack Kemp and a pair of touchdown runs from the Buffalo quarterback to post a 24–14 victory over the Patriots, clinching the division for the Bills.

The 1963 and 1964 seasons would represent the high points of the franchise's first decade and a half. After one appearance in the AFL title game and getting one win away from making it back-to-back championship contests, the team would not appear in an AFL or NFL postseason game for another 13 years. The 8–4–2 finish in 1966 marked the only season between 1965 and 1975 in which the Patriots posted more wins than losses.

As other cities were celebrating gridiron heroes like Bart Starr, Johnny Unitas, and Gayle Sayers, the Patriots were caught in a mostly downward spiral through the mid- to late 1960s—and certain moments played out as surreal theater, a mix of the absurd, humorous, and flat-out bizarre.

RUSH SPARKS DOWNWARD SPIRAL

Coach Clive Rush, who took over for Mike Holovak following the 1968 season, never failed to disappoint. One month after getting the head coaching job, Rush made an early imprint on the team at the introductory press conference for general manager George Sauer Sr. While grabbing the microphone, Rush received a five-second electrical shock that left him briefly stunned. At one point during his tenure, Rush reportedly was convinced that the opposing team had bugged his locker room. Hoping to confuse the alleged spies, he would loudly announce blocking assignments and other plays, all while shaking his head "no" to the players. He tried to implement the "Black Power Defense," boasting that he would be the first coach in the history of pro football to start 11 black players at the same time—but he failed to remember that he didn't have 11 black defensive players on the roster. Then, there was the time the team was returning to its hotel from a game at the Astrodome in Houston. Convinced the driver was taking them on a circuitous route, Rush started to complain angrily. "You don't know who you have on this bus!" he thundered. "We can go any route we want!" Rush got off the bus, stopped oncoming traffic, and waved the bus down a one-way street—the wrong way.

Rush was part of another ignominious moment in franchise history before the 1970 season opener. Running back Bob Gladieux was cut by the coach the Thursday before the opener, but Gladieux still decided to attend the game at Harvard Stadium against the Dolphins. While sitting in the crowd with the rest of the fans, Gladieux was summoned over the loudspeaker to report to the team locker room. It turns out that Rush had suddenly and unceremoniously cut defensive back John Charles just before the game, leaving an empty roster spot, which the unsuspecting Gladieux was asked to fill then and there. Gladieux made the tackle on the opening kickoff and ended up playing eight games for the Patriots that season. Rush himself was fired midway through the 1970 season and replaced by John Mazur.

Sullivan and his family dearly loved their team, but they were unable to compete with their more affluent counterparts in New York and Los Angeles,

BOB GLADIEUX

Bob "Harpo" Gladieux was a star halfback and return man for Notre Dame under Ara Parseghian, and he finished his collegiate career with the Fighting Irish with 263 carries for 1,208 yards and 20 touchdowns. In addition, he caught 72 passes for 947 yards and 6 TDs, and his all-purpose yardage total of 2,575 yards was a Notre Dame record that stood for 15 years.

An eighth-round pick of the Boston Patriots in 1969, Gladieux was on the bubble for much of his first two seasons with the team. As a rookie, he said he was cut shortly before the start of the season and then was re-signed shortly afterward—because, as he later told reporters, the team owed him a $2,000 bonus if he was on the opening day roster. He ended up sticking around and having a good rookie season, but he was on the bubble again the following year, and this time, he was cut. In a fit of nostalgia, he went to the opener against the Dolphins with a friend—with a six-pack of Schlitz and a quart of homemade port wine. "I was having one and chasing it with the other," he recalled.

But before he knew it, he heard announced over the public address system, "Will Bob Gladieux please report to the Patriots dressing room?" After a bit of an internal struggle, Gladieux decided to head down to the locker room, where an assistant coach told him to get dressed.

According to Gladieux, John Charles, who had been the team's top pick in 1967 out of Purdue, was up for contract renewal. "The team went out and warmed up," Gladieux wrote for DomerConnect.com, "and as they returned to the locker room prior to kickoff, [the team] tried to use it as leverage to force him to sign the new contract. He said no, no way, and they cut him right there five minutes before kickoff. What a great organization!"

Gladieux was part of the special-teams unit, and he made the tackle on the opening kickoff.

"And I tell you I had more fun that day than I probably ever had in any ball game because I played care free and knew I didn't have anything to worry about, and we ended up beating the Dolphins," he wrote. "And then we had a little celebration after that. It was one day in my life that as each year goes by and each time that I go up and I sit down in my seat to watch a game, I think to myself of that day and wonder how did I do that. Well, when you're young and dumb and you love the game of football like I do—what do they say today, impossible is nothing."

Gladieux ended up playing four years in the NFL, with the Patriots from 1969 to 1972 and a portion of the 1970 season with Buffalo. His best season was with the Patriots in 1971, when he finished with 175 rushing yards.

Bob Gladieux, circa 1970.
Pro Football Hall of Fame/
Getty Images

and they occasionally had to cut corners. For example, there was no one staffing the Patriots' switchboard. Cappelletti recalled watching game film while sitting on milk crates in the bowels of a high school stadium. "We hung bed sheets over water pipes," Cappelletti said, "and we'd show the film against those sheets." Without a permanent home of its own, the team sometimes had trouble even finding a practice field. When the Patriots managed to get permission to use a public school field in East Boston, local politicians accused them of depriving the kids of a playground.

Although the Patriots struggled as a team through the latter half of the 1960s, that didn't mean New England fans didn't have the opportunity to cheer on some great individual performers. On the offensive side of the ball, Cappelletti set the pace when it came to scoring—a wide receiver and placekicker, he retired as the franchise's all-time leading scorer with 1,130 points. Parilli, who played with the Patriots from 1961 until 1967, passed for more than 22,000 yards in his 15-year pro career. Fullback Jim Nance, a smashmouth ball carrier who wore a Patriots uniform from 1965 until 1971, led the AFL in rushing yards in 1966 and 1967, and he still holds the franchise record for rushing touchdowns with 45.

On defense, Patriots fans were treated to the ferocious approach of Nick Buoniconti, a savage tackler who played for the Pats from 1962 until 1968 and recorded 24 interceptions with the franchise before going on to be a part of the undefeated Miami Dolphins in 1972. There was the durable Bob Dee, a Holy Cross product who never missed a game in his eight-year career with the Patriots (1960–1967) and made four AFL all-star teams, as well as defensive tackle Jim Lee Hunt, an original member of the 1960 Patriots who also made four AFL all-star teams by the end of his career in 1970.

As goofy as things got for the Patriots, in many ways they were one of the more stable franchises during the AFL's first decade. The Chargers suffered serious financial losses in their only year in Los Angeles and were forced to move to San Diego. Buffalo owner Ralph Wilson loaned hundreds of thousands of

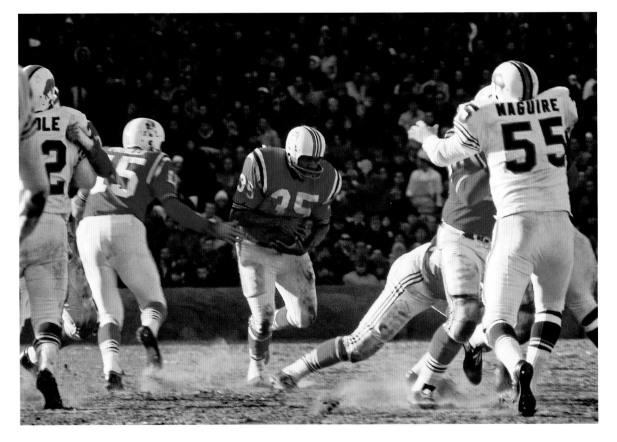

Jim Nance, seen here gaining yards during a late-season game against Buffalo in 1966, led the AFL in rushing in 1966 and 1967 while earning two straight All-Pro selections. *Herb Scharfman/Sports Illustrated/Getty Images*

Mike Taliaferro was under center for Boston in the late 1960s, and he completed an All-Pro season in 1969 with 2,160 passes—despite the team winning only four games that year. *Dick Raphael/Sports Illustrated/ Getty Images*

The Patriots forced a fumble on the opening kickoff of the first game of the 1970 season and went on to win, 27–14. It was all downhill from there, as Boston lost 12 of the 13 remaining games.
AP Images

dollars to the Oakland ownership group to keep the Raiders solvent. (Meanwhile, Wilson's Bills traveled to Hamilton, Ontario, for a much-hyped battle with the Canadian Football League's Tiger Cats in an attempt to show the AFL was just as competitive as any league in North America. Buffalo lost, 38–21.) Attendance was so low at Titans games that team owner Harry Wismer had fans move to seats closer to the field to give the illusion of a fuller stadium on television. Wismer eventually failed to meet payroll, and the league had to take control of the Titans. (They were later sold to Sonny Werblin and became the Jets.) And the Dallas Texans, the team owned by league cofounder Lamar Hunt, won the AFL championship in 1962—and promptly relocated to Kansas City in 1963, as the Texans struggled to compete with the NFL's expansion team in Dallas, the Cowboys. It was clear the younger league needed more cash to survive.

Enter NBC. On January 29, 1964, the AFL signed a lucrative $36 million television contract with the network, providing the league with much-needed revenue to compete with the NFL for talent. And the race was on. Teams started to aggressively go after the top college prospects, and many times they came away with them. A couple of years later, the AFL got so bold that teams started targeting NFL players—and the players often used an AFL offer as leverage to get a new contract or make the jump to the rival league.

The NFL owners soon realized that a prolonged bidding war for players would be bad for business, and they approached the AFL about a merger. A deal was worked out whereby the two leagues would play a championship game beginning in 1967, which would ultimately lead to a full merger between the leagues in 1970.

HOMELESS IN NEW ENGLAND

The lack of a permanent stadium meant little stability for the Patriots. While other AFL teams had been able to land suitable stadiums and were becoming entrenched in their communities, a distinct lack of security permeated the Patriots franchise. If New England was going to level the playing field with its competitors and be a suitable part of the AFL-NFL merger—which was coming at the start of the next decade—the Patriots would have to stop wandering through professional football's wilderness and find themselves a permanent home.

Throughout the 1960s, the Patriots played home games at Boston University's Nickerson Field (the old Braves Field), Fenway Park, Harvard Stadium, Boston College's Alumni Stadium, and even one game at Birmingham, Alabama's Legion Field because of a scheduling snafu at Fenway involving the Red Sox.

"We really didn't know whether we'd play at Fenway, BC, or Harvard," said Pat Sullivan. "So we printed tickets for all three venues to send to season-ticket holders."

From 1963 to 1968, the Patriots played at Fenway, home of the Red Sox. While the atmosphere was nice, the facility was poorly suited as a football venue and had a capacity of only about 40,000. "The Patriots make money, but they are not making friends around the American Football League," wrote Mark Mulvoy in *Sports Illustrated* in June 1967. "Since their home park has the smallest seating capacity in pro football, the Pats give visiting teams consistently small take-home checks. This rankles other AFL owners, not to mention NFL owners, who will have to play in Boston when the pro football merger goes into full operation in 1970." Mulvoy quoted Sullivan as saying, "I don't see how you could expect Cleveland, with 80,000 seats, or St. Louis, with 50,000, to want to play us on a home-and-home basis every year."

So the search for a larger, permanent venue was on. After getting the boot from Fenway at the end of the 1968 season, the Patriots played the 1969 season at Alumni Stadium in Chestnut Hill and the 1970 season at Harvard Stadium in Cambridge before succeeding in getting a home of their own.

In New England, the looming merger forced the Patriots to get their act together. The AFL was preparing for a new era, and teams were starting to shape up. There was to be no more foolish club. This was the NFL we're talking about here: New stadiums went up all over the AFL, new head coaches were installed, and new attitudes were adopted. The AFL was playing with the big boys now, and the owners wanted to make sure they would be taken seriously. In New England, the biggest priority became securing a permanent stadium. Sullivan had gone to the legislature in the late 1960s, but no one on Beacon Hill wanted to buy what he was selling. He would have to get creative with his financing.

"I think if you talked about the darkest hours," Pat Sullivan said in a 2009 interview, "it was probably in the late sixties when one stadium after another got shot down for various reasons. It wasn't until we ended up building in Foxborough that we had a clear path to keep the franchise here, because the league mandated that we have a stadium with at least fifty thousand seats."

FINALLY, A HOME OF THEIR OWN

1971–1974

It wasn't much, but Schaefer Stadium was home. After a decade of wandering the countryside, the Patriots finally found a permanent place to hang their collective hat, a little patch of land to call their own in the bucolic Massachusetts town of Foxborough.

As cities went about erecting stadiums at a record pace in the late 1960s and early 1970s—all of them two-sport facilities built almost entirely with state funds, including venues in Washington, D.C. (RFK Stadium), New York (Shea Stadium), Atlanta (Fulton County Stadium), Houston (the Astrodome), Cincinnati (Riverfront Stadium), St. Louis (Busch Memorial Stadium), Pittsburgh (Three Rivers Stadium), and Philadelphia (Veterans Stadium)— the Patriots continued to face opposition.

The impending merger between the AFL and NFL necessitated that the AFL teams dance to the

The Patriots' very own Schaefer Stadium in Foxborough, Massachusetts. *Focus on Sport/Getty Images*

NFL's tune, and that included finding a venue with at least 46,200 seats by the spring of 1970. Sullivan had initially proposed moving into Harvard Stadium and expanding the capacity from 40,000 to the NFL minimum, but Harvard wanted no piece of the Patriots. The Red Sox were agreeable enough land-lords throughout the 1960s, but like Harvard, they wanted no part of a proposed expansion of Fenway Park for permanent football use.

Boston city fathers would have loved to have an NFL team in town, but they didn't want to pay for a stadium. Without a suitable venue, it looked like the Patriots might be headed elsewhere. Tampa, Memphis, Seattle, Portland, and Jacksonville were among the cities that were flirting with Sullivan about a possible move, and things looked bleak after a deal brokered by former White Sox owner Bill Veeck (the owner of Suffolk Downs) was shot down by the Massachusetts legislature.

But in the spring of 1970, E. M. Loew, movie-theater kingpin and owner of the Bay State Raceway, said he would be willing to donate to the team a stretch of land next to his racetrack in Foxborough if the Patriots would recip-rocate with a share of the parking profits. The town approved the move, and ground was broken in September 23, 1970, in the sleepy town of Foxborough, located midway between Boston and Providence. A mild win-ter and the basic stadium structure allowed the job to be completed 11 months later at an announced cost of $4 million (later determined to be about $7.1 million).

Built on the cheap because the Patriots received no city or state funding, the facility had none of the modern amenities found in most other stadiums built during the same era, things such as individual seating (only 5,600 of the seats had backs) as well as club seats and luxury suites. Parking was often a mess. Players didn't have it much better: The artificial turf was noted as one of the toughest surfaces in the league to play on, there were no extra practice fields, and there were no deluxe, NFL-style locker rooms for the teams.

1971 PATRIOTS NEWS MEDIA GUIDE

UPTON BELL

Upton Bell had deep roots in professional football. The son of former NFL commissioner Bert Bell, he gained a measure of fame in the football world for his work in helping to assemble the Baltimore Colts roster that ultimately defeated the Dallas Cowboys in Super Bowl V. He was hired as the general manager of the Patriots in 1971 at the age of 33, and his tenure with the franchise never lacked for drama. He was there when Schaefer Stadium opened, and he feuded with Coach John Mazur—most notably over the choice between Duane Thomas and Carl Garrett—but he did a lot to bring the franchise into the modern era. He created a workable front office, hiring capable and talented assistants, such as Peter Hadhazy. Rommie Loudd, a former Patriot linebacker and the AFL's first black assistant coach when he joined the Patriots' staff in 1966, was named director of pro personnel, while the well-respected Bucko Kilroy was put in charge of college scouting. Bell also furiously scoured the wires for talent and lowered the team's average age from 28 to 25.

He also always managed to leave people laughing with his sharp wit. When asked about negotiating with some of his Ivy League players, Bell replied, "When some guys come in to talk contract, I may be reading a paperback. When those guys come in, I'm reading Dostoevsky." On another occasion, he was asked about the occasionally spotty history of a franchise that played a sizable portion of its games at Fenway Park and still had an office there even after the team moved to Foxborough: "This franchise has been in left field for a long time—both literally and figuratively," he told reporters. He recalled seeing so many lights during the infamous traffic jam the night the stadium opened, he said, "I felt like Nero."

He was able to turn that quick wit into a lucrative post-football career, working for several media outlets in New England. As of 2009, he hosted a radio show in Worcester.

Fans flocked to Schaefer Stadium during its inaugural season, and the team posted a 5–2 record at home in front of mostly packed crowds. *AP Images*

"Everyone knocked the hell out of it, but I didn't think it was that terrible," said Jack Grinold, a season-ticket holder from 1960 until 1982. "When it was being built for [$7.1] million, they were renovating Yankee Stadium for $120 million. That's a pretty good deal—a good example of some *real* Yankee ingenuity." And that ingenuity allowed it to remain as the Patriots' home for 30-plus years.

The stadium was a rare project among all American professional sports because it cost so little to build and the naming rights were sold. Stadium naming rights were mostly unheard of in the 1960s and 1970s, but Sullivan saw an opportunity to defray building costs if he partnered with the New England–based

Schaefer Brewery. The agreement netted the Sullivans an extra $1.4 million toward construction costs, and the brewery got a stadium named after it.

NEW STADIUM, NEW NAME, NEW TEAM

The move out of Boston also led Sullivan to make a change in the team name. He initially decided on Bay State Patriots, but that lasted about two weeks, until someone noted the headline opportunities with a team named the "BS Patriots." They quickly made the change to New England Patriots.

The new stadium deserved a centerpiece, a crown jewel to show off to the masses that made the trek down from Boston or up from Providence.

JIM PLUNKETT

He was the quarterback who was going to make people forget about the offensive ineptitude of the previous five seasons. He was the quarterback who was going to lead the Patriots out of the wilderness and into NFL relevance. He was the quarterback who was going to be able to fire laser beams all over brand-new Schaefer Stadium with his rocket right arm.

The first pick in the 1971 draft, Jim Plunkett arrived in New England with a ton of expectations, and for a year or two, he managed to live up to the hype, throwing for 19 touchdowns and 2,158 yards as a rookie and being named the AFC Rookie of the Year. With Plunkett under center, the Patriots had their chance to affect the AFC playoff picture—his 88-yard fourth-quarter bomb to Randy Vataha on the final day of the season lifted New England to an unlikely victory and dropped the Colts to a 10–4 record and into second place in the division behind the 10–3–1 Dolphins. (Two weeks before the Patriots defeated the Colts, Plunkett engineered a 34–13 victory over Miami.)

"I thought it was very exciting going to a city like Boston where there were a lot of young people and a lot of historic places," Plunkett later told reporters. "I really enjoyed myself the first few years I was there, and in some respects, I had the time of my life.

"The first year was fun," he said. "The second year was awful, and then [Chuck] Fairbanks came in. In 1974 we started out 6–1, and then everyone got hurt. And by 1975, I was hurt. By then, I was beat to hell, and it was time to go."

Things went south pretty quickly for Plunkett, who struggled with injuries to his shoulder, neck, and knees, as well as a poor offensive line. With the emergence of Steve Grogan, Plunkett was dealt to San Francisco for a bunch of draft picks, where he continued to struggle.

"I took a lot of beatings playing for New England and San Francisco," said Plunkett, who in 61 games with the Patriots was sacked 146 times.

"There's a big difference getting beaten up when you're losing than when you're winning."

Plunkett eventually found happiness and success in his third stop: Oakland. Signed as a free agent in 1978 by Al Davis, Plunkett completed 960 passes for 12,665 yards and 80 touchdowns and won two Super Bowls with the Raiders.

He is the only retired quarterback to start and win two Super Bowls who is not also in the Pro Football Hall of Fame.

Jim Plunkett, early 1970s. *Focus on Sport/ Getty Images*

Top draft pick Jim Plunkett didn't have a lot to work with when he came to New England as a rookie, but he helped turn the Patriots from a two-win team in 1970 to a six-win team in 1971. *Focus on Sport/Getty Images*

Enter Jim Plunkett, the No. 1 pick in the 1971 draft out of Stanford. Plunkett joined the Patriots with no small measure of fanfare—1970 was billed as the year of the quarterback in college football, and Plunkett was the best, beating out Joe Theismann, Archie Manning, and Dan Pastorini to take home top honors. As a senior, Plunkett had 2,715 passing yards, as well as 18 passing and 3 rushing touchdowns, in his Heisman Trophy–winning campaign. UCLA coach Tommy Prothro called him the "best pro quarterback prospect I've ever seen," while Washington State coach Jim Sweeney called Plunkett "the best college football player I've ever seen."

Unfortunately for Plunkett, there wasn't much talent around him when he arrived in New England. In the first year of the merged leagues, the Patriots finished the season with a 2–12 record—worst in all of football in 1970. Quarterback Joe Kapp completed just 45 percent of his passes and had an ungodly poor touchdown-to-interception ratio that year: 3 to 17. The Patriots cracked double digits in scoring in only 8 of their 14 games, sent just one player to the AFL All-Star Game (center Jon Morris), and finished dead last in the AFC East Division.

The Patriots initially believed they had a world-class running back to go along with their star rookie quarterback heading into the 1971 season. As a rookie in 1970 out of West Texas State, Duane Thomas led the Dallas Cowboys in rushing with 803 yards (good for eighth in the league) on 151 carries (5.3 yards per carry) while scoring 5 touchdowns. After he became embroiled in a contract dispute with Cowboys management, the Patriots volunteered to take him off their hands, and in July, Dallas dealt Thomas to New England. It quickly became clear that things weren't going to be any easier between Thomas and the Patriots than they had been in Dallas with the Cowboys. On the second day of practice, Patriots coach John Mazur asked Thomas to get into a three-point stance. Thomas refused, and Mazur ordered him off the field.

"I was in a two-point stance because it gives a better view of a handoff," Thomas explained in a 2003 interview with the *Boston Globe*. "I was behind Jim Nance, and I couldn't see. His ass was the size of a volleyball court."

"I was putting in an I formation," Mazur told the *Boston Globe* in a 2005 interview. "It was sort of new. He [Thomas] got in his stance, and I said 'That's not the right stance.' I told him I wanted him in this other [three-point] stance, and he said, 'I'm me, man. I do what I do, man.' I said, 'You do like hell. Get your [butt] off this field.' So he went in." Center Jon Morris was in the locker room, and according to Mazur, the two were taking bets on whether the coach would fire Thomas or Thomas would get Mazur fired.

The Patriots, claiming that Thomas had failed his physical, got the league to void the trade. After a few days, he was sent back to the Cowboys.

"Mazur stood there and lied, and everybody believed it," recalled Thomas. "He said, 'Duane did not pass the physical.' I was sent back to Dallas. That was the year we went to the Super Bowl. If I didn't pass the physical in Boston, how did I pass the physical in Dallas?"

Thomas became a sort of counterculture hero, and he helped the Cowboys to a win in Super Bowl VI in January 1972. That season, he led the league in touchdowns with 13 while also leading Dallas in rushing with 793 yards on 175 carries.

AN INAUSPICIOUS BEGINNING

While the record shows that Schaefer Stadium opened to the public on August 15, 1971, in actuality, the first game on the field took place about a month before that. Chuck Sullivan recalled to the *Boston Globe* in 2001 that his father, the owner, set up a game between the carpenters and metal workers to decide who was going to erect the goalposts in the new stadium. "There was a jurisdictional dispute between the carpenters and the metal workers over who should put up the goalposts," Sullivan told Will McDonough. "Traditionally, goalposts were made of wood, and the carpenters had the rights. But in this stadium, the goalposts were made of aluminum, so the metal workers said they should do it. My dad figured out a way to settle it. He got a football, gave it to the two sides, and told them to play a game [of touch football] and the first team to score got the job. So they played the game, but I don't remember who won."

The goalposts were raised, and the field opened in spectacular fashion. On a bright, beautiful summer

Center Jon Morris (56), seen here following a game against Miami, had just completed his seventh straight all-star season when the Patriots debuted at their new stadium in 1971. *Al Messerschmidt*

afternoon, the U.S. Marine Band gave a halftime concert, a barbershop choral group performed, and a brief moment of silence was held to remember the recently deceased Vince Lombardi. Behind Plunkett and Cappelletti, the Patriots beat the New York Giants, 20–14. (Emboldened, a sports talk show in Boston called New York–area funeral homes asking if they wanted the Giants' body.)

For the first time in years, a real feeling of optimism surrounded the team, and the Patriots were starting to get some national attention, too. In the October 18, 1971, issue of *Sports Illustrated* in a story entitled "There's No Need to Pity the Pats," writer Robert H. Boyle took note of the buoyant new attitude: "Some of this enthusiasm can be attributed to the opening of Schaefer Stadium in Foxborough, midway between Boston and Providence, and named for the beer company that contributed $1.4 million toward its construction. This is the first real home the Pats have had in their 12-year history, and season ticket sales have gone from 9,000 to 45,000 in the past 18 months. No wonder that team president Billy Sullivan, who was thwarted in his attempts to build a stadium in Boston, now moves through the crowd beaming like a bishop who has won the Cadillac in the diocese raffle."

"For the first time, I feel like I'm in the big leagues," Jon Morris told reporters shortly after the stadium opened. "I never thought of myself in those terms until this year. We were the laughingstock of the league. Before, we'd get behind, then fold our tents and watch the clock run out. No more."

The new stadium's security was no laughing matter either. In a story that appeared in the *Boston*

Globe shortly before the stadium's final game, long-time offensive linemen Bill Lenkaitis revealed that the place was locked up pretty tight, at least after hours. "The first year we were in the stadium, we had a defensive coach we nicknamed 'Big Bird.' His real name was Dick Evans," Lenkaitis said. "One night he left the stadium late, got home, and realized he had left the film he wanted to see back on his desk. He drove back to the stadium. It was locked, and he didn't have a key. So he decided to climb over the fence. He forgot about the attack dogs. They got him. Ripped the seat right out of his pants. The next day he came in showing all of us the bite marks he had on his rear end."

While security was tight, transportation was another matter. The day of the first game, there was an absolutely horrific traffic jam along Route 1, with cars backed up for miles before and after the game. The

small town of Foxborough simply didn't have the necessary infrastructure to support the influx of 60,423 fans who showed up on game day.

The stadium's plumbing system was another nightmare during the exhibition opener, eventually giving way that afternoon and causing backups all over the facility. Sinks and toilets began to overflow, forcing people to find emergency bathrooms. One fan at the game later recollected how he was led into a dark room and told to pee against the wall.

The board of health threatened to shut down the stadium just weeks before the regular-season opener, and ownership raced against the clock to make sure it would be ready on time. When everything was set, the team organized something called the Great Flush: Members of the Patriots front office, stadium workers, and local journalists split into teams and were positioned throughout the stadium. At the sound of the

Jim Plunkett hands off to running back Odell Lawson during New England's 20–6 upset victory over the Oakland Raiders in the opening game of the 1971 season in Foxborough.
AP Images

scoreboard horn, the participants ran around flushing *every* toilet to prove to the board of health that back-ups wouldn't happen again. The board of health gave the OK, and the stadium was cleared to open. That wasn't the end of the troubles, however. In the regular-season opener against the Raiders, the pipes burst in the visitors' locker room, dumping sewage on some of the Oakland players.

The Patriots' 1971 schedule opened with four straight home games, which they split to start the season 2–2, including a 20–6 win over Oakland in the opener. They won their three remaining home games to post a 5–2 record at Schaefer Stadium in the first season in Foxborough; they went 1–6 on the road to finish the season at 6–8 under Mazur, the team's best record since 1966.

Mazur, who had replaced Clive Rush midway through the 1970 season, was a football lifer, having played in the Canadian Football League and coached at several colleges, including Tulane, Marquette, and Boston University. He had an extensive resume as an assistant in the pro ranks and achieved his greatest success as an offensive coordinator with Buffalo, where he spent seven years and helped the Bills capture AFL titles in 1964 and 1965.

Any coach would be a welcome change from the occasionally nutty Rush, and the New England organization and players responded well to Mazur. The Patriots posted big wins over the New York Jets (always a good thing), Buffalo, Miami, and Baltimore in 1971, sparking more optimism around the team—enough for the ownership to reward Mazur with a new contract that included a pay raise. Plunkett finished with 2,158 passing yards, his former Stanford teammate Randy Vataha led the team with 872 receiving yards and 9 touchdowns, and

Randy Vataha pulls in a 25-yard touchdown pass from Jim Plunkett against the Dolphins on December 5, 1971. It was Vataha's second score of the game, a 34–13 win over the eventual AFC champions. *AP Images*

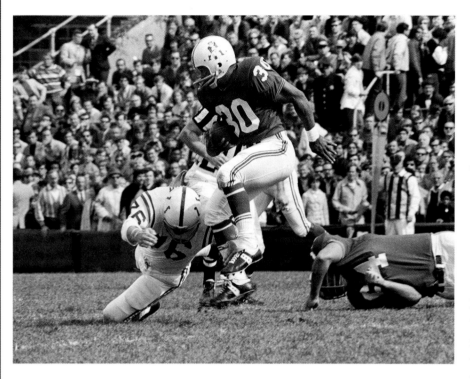

Carl Garrett, seen here gaining yards against Baltimore, had been an all-star in 1969 and was the team's top rusher in 1971, but his habit of skipping practices proved to be a distraction. *A. E. Maloof/ AP Images*

running back Carl Garrett led a ground attack with 784 rushing yards.

The excitement would be short-lived, however, as the Patriots won only two of their first nine games in 1972. In many ways, the team was a mess that season. In mid-November, general manager Upton Bell announced that star running back Carl Garrett had been suspended for missing his twelfth practice of the year.

"I've learned never to say never, but right now Carl Garrett is finished for the rest of the season," Bell told reporters.

Shortly after the decision, Sullivan reinstated Garrett, making Bell appear weak and ineffectual. Things went from bad to worse for Bell when Garrett proclaimed, "I don't think you have to practice to be perfect. I can do my thing on Sundays without practice. It doesn't say in any contract that you have to practice. All it says is that you have to play those fourteen games."

Later that same month, before a contest with the Colts, the Patriots staged one of the most dramatic promotions in team history: Sullivan signed Jumpin' Joe Gerlach for a halftime appearance. Gerlach was a daredevil who dove 100 feet out of

a hot-air balloon onto a pile of mattresses for a living. The Patriots wanted to make sure that Gerlach was on the level, and so they had him do a trial jump the day before the game. Gerlach jumped from the top of the Schaefer Stadium press box onto a stack of mattresses. Satisfied, Sullivan agreed to the jump the next day.

However, things were different the next night. Windy conditions made for a shaky ride for Gerlach and his balloon, as the basket rocked back and forth. He took a long time trying to get just the right spot to launch himself—so long, in fact, that the Colts and Patriots had come back out on the field, where Gerlach's pile of mattresses lay on the 50-yard line.

Gerlach jumped. When he hit, it triggered a huge explosion—he had some sort of firecrackers under the mattresses. No one could see him for a few moments, and no one was sure if he had survived the jump. When the smoke cleared, Gerlach was lying there motionless. According to eyewitnesses, half of him was hanging over the edge of the mat. Suddenly, he leapt into the air and jumped onto the field. The crowd went crazy, and the Patriots had their promotion.

Mazur wouldn't be as lucky. He resigned on November 13, 1972—one day after a humiliating 52–0 shutout at the hands of Don Shula and the Miami Dolphins—and was replaced by former Lombardi assistant coach Phil Bengston. Bengston finished the season as the interim head coach with four losses in the last five games, completing a two-year stretch in which the team won just nine games and finished no higher than a tie for third place in the AFC East. Although his coaching days were limited, Bengston was later named the team's director of pro scouting and stayed with the organization through the 1974 season.

FAIRBANKS, KILROY LEAD TURNAROUND

The on-field product eventually did start to improve, in large part due to new head coach Chuck Fairbanks. The former Oklahoma coach, who led the Sooners to a 52–15–1 record in six years, was hired by Sullivan (instead of Penn State's Joe Paterno or Southern Cal's John Robinson) on January 26, 1973. Fairbanks became the sixth head coach in franchise

Plunkett goes deep against Miami on November 12, 1972. The second-year quarterback completed only seven passes in a 52–0 rout by the eventual world champion and undefeated Dolphins. *Kidwiler Collection/Diamond Images/Getty Images*

history while assuming the dual roles of coach and general manager.

Fairbanks was a forward-thinker—he was an early believer in the success of the 3–4 defense, among others. Years later, several successful coaches would cop to imitating his schemes, as well as his terminology, including future Patriots coach Bill Belichick.

"I think Chuck has had a tremendous influence on the league as well as this organization in terms of nomenclature and terminology and those kinds of things," Belichick said more than 30 years later. "I'm sure Chuck could walk in and look at our playbook and probably eighty percent of the plays are the same terminology that he used—whether it be formations or coverages or pass protections. . . . All of the stuff that was really the fundamentals of his system are still in place here even, again, to the way we call formations and plays and coverages and some of our individual calls within a call."

Fairbanks wasn't alone in trying to craft a winner in New England. Francis "Bucko" Kilroy took over as the Patriots' personnel director in 1971, and he began the long process of turning the team into a champion. One of the most respected men in the game, Kilroy played in the league for 13 years, winning All-Pro honors six times as an offensive line-man with Philadelphia and spending his last three seasons with the Eagles as a player/coach before becoming a full-time assistant coach and, later, Philadelphia's player personnel director. After his days with the Eagles, Kilroy was hired as director of player personnel for the Redskins in 1962, and he later served as a super scout for the Dallas Cowboys from 1966 to 1970 before joining the Patriots in 1971.

That 1973 draft was where it all started to come together. With the fourth overall pick, the Patriots took future Hall of Famer John Hannah. A nasty offensive lineman out of Alabama, Hannah was consensus All-America as a senior playing for legendary Crimson Tide head coach Paul "Bear" Bryant, who once said of Hannah, "He was the greatest lineman I ever coached." He was an eight-letterman star in football, track, and wrestling.

Football ran in the family. His father, Herb Hannah, played offensive tackle one season with the Giants. His uncle, Bill, played guard at the

JOHN HANNAH

John Hannah, 1983. *Andrew D. Bernstein/Getty Images*

Hannah spent his entire Hall of Fame career with the Patriots, clearing the way for running backs and protecting quarterbacks for 13 seasons. *Bruce Bennett Studios/Getty Images*

The fourth overall pick in the 1973 draft out of Alabama, John Hannah maintained a level of excellence and durability at the guard position, despite playing on some mediocre teams over the years, that allowed him to go on to become the first player who played his entire career with the Patriots to become enshrined in the Pro Football Hall of Fame.

Over the course of his 13-year professional career, Hannah missed only five games due to injury (he also missed three games due to a contract dispute at the start of the 1977 season), building a resume worthy of a Hall of Famer. He made nine Pro Bowls and is one of the few players to have been named to the NFL All-Decade Team twice—he was selected for both the 1970s and 1980s squads. Hannah was also selected to the NFL's 75th Anniversary Team, being the top guard on the team.

Hannah was a true throwback, someone who believed that football was a physical sport that wasn't for the weak. (He once suggested that his own quarterback Tony Eason put on a dress.)

"I played hurt because of a sense of ego, macho," Hannah told the *Boston Globe* in an interview prior to his induction into the Pro Football Hall of Fame. "I don't know what to call it. It was part of the image that I grew up with. That's what football players were. If it was just pain, you played. So long as the injury wouldn't get worse, you're supposed to play.

"You did everything you could to be on the field. It was just part of the philosophy of the game. To be honest with you, guys around you would look down on you if you didn't. I think it was peer group pressure somewhat, but mostly it was a sense of pride. Go out there and play hurt and you feel good about yourself. 'I can suck it up. I can beat my body. I can control me.'"

University of Alabama. His brother Charley had a 12-year NFL career as an offensive lineman for Tampa Bay and the Los Angeles Raiders. Another brother, David, had his football career cut short by a knee injury at Alabama.

With the 11th pick in the draft, the Patriots selected Sam "Bam" Cunningham, a running back out of Southern Cal and another All-American in 1972, the same year his USC Trojans won the national championship. In his final collegiate game, Cunningham scored four touchdowns in a 1973 Rose Bowl win over Ohio State, which still stands as a modern-day Rose Bowl record. (While Cunningham put up sensational numbers throughout his career with the Trojans, he is perhaps best remembered for his performance against Alabama that may have changed the history of college football. On September 12, 1970, he ran for 135 yards and two touchdowns against an all-white Crimson Tide team, sparking USC to a 42–21 win. Legend has it that, as a result of Cunningham's performance, Bryant decided to integrate his football team.)

With the 19th overall selection in the 1973 draft, New England took wide receiver Darryl Stingley out of Purdue. A former high school running back, Stingley possessed breakaway speed and terrific hands.

The Patriots added a fourth eventual regular to the roster that weekend when they selected Oklahoma's Ray "Sugar Bear" Hamilton in the 14th round. It was a reunion of sorts for Hamilton and Fairbanks, as the two had been together at Oklahoma.

The moves didn't pay dividends immediately, and things were a little rough in the first season under Fairbanks. Losers of seven of their first nine games, the 1973 Patriots didn't look much different than their predecessors.

The sluggish start included a season-opening performance that is still in the history books, but for all the wrong reasons for New England. Buffalo's O. J. Simpson put forth one of pro football's greatest rushing efforts, gaining 250 yards to kick-start what would be the first 2,000-yard rushing season in NFL history.

New England's 31–13 loss to Buffalo in the 1973 opener was the start of a three-game losing streak, but three wins in the last five games

First-round pick Sam "Bam" Cunningham confers with new Patriots coach Chuck Fairbanks during the opening practice session of the 1973 season. *AP Images*

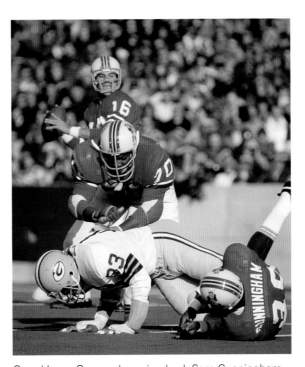

Guard Leon Gray and running back Sam Cunningham provide protection for Jim Plunkett during New England's 33–24 win over Green Bay in November 1973. Plunkett threw for 348 yards to lead the Pats to their third win of the season. *Vernon Biever/NFL/ Getty Images*

CHUCK FAIRBANKS

While the Patriots did have successful coaches throughout the first 10 or so years of their existence, Chuck Fairbanks was the first truly successful coach after the franchise made the jump from the AFL to the NFL. He helped modernize the front office, working with a brain trust that included Bucko Kilroy, and helped bring real change to Foxborough. He was the first coach/general manager in the history of the franchise, making personnel decisions and building a roster that was chock full of Pro Bowlers throughout the 1970s. As a head coach, Fairbanks spearheaded New England to a 46–40 record, including 31 wins in his final 44 regular-season games with the Patriots. In addition, he guided them to the first home playoff appearance in franchise history, a 1978 date with the Oilers in Foxborough.

But Fairbanks is also remembered as the man who ditched the team on the eve of that historic game to take a job with the University of Colorado. Late in the 1978 season, Colorado booster Jack Vickers visited Fairbanks and offered him a deal to coach at the school—a $45,000-a-year salary, with other potential revenue sources that could bring him $150,000 a year.

Chuck Fairbanks addressing the media, early 1970s.
Pro Football Hall of Fame/Getty Images

Fairbanks denied the report when it initially surfaced, but late in the season, Fairbanks called Chuck Sullivan and told him he wanted out of the last four years of his $150,000-per-year contract with New England. He would, he said, continue to coach the Patriots through the postseason. Sullivan fired him on the spot, but he reinstated him before the playoff game, only to see his team get beaten badly by Houston in the first round.

"I don't have any way of measuring the effect," Fairbanks told reporters after the game. "I thought during the week's preparation the squad was in good form. I'm sure there was some measure of distraction for me, but I tried to prepare as hard as I ever have. I tried to shelter myself from distractions."

After a protracted legal battle, Fairbanks won the right to go to Colorado. The decision to leave New England left a stain on his legacy with the Patriots, and it didn't do much for his coaching career—in three seasons in Colorado, Fairbanks posted a 7–26 record and was fired following the 1981 season. (After a rough start in his first season with the Buffaloes, syndicated sports columnist Steve Harvey ranked Colorado No. 1 in his "Bottom Ten" ranking, writing: "There's just no telling how poorly Colorado would be faring this season if the school hadn't had the good sense last December to lure Coach Chuck Fairbanks away from the New England Patriots.")

Fairbanks wrapped up his coaching career in the United States Football League (USFL) leading the 1983 New Jersey Generals to a 6–12 season.

that year and five consecutive victories to start the 1974 season caused the rest of the NFL to sit up and take notice. It felt like professional football had truly arrived in New England. "From that wonderful land that gave you statesmanship, rusted anchors, America, intellectuals, banking, town houses, landscape painting, Ted Williams, Bill Russell, and Bobby Orr, there now comes football. A new kind of madness is sweeping New England," wrote Dan Jenkins in an October 1974 story for *Sports Illustrated*. "Four weeks deep into the season some guys known as Patriots instead of your basic Celtics or Bruins or Red Sox or Political Activists or Scrods just happen to be undefeated and untied and unafraid, and if this sort of thing continues much longer, there is the possibility that someone sitting around Harvard Square discussing Sanskrit poetry as it applies to the works of Joan Didion may even look up from the water pipe and ask who Chuck Fairbanks and Jim Plunkett are."

Although the Patriots lost six of their last seven games, the 1974 season was a memorable one for the franchise. The 7–7 final record marked New England's first non-losing season since 1966, and the team posted wins over the Dolphins, Rams, and Vikings, all division champs in 1974, as well as the rival Jets. In one two-game stretch, they outscored the Colts and Jets by a combined score of 66–3. Sure, they ended up losing their last three, but that could be explained away by looking at the number of injuries the team took down the stretch.

It was becoming clear that, under Fairbanks' leadership, the real glory days for the Patriots were just around the corner.

O. J. Simpson (32) and the Bills beat the Patriots 30–28 on October 20, 1974, but New England's running back outplayed Buffalo's future Hall of Famer. While Simpson gained 122 yards on 32 carries, Sam Cunningham ran for 125 yards on just 11 carries and scored three touchdowns. *Diamond Images/ Getty Images*

3

REVOLUTIONARY

1975–1978

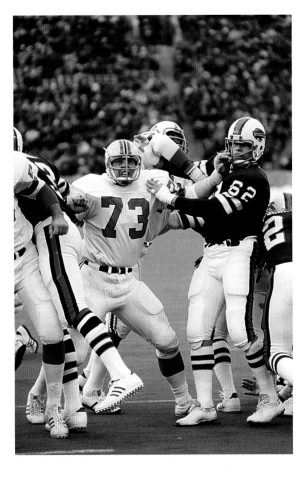

Center John Hannah tried to hold things together on the frontlines, as New England's offense took a big step backward in 1975. *Tony Tomsic/Getty Images*

As the 1975 season dawned for the Patriots, it appeared that all the pieces were in place for a big year, maybe the biggest in a decade. They were coming off their first season at .500 or better since 1966. They had a talented, innovative coach who had support from the ownership. They had a stable of young players on both sides of the ball. And they had a new stadium, a loyal fan base, and an ownership that was willing to invest the money it had back into the franchise. After years of foolishness, it looked like the Patriots were finally approaching the NFL elite.

The team of Bucko Kilroy and Chuck Fairbanks were coming off their third consecutive good draft. After selecting future Pro Bowl linebacker Steve Nelson and running back Andy Johnson in 1974, in the 1975 draft the Patriots nabbed two players who would go on to become pillars of the organization: first-round selection Russ Francis out of Oregon and fifth-round pick Steve Grogan out of Kansas State. A Hawaiian native, Francis was something of a free spirit—he had been known to try and invoke the names of ancient Polynesian shamans while on the sidelines—but he also had the chops to make it in professional football, particularly as a pass-catcher. As a senior at Oregon in 1974, he was named first team All-Pac 8 and an honorable mention All-American while ranking third in the conference with 31 catches (495 yards).

Sam Cunningham and the rest of the Patriots stumbled out of the gate in 1975, losing their first four games. Cunningham led the team with a lowly 919 total yards from scrimmage during the year. The running back also coughed up a league-worst 12 fumbles. *Focus on Sport/ Getty Images*

While there were others who were more talented and went on to achieve greater success, no one player was more identifiable as the face of the Patriots franchise over several decades than Grogan. A lean, quick Midwesterner, he started for Kansas State as a junior and senior and was known as a run-first, pass-second quarterback. As a collegian, Grogan finished with 2,214 passing yards and had 12 touchdowns and 26 interceptions, but he ran for an additional 585 yards and 6 touchdowns during that same span. He wouldn't get the starting job right away in New England—that still belonged to former Heisman Trophy–winner Plunkett, despite a season in which he completed only 49 percent of his passes and took more sacks (21) than touchdown passes (19).

Most observers believed that there was no reason to think that the 1975 Patriots wouldn't match or surpass the .500 record of the previous season. Plunkett was still under center, and most expected him to bounce back from his subpar 1974 performance. In addition, there were budding young offensive stars

Mack Herron was expected to be a central player in the Patriots offense in 1975, and although he pulled in a career-high 119 yards receiving against Cincinnati in Week 4, Herron was sent to Atlanta before the season was over. *Clifton Boutelle/NFL Photos/ Getty Images*

RUSS FRANCIS

For a franchise that has had more than its share of unique players over the years, Russ Francis might be the biggest free spirit in the 50 years of the franchise. In the offseason, the longtime Hawaii resident loved to hang-glide. He used to wrestle professionally for his father, wrestler and wrestling promoter Big Ed Francis. Halfway through his senior season at Oregon, Russ quit, angry that his old coach had been fired. He entertained ideas about law school or working as a vet. He loved skydiving and started an air-charter business in Hawaii.

Not all of his teammates appreciated the antics, including one future Hall of Famer.

"To the press and fans, it's Russ Francis this, Russ Francis that. But here's a guy with more talent in his finger than I have in my whole body, who doesn't use it," John Hannah told reporters in 1979. "If Russ would bust his hump, nobody would know who Dave Casper was. But he doesn't."

After six years with the Patriots, Francis went into voluntary retirement after the 1980 season. It was believed he started to sour on the game following the 1978 hit on Darryl Stingley—his former roommate with the Patriots—and later said he had a "dislike for the malicious intent of violence rather than just good, clean hard-hitting football." San Francisco coach Bill Walsh convinced Francis to come out of retirement in 1982, and the tight end joined a group of overwhelming offensive options in Joe Montana, Wendell Tyler, and Roger Craig. In 1985, Francis was the starting tight end for the 49ers, who beat the Dolphins 38–16 in Super Bowl XIX.

After spending six seasons with San Francisco, Francis returned to New England and retired as a member of the Patriots after the 1988 season.

Russ Francis, circa 1978.
Al Messerschmidt/Getty Images

The Patriots of '76

like Sam Cunningham, who had rushed for 811 yards in his second full season in the pros, and Darryl Stingley and Mack Herron, who were part of an impressive nucleus around him. But four straight losses to open the 1975 season soured any sort of optimism. The string included a 36–7 pasting at the hands of the Jets and Joe Namath, who tossed four touchdown passes as New York coasted to the victory.

A chasm started to develop between the coach and the quarterback, the latter of whom bristled openly at the play selection. After the 1–4 start, Fairbanks had no concerns about pulling the plug on Plunkett and going with Grogan, who had no such qualms about Fairbanks. ("I think I've called the plays in

only one game in my life," he told reporters early in his career.) The switch paid off immediately. Taking over for Plunkett early in a game against the 49ers in Foxborough, Grogan tossed a pair of touchdowns on the way to a 24–16 victory. Things went a little rougher in his first start a week later—Grogan threw a pair of interceptions in a 24–17 loss to the Cardinals in St. Louis—but it was clear a new era had dawned in New England. The Patriots were now Grogan's team. He was not the most polished quarterback, but he had a way with his teammates that other stars did not. They liked him and wanted to win for him.

"He was the kind of guy you wanted to protect," Hannah later recalled, "the kind of guy you wanted to play for."

media guide

GROGAN TAKES CHARGE

The team finished the 1975 season with a 3–11 record, a step backward from 1974, but they were clearly headed in the right direction. Fairbanks had completely turned the team over to the youngsters. Cunningham led the team in rushing, and the rookie Grogan threw for 1,976 yards and 11 touchdowns while winning the hearts and minds of his teammates with his guts and attitude. "Quarterbacks are supposed to be these guys with California attitudes. Not Steve, man. He would get fired up," Hannah said. "He believed that quarterbacks should be football players and not wear a skirt."

The Patriots ultimately dealt the unhappy Plunkett to San Francisco on April 5, 1976, in exchange for backup quarterback Tom Owen and four draft picks—two first-round selections later that month and a first- and a second-round pick in 1977. As had been the case in 1973, the Patriots were in possession of three first-round picks in the 1976 draft, and again Kilroy and Fairbanks hit the jackpot, delivering three more players who would be cornerstones of the team for years to come. Defensive back Mike Haynes (a three-year All-WAC star at Arizona State), center Pete Brock (out of Colorado), and defensive back Tim Fox (a consensus All-American out of Ohio State) would become integral to the success of the franchise for the better part of the next decade. Plunkett eventually went on to win a Super Bowl with the Raiders, but the four players acquired via the draft—the Pats added Texas defensive back Raymond Clayborn and Oklahoma running back Horace Ivory in 1977—were a significant part of the turnaround the New England franchise would enjoy in the latter part of the 1970s.

The departure of Plunkett left Grogan as the unequivocal No. 1 quarterback in New England. He later said that he had heard about the Plunkett trade from a reporter and sounded nonplussed when informed of the situation. "We had a spring camp in late May," Grogan later told reporters, "and when I came in, I was the only quarterback who had been here last year. So I was the only one who knew what was going on. I figured I was number one until someone came up and told me to get out."

Coach Chuck Fairbanks (right) put the team fully in the hands of quarterback Steve Grogan in 1976, and the Patriots responded with its first postseason appearance in more than a decade. *AP Images*

Defensive end Julius Adams contributed to a re-energized Patriots defense in the mid-1970s. New England held opponents to a then-franchise-low 16.8 points per game in 1976, which they improved to 15.5 points in 1977. *George Gojkovich/Getty Images*

STEVE GROGAN

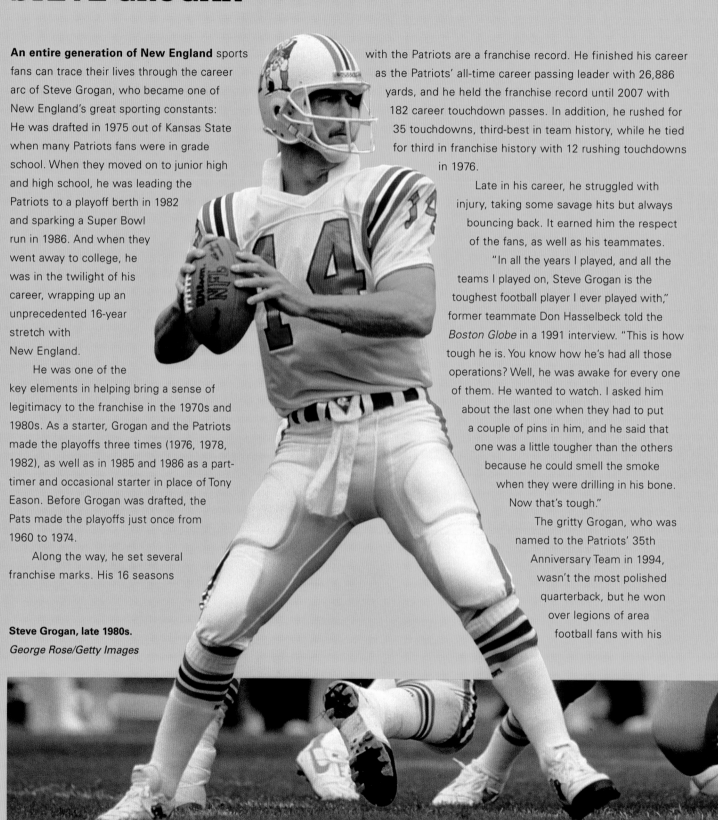

An entire generation of New England sports fans can trace their lives through the career arc of Steve Grogan, who became one of New England's great sporting constants: He was drafted in 1975 out of Kansas State when many Patriots fans were in grade school. When they moved on to junior high and high school, he was leading the Patriots to a playoff berth in 1982 and sparking a Super Bowl run in 1986. And when they went away to college, he was in the twilight of his career, wrapping up an unprecedented 16-year stretch with New England.

He was one of the key elements in helping bring a sense of legitimacy to the franchise in the 1970s and 1980s. As a starter, Grogan and the Patriots made the playoffs three times (1976, 1978, 1982), as well as in 1985 and 1986 as a part-timer and occasional starter in place of Tony Eason. Before Grogan was drafted, the Pats made the playoffs just once from 1960 to 1974.

Along the way, he set several franchise marks. His 16 seasons

Steve Grogan, late 1980s.
George Rose/Getty Images

with the Patriots are a franchise record. He finished his career as the Patriots' all-time career passing leader with 26,886 yards, and he held the franchise record until 2007 with 182 career touchdown passes. In addition, he rushed for 35 touchdowns, third-best in team history, while he tied for third in franchise history with 12 rushing touchdowns in 1976.

Late in his career, he struggled with injury, taking some savage hits but always bouncing back. It earned him the respect of the fans, as well as his teammates.

"In all the years I played, and all the teams I played on, Steve Grogan is the toughest football player I ever played with," former teammate Don Hasselbeck told the *Boston Globe* in a 1991 interview. "This is how tough he is. You know how he's had all those operations? Well, he was awake for every one of them. He wanted to watch. I asked him about the last one when they had to put a couple of pins in him, and he said that one was a little tougher than the others because he could smell the smoke when they were drilling in his bone. Now that's tough."

The gritty Grogan, who was named to the Patriots' 35th Anniversary Team in 1994, wasn't the most polished quarterback, but he won over legions of area football fans with his

Grogan during the 1976 Divisional Playoffs.

Michael Zagaris/Getty Images

Grogan was a threat running the ball as well as passing it. Here he heads to the end zone for his second touchdown run of the day against the Saints on December 5, 1976. The Patriots won, 27–6, to put the team in first place.
AP Images

heart and desire. They saw the native Midwesterner as one of their own.

"Let's face it—I wasn't the best football player who ever lived. Far from it," Grogan told reporters after he retired. "But I think people appreciated the fact I did the best I could. Don't misunderstand, I have regrets, too. I don't think anybody who's truly honest looks back with no regrets. There are things I'd love to go back and change, but I can't. None of us can. That's why it's so important to be able to live with what we did and I can do that. I did the best I could for as long as I could. That's not a bad legacy, is it?"

No one was telling Grogan to get out. He was now the man in command and a large reason why the Patriots turned a 3–11 mark in 1975 into an 11–3 record the following season. It was a great time to be a New England football fan—the spirit of '76 had energized the franchise. Among the memorable moments that season were wins over the defending Super Bowl champion Steelers in Pittsburgh and traditional powerhouses Miami and Baltimore, and a stretch of eight wins in their last nine games.

Without the rifle-armed Plunkett, New England didn't offer much of an air attack. Instead, the real success came on the ground. Behind a peerless offensive line, the Patriots rushed for 2,957 yards as a team—then the fifth-highest total in NFL history—and gained a league-best average of 5 yards per carry. A late November win over the Broncos saw the team gain 332 yards on the ground. Three players rushed for at least 699 yards on the year—Cunningham (824), Don Calhoun (721), and fullback Andy Johnson (699). Grogan's 12 rushing touchdowns still stand as the most by a quarterback in one season. The Patriots

STEVE NELSON

A durable inside linebacker who became one of the cornerstones of the franchise for the better part of a decade, Steve Nelson—or, as almost everyone calls him, "Nellie"—played for the Patriots from 1974 until 1987, spending his entire career in Foxborough. The three-time Pro Bowler led the team in tackles 8 of his 14 seasons, and he recorded more than 100 tackles nine times over the course of his career, including in 1984 when he was credited with an amazing 207 tackles, an unofficial franchise record.

He provided a rare dose of stability through some crazy stretches, including some of the highest highs (he was part of a team that won the 1985 AFC Championship) and the lowest of lows (he was also part of the 1981 team that went 2–14). Through it all, Nellie was a rock-steady presence at linebacker for the franchise.

"It's been a great ride," Nelson told reporters at a news conference when he announced his retirement. "My dance card is filled. I'm really not questioning what I've decided."

The Patriots retired his No. 57 jersey, and he was later named to the Patriots' Team of the Century in 2000. For several years, he served as the athletic director at Curry College, and he has done a lot of work as a football analyst for Sportsradio 850 WEEI and New England Cable News.

Steve Nelson, circa 1978. *George Gojkovich/Getty Images*

did just enough passing to keep opposing defenses honest—Grogan had just 1,903 passing yards on the season, and only one receiver ended up with more than 300 yards receiving. But it all worked.

"With Grogan in the game, we're not going to try to bomb them," Cunningham told reporters late in the season. "When Plunkett was our quarterback, he had a very good arm and we had to utilize it. But the thing is, you've got to set up the arm with the run. We know that with Grogan we're going to make the defenses run-conscious and then work them with the pass."

Among their wins that season was a 48–17 blowout of the Raiders, the only regular-season defeat suffered by Oakland. It was a shock to Raiders coach John Madden, who told reporters he had never seen such blocking. "They have five offensive linemen who can block, a fullback who can block, and a tight end who can block," Madden said. "It's like playing against a seven-man line all day. Devastating."

New England ended up meeting the Raiders again in the first round of the playoffs in Oakland. The Patriots charged to a 21–10 lead after three quarters on a pair of rushing touchdowns plus a 26-yard touchdown pass from Grogan to Francis. In the fourth quarter, the Raiders cut the lead to 21–17 and were driving for another score with time winding down in regulation when referee Ben Dreith flagged Ray "Sugar Bear" Hamilton for a highly questionable roughing the passer call after a third-down pass from Oakland quarterback Ken Stabler fell incomplete. (Replays showed there was no illegal contact.) The call gave the Raiders' drive new life, and they took advantage, eventually scoring on a 1-yard scramble by Stabler with less than a minute left to give the Raiders a 24–21 win. Partly because of the controversial call, the league never assigned Dreith to officiate another Patriots game.

Russ Francis heads into the end zone to give New England a 14–10 lead in the third quarter of the 1976 AFC Divisional Playoffs against Oakland.
AP Images

"GOODBYE, CHUCKY"

Even in the wake of the bitter postseason defeat—and the sight of the Raiders going on to win the Super Bowl—there was every reason to feel good again about the state of the Patriots in 1977. Everyone was returning from one of the best young teams in the league. But Pro Bowl offensive linemen Hannah and Leon Gray walked out at the start of the 1977 season over a contract dispute. The pair, a sizable reason the New England running game had been as unstoppable as it was over the previous few seasons, missed three games in their holdout, during which the Patriots went 1–2.

During the holdout, the initial seeds of discord between Fairbanks and the Sullivan family were sown when Fairbanks thought he had Hannah and Gray signed to a deal that would bring them back into the fold sooner rather than later, only to see the deal rejected by Chuck Sullivan. According to players from that era, it wasn't the first time Sullivan had bollixed a deal, and it wouldn't be the last.

"There was just one guy who kind of goofed it up on that side of things, and that was . . . Chuck," recalled Russ Francis. "[He] may have meant to do

A stunned Patriots defense heads to the sideline after Oakland quarterback Ken Stabler tumbled into the end zone with the game-winning score during the 1976 playoffs—a disappointing end to a promising season. *AP Images*

what was best for his father, but sure didn't. . . . With the way that Chuck Sullivan dealt with the players, dealt with Chuck Fairbanks, the head coach who was supposed to be running the team—Chuck Sullivan clearly interfered with that. That was the beginning of the end. The team he interfered with . . . would have gone on to win Super Bowl championships."

The bitterness that emerged out of that holdout gave rise to many of the problems the team would suffer in the latter years of the 1970s. The relationship between Fairbanks and the Sullivan family continued to sour. The players started to see the writing on the wall. Hannah, one of the greatest players in the history of the franchise, became alienated by the experience, and he later told reporters, "I'll never sign another Patriots contract." Gray, a two-time Pro Bowl tackle, was eventually traded to Houston for a pair of draft picks, breaking up one of the finest guard-tackle combinations in the league. ("Leon

The preseason contract holdout by All-Pro offensive linemen John Hannah (left) and Leon Gray brought added tension and frustration to the Patriots heading into the 1977 campaign. *AP Images*

and John Hannah, that's as good a left side as you can get," Bill Belichick remarked after Gray passed away in 2001.) Cornerback Haynes, a future Hall of Famer, announced before the 1979 season that he would play out his option.

Despite the turmoil, there was some on-field drama that 1977 season. After the slow start, the team took off toward the middle of the season, winning four straight games on a pair of occasions. A loss in the season finale to the Colts in Baltimore did the Patriots in, however, and they missed out on the postseason by a single game after finishing with a 9–5 record.

While great success came in the years following the playoff defeat to Oakland in December 1976, real tragedy also touched the franchise. During a 1978 preseason game, talented young wide receiver Darryl Stingley was paralyzed after a frightening hit from Raiders defensive back Jack Tatum. Stingley would never recover from the blow, and he remained a quadriplegic the rest of his life. It snuffed out what could have been an exceptional career. Just 26 years old at the time of the incident, Stingley was coming off a season in which he had 39 catches with a 16.8 average and 5 touchdowns, terrific numbers for an era when defensive backs were allowed to hit receivers all over the field and linemen couldn't use their hands to block. Stingley later wrote a book about his experience, *Happy to Be Alive*, and eventually worked as a consultant for the team.

"I remember thinking, 'What's going to happen to me? If I live, what am I going to be like?'" Stingley said of the injury in a 1988 interview with the Associated Press. "And then there were all those whys, whys, whys. . . . It was only after I stopped asking why that I was able to regroup and go on with my life."

The Stingley tragedy notwithstanding, there was a real sense of optimism when the 1978 season kicked off in Foxborough—in fact, there was a belief that the team might be good enough to go all the way. The franchise introduced a new mascot, named Superpatriot, who was billed as a combination of Paul Revere and Superman. The Patriots also circulated a team picture boldly inscribed "The 1978 Superpatriots"—which was meant to suggest, of

course, a succession of super Sundays leading ultimately to the Super Bowl. Fairbanks told reporters, "We can beat any team in this league consistently with the players we have right now." All that being the case, the team lost two of its first three, and the fans, who had gotten used to some success during the previous seasons, started to get ugly with the team. (Grogan reportedly had a beer dumped on his head after an early season loss to Baltimore.)

But the Patriots' legendary running game again provided a jumpstart. New England ended up with four players—Cunningham, Horace Ivory, Johnson, and Grogan—who rushed for at least 500 yards that season; as a team, the foursome accumulated 3,165 total rushing yards, a colossal point of pride for the offensive line. After the penultimate regular-season game against the Bills—a 26–24 win during

which New England posted an amazing 249 rushing yards and broke the NFL record for most rushing yards by a team in a single season—Patriots offensive line coach Jim Ringo poured congratulatory shots of Johnnie Walker Red for his players. For more than an hour, they sat together, drinking in their triumph and their scotch. "That season, that day, was as good as it got for me in pro football," Hannah later said. "Our mark [of 3,165 yards] still stands. It was a total team effort."

Buoyed by their ferocious ground attack, the Patriots rebounded from the 1–2 start to win seven straight, claiming sole possession of first place after an October win over the Dolphins. When the Patriots entered the regular-season finale with the Dolphins in Miami, they had an 11–4 record and were feeling pretty good about their chances.

The 1978 season got off to a tough start when receiver Darryl Stingley was struck with a devastating hit by Oakland's Jack Tatum during a preseason game on August 13. Stingley was taken off the field on a stretcher, paralyzed from the neck down. *AP Images*

Sam Cunningham goes up and over the Miami defense to score a touchdown in New England's 14–10 win over the Dolphins on December 11, 1977. The victory put the Patriots in a three-way tie for first with Miami and Baltimore with one game left to play before losing to Baltimore in the finale. *AP Images*

MIKE HAYNES

It didn't take long for Mike Haynes to make an impact with the Patriots. The fifth player and the first defensive back taken in the 1976 draft out of Arizona State, he lit up Schaefer Stadium as a rookie with 8 interceptions and an AFC-leading 608 yards on 45 punt returns. That season, Haynes gave the Patriots their first-ever touchdowns on punt returns with 89-yard and 62-yard returns, and he made the first of nine trips to the Pro Bowl.

Over the course of his seven-year career in New England, Haynes recorded 28 interceptions (fifth all-time in franchise history), as well as 1,159 yards on punt returns (second-best in team history). However, after a holdout in 1983, his contract was awarded to the Los Angeles Raiders in a settlement that gave the Patriots a No. 1 draft choice in 1984 and a No. 2 pick in 1985. He had a great second half of his career, eventually finishing with the Raiders in 1989, and in 1997, he became just the second member of the Patriots—after John Hannah—to be elected to the Pro Football Hall of Fame.

Any bitterness Haynes may have felt toward the franchise evaporated a long time ago, according to a 2004 interview with the Pro Bowler, who was part of the NFL's 75th Anniversary Team, the All-Decade Team for the 1980s, and the Patriots' Team of the Century in 2000.

"I definitely enjoyed my experience [with the Patriots] and felt like I was fortunate to play with a lot of talented guys," Haynes told the *Boston Globe*. "It was the days when we had a lot of top draft choices on the team and a lot of great athletes. There were a lot of great coaches where many of them went on to become head coaches in the NFL or college and had success. More than anything else, I was in the right place at the right time."

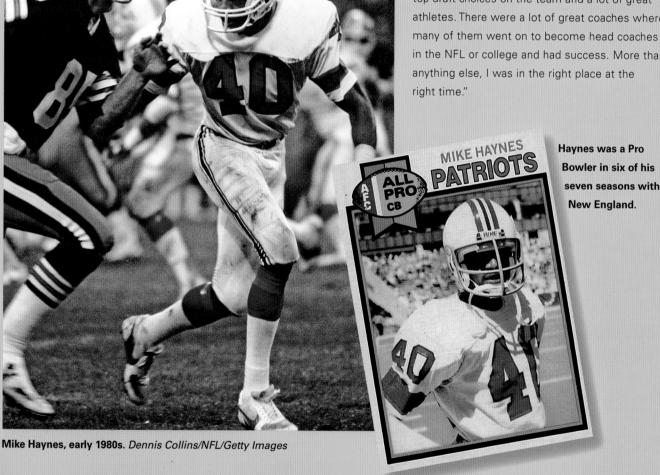

Mike Haynes, early 1980s. *Dennis Collins/NFL/Getty Images*

Haynes was a Pro Bowler in six of his seven seasons with New England.

While Steve Grogan, Sam Cunningham, and others paced a record-setting offense in New England, cornerback Mike Haynes was the team's defensive Pro Bowler in 1978. Here he intercepts a pass during a key late-season game against Buffalo.
David Tenenbaum/AP Images

Then, Fairbanks dropped a bombshell. Hours before the game against the Dolphins, he announced he was leaving the Patriots to take over the head coaching job at Colorado. The outraged Sullivan fired Fairbanks on the spot and named co-coaches to take the reins for the Miami game: offensive coordinator Ron Erhardt would run the offense, while defensive coordinator Hank Bullough handled the defense. Predictably, the Patriots were thrashed that evening, 23–3.

"We were orphans tonight," Hannah told reporters after the game. "I felt like a fatherless child."

The two sides quickly made peace: Sullivan reversed his decision two days later after Fairbanks agreed not to have any dealings with Colorado until after the Patriots' season ended. Meanwhile, Sullivan made public statements that seemed to suggest the two sides could work out some sort of deal whereby Fairbanks could forego Colorado and return to New England. But the damage Fairbanks created with his announcement fostered ill will among players, coaches, and the front office. His players didn't know where his allegiances lay. His assistants suddenly had little job security. And the front office was faced with the specter of trying to win over a coach who still had four years left on his current contract that paid him $180,000 a season. The mood around the team, which had been so bright a few weeks before, darkened.

All of this played out against the backdrop of New England's preparations for the first home NFL playoff game in franchise history. The Patriots would host Earl Campbell and the fifth-seeded Houston Oilers at Schaefer Stadium on New Year's Eve, and despite the public flap, it was believed that New England had a good shot to win the game. The second-seeded Patriots had a powerful offense, and if they could keep Campbell in check (easier said than done), they were facing a quarterback in Dan Pastorini who had suffered a brutal rib injury and was questionable as the game approached. However, Pastorini—wearing the prototype for what would become the modern-day flak jacket—did play. With his ribs protected, he had little to worry about, and he went out and lit up the Patriots, throwing three touchdowns in a 31–14 blowout. At the end of the game, as he walked toward the tunnel that led off

The New England defense could not slow down Houston's All-Pro running back Earl Campbell during the 1978 Divisional Playoff Game at Schaefer Stadium. *Heinz Kluetmeier/Sports Illustrated/Getty Images*

the field, Fairbanks was serenaded with singsong jeers of "Goodbye, Chucky, we're glad to see you go" and "We want Shula!"

"Our talent is as good as any team's," safety Tim Fox told reporters after the loss to the Oilers. "But for some reason, we never play to our capability."

Fairbanks exited the franchise under a dark cloud—the Patriots eventually sued him for breach of contract, and he eventually admitted to working for Colorado while still under contract with the Patriots, helping smear a once-great reputation. (Colorado eventually bought out Fairbanks' contract.) In three seasons in Colorado, Fairbanks had a 7–26 record.

The Patriots of the mid-1970s had enjoyed a remarkable run of success. From 1974 through 1978, they won 41 games and made a pair of postseason appearances. They had a run of solid drafts and enjoyed a good nucleus of young players to build on going forward, with many of those good young players becoming annual participants in the Pro Bowl. But in terms of overall, franchise-wide success, the departure of Fairbanks triggered a series of events that meant the Patriots would go the better part of the next decade without being able to recapture the achievements of the mid-1970s.

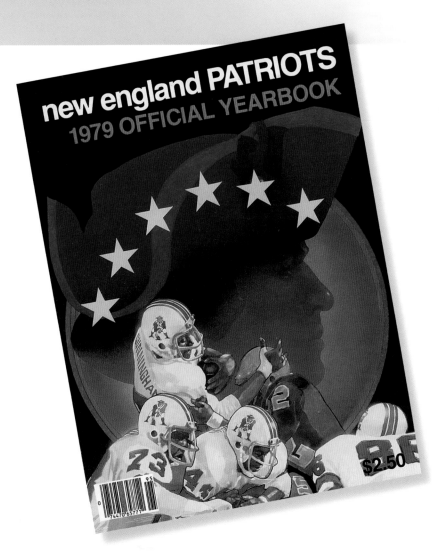

In the late 1970s and early 1980s, the Patriots wouldn't get as close to a title as they had in 1976, but they did have their share of success. A collection of stars on both the offensive and defensive side of the football kept the Patriots competitive throughout much of the late 1970s and early 1980s.

Among New England's star talents, none was bigger than John Hannah. Hannah set the standard for offensive linemen throughout the NFL during this era. A 1981 story in *Sports Illustrated* lionized Hannah as not only the best offensive lineman in NFL history but one of the best ever to play the game. "The greatest offensive lineman in history is playing right now and probably hasn't even reached his peak," wrote Paul Zimmerman for the August 3, 1981, issue. "He is John Hannah, the left guard for the New England Patriots, out of Alabama. He stands six feet, two and a half inches and his weight fluctuates between 260 and 270 (no lineman can honestly claim only one weight). He is 30 years old and is in his ninth year and is coming off the best season he ever had."

In New England, Hannah was joined by the likes of future Hall of Fame cornerback Mike Haynes, who pulled in 22 interceptions in his first four seasons in a Patriots uniform and was eventually named to the NFL's 75th Anniversary Team. Helping to bolster the defense was linebacker Steve Nelson, a three-time Pro Bowler who led the team in tackles in 8 of his 14 seasons in New England. And in 1982, the Patriots got themselves another future Hall of Famer when pass-rushing demon Andre Tippett was drafted out of Iowa. By the time his career was done, Tippett had played in five Pro Bowls and finished his career with 100 sacks. His 35 combined sacks in 1984 and 1985 still stands as the best two-year sack total by a linebacker in NFL history.

On offense, leading the way was Russ Francis—dubbed an "all-world" tight end by Howard Cosell. The occasionally flaky pass-catcher marched to the beat of his own drummer, but he was good enough to be a three-time Pro Bowler in his six seasons with the Patriots. Wide receiver Stanley Morgan stretched the field like no other—his career average of 19.2 yards per catch is the best in the history of the league among wide receivers with at least 500 career receptions. Tying everything together on offense was Steve Grogan, an eternally stalwart presence under center who spent 16 seasons with the franchise.

This bunch made sure the Patriots were a competitive team throughout the late 1970s and early 1980s—New England was .500 or better in every year between 1976 and 1988 except 1981. But in the competitive AFC East, those plus-.500 years didn't always lead to the playoffs, and some late-season collapses kept them out of the division elite.

While the player talent was solid, coaches shuffled in and out of Foxborough during this period. Following Chuck Fairbanks' departure, offensive coordinator Ron Erhardt was named head coach on April 6, 1979. A well-respected assistant, Erhardt started with the franchise in 1973 as backfield coach, a job he held for four years before being promoted to offensive coordinator under Fairbanks in February 1977. Erhardt's only previous experience as head coach had been in the 1960s at North Dakota State, where he compiled a 61–7–1 record in seven years at the helm. Noting his history, he had reason to feel confident heading into his head coaching stint with the Patriots. "I've never been a loser in football, and I don't intend to start now," he told reporters at his first press conference.

Under Erhardt, the Patriots offense enjoyed a field day. In 1979, the team scored 411 points and twice scored at least 50 in a game. Wide receivers

SI Cover/Sports Illustrated/Getty Images

RAYMOND CLAYBORN AND WILL McDONOUGH

During the 1979 season, the Patriots locker room was the setting for one of the most surreal moments in the history of the franchise—a fight between a sportswriter and a player.

On September 9, New England had just finished a 56–3 pasting of the Jets when Patriots cornerback Raymond Clayborn was just stepping out of the postgame shower and was on his way back to his locker. His space abutted one of the big stars of the afternoon, wide receiver Harold Jackson, and Clayborn grew angry as reporters continued to spill over into his locker area, and he took issue with the media.

Boston Globe writer Will McDonough answered, and things escalated pretty quickly between the two. According to writers who were there, Clayborn poked McDonough in either the eye or the chin, and McDonough took a swing, knocking Clayborn back into his locker. McDonough landed a second shot, and sportswriters and players were all drawn into the fray. In the midst of the brawl, owner Billy Sullivan was dumped backward into a canvas laundry bin.

"Clayborn came out of the shower and had trouble getting to his locker, and [he] started yelling and screaming and pushing his way through people," recalled former *Boston Globe* writer Leigh Montville. "McDonough kind of said something to him like, 'Straighten up and don't be an idiot' or something like that. . . . Clayborn started talking to McDonough and he meant to put his finger in his chest, and it slipped and went into McDonough's eye. McDonough then just grabbed him and threw him into a locker."

Clayborn—who had gotten into a dustup earlier in the season with a writer from the Associated Press—was fined $2,000 for the incident for what NFL Commissioner Pete Rozelle called "conduct involving members of the news media." McDonough gained a sizable level of fame among the fourth estate for his involvement in the fight, cementing his reputation as a tough guy among sportswriters.

The day after the fight, a contrite Clayborn held a press conference and offered a public apology. "I don't plan to have any more temper tantrums," Clayborn said.

Morgan and Harold Jackson became the first and second receivers in franchise history to surpass the 1,000-yard receiving mark in a single season. The team looked good out of the gate, shooting to a 6–2 record to start the season, thanks largely to the play of Hannah, Haynes, and Morgan, all of whom would go on to make the Pro Bowl. But a late-season slide saw New England lose three of its final four games—including an overtime defeat at home against the Bills and a one-point loss to the Jets at the Meadowlands—to finish 9–7 and on the outside looking in at the playoffs, one game out.

In 1980, it was the same story, as the team got off to a strong 7–2 start. The offense took it up a notch, finishing the year with a league-high 441 points—a franchise single-season mark that stood until 2007. Seven guys were named to the AFC's Pro Bowl squad. Joining returning Pro Bowlers Hannah,

Haynes, and Morgan in Hawaii were defensive end Julius Adams, free safety Tim Fox, linebacker Steve Nelson, and kicker John Smith.

Once again, however, things went sour in the second half of the season. The slide started in early November, and the Patriots won just three of their final seven games. On November 10, they lost a 38–34 shootout against an Oilers team that featured many familiar faces who had tormented New England as members of the Oakland Raiders, namely Ken Stabler and Dave Casper. On December 8 against the Dolphins in Miami, Uwe von Schamann booted a 23-yard field goal in overtime to hand New England another loss. (The game was secondary for many, however, because of the news, announced by Howard Cosell during the broadcast, that John Lennon had been shot and killed that night in New York City.) In the end, the Patriots lost their last four

Matt Cavanaugh (12) got the start at quarterback against Miami on December 8, 1980, and completed 12 of 16 passes, but the Patriots lost in overtime, 16–13. *Al Messerschmidt/Getty Images*

games by a combined 14 points, which resulted in a 10–6 record and another postseason miss by a single game.

Unfortunately, as the Patriots offense was putting up astronomical point totals, so were opposing offenses. In 1979 and 1980, New England held opponents in single-digits in scoring on only five occasions. The Patriots fell hard in 1981, slumping to a 2–14 finish. Citing the fact that Erhardt was "just too nice a guy," general manager Pat Sullivan dismissed the head coach on December 22, two days after the conclusion of the season.

MEYER TAKES CHARGE

The pendulum swung in the other direction with the hiring of Ron Meyer, who on January 15, 1982, became the eighth head coach in the history of the team. Meyer quickly turned things around,

Although the game was all but decided at this point, Don Hasselbeck pulls in a fourth-quarter touchdown pass in the Wild Card Playoff Game on January 8, 1983. The tight end had been the team's leading receiver in 1981, but he saw relatively little action in 1982 and was traded away a year later. *Al Messerschmidt/Getty Images*

transforming a 2–14 franchise into a playoff team in his first season at the helm, winning AFC Coach of the Year honors along the way. The 1982 Patriots finished 5–4 in a strike-shortened campaign and won three of their last four to claim their first post-season appearance since 1979. A 28–13 defeat to the Dolphins in Miami brought a quick end to that postseason honeymoon.

One highlight of the 1982 season came in a game against the Dolphins on December 12 at Foxboro Stadium. Playing in cold, snowy conditions, the two teams were locked in a scoreless stalemate

deep into the second half. With just under five min-utes remaining in the game, the Patriots were able to maneuver into field-goal range, and Coach Meyer called on snowplow driver Mark Henderson to clear a spot for kicker John Smith. Henderson (who was working as part of a work-release program from a local prison) brushed off a spot, and Smith connected on the 33-yard field goal, providing the only scoring for the afternoon. Don Shula and the Dolphins were furious, but Henderson and his plow achieved a spe-cial place in New England sporting lore. (When the stadium closed after the 2001 season, Henderson

MARK HENDERSON

On the afternoon of December 12, 1982, Mark Henderson etched himself a place in New England sports history. That day, Henderson was a convicted burglar out of prison on a work-release program and working on the Patriots' grounds crew for the New England-Miami game at Foxboro Stadium. It was a brutal afternoon for football, with record low temps across the Northeast and blizzard conditions in many parts of New England. As a result of the awful conditions, the Patriots and Dolphins went deep into the fourth quarter locked in a scoreless duel.

With 4:45 left in regulation, the Patriots called timeout before attempting a 33-yard field goal. Patriots coach Ron Meyer spotted Henderson sitting on the sidelines atop a tractor that had a broom attached to the front.

While Miami coach Don Shula fumed, Henderson was waved onto the field by Patriots coach Ron Meyer to clear a path four feet wide for New England kicker John Smith.

"He was waving and screaming, and he said, 'Get on that thing and do something,'" Henderson told the *Boston Herald* years later. "The tractor was still running. So I went out on the twenty-yard line like I was going to do my normal thing, which was to clear the yard markers, and I swerved over where Matt Cavanaugh was. I turned on the brush and I made what looked like a sidewalk of green."

Smith's kick was good and gave New England a 3–0 win.

Henderson was told to avoid the media after the game, but his tractor stalled out on the way off the field and

Mike Kullen/AP Images

reporters converged on him. When a Miami sportswriter told him that Coach Shula was livid about the incident, Henderson fired off the line of the afternoon: "Well, what are they going to do, throw me in jail?"

Shula remains bitter about the incident. "When I saw Ron Meyer signal that convict to the field, I should have thrown myself in front of that plow," he later told reporters.

The broom was retired when the Pats switched from turf to grass in 1991. While the Patriots continued to use the tractor to tow various things—tarps, watercoolers, and so on—the broom is hanging from the rafters in the Hall at Patriot Place.

RON MEYER

Ron Meyer was a take-no-prisoners coach who might have been the perfect coach for the perfect time in Foxborough. After the Patriots finished with a 2–14 mark in 1981, Meyer was brought in to clean things up, and he turned New England into a playoff team a year later—the strike-shortened 1982 season saw the Patriots post a 5–4 mark and make the playoffs. The following season, the team took a brief step back, finishing 8–8. But even with the improvement, it was clear the players were chafing under Meyer's hard rule, and midway through the 1983 season, he was fired.

General manager Pat Sullivan later revealed that Meyer had wanted to deal away almost half the roster, but he was overruled, leading to conflict with the ownership. Sullivan told reporters that Meyer wanted to trade Hall of Fame left guard John Hannah, tailback Tony Collins, defensive end Julius Adams, free safety

Ron Meyer, 1982. *Paul Benoit/ AP Images*

Rick Sanford, and running backs Robert Weathers and Mosi Tatupu, among others.

"I overruled him," Sullivan told reporters. "He wanted to flush everyone down the toilet and rebuild from the ground up. OK, maybe when you're a 2–14 club there's some justification for something like that, but I felt we were a darn good team with playoff-caliber material. I didn't want to see everything torn apart."

But Meyer's reputation as a fix-it man followed him to Indianapolis. After spending a year out of coaching, he was hired by the 0–13 Colts. Meyer promptly led the Colts to three straight victories to finish 3–13. A year later, he won the AFC East Division title with the Colts, where he once again was named the AFC Coach of the Year. But as was the case in New England, the players quickly grew tired of his approach, and after the Colts started 0–5 in 1991, he was again let go.

returned as an honored guest at the last game and received a loud ovation from the fans.) In 1983, the NFL banned the use of snowplows on the field during a game.

A coach with a reputation as a tough guy, Meyer was also seen as a rigid, dogmatic leader who wouldn't listen to the concerns of his players. (Trying to downplay the importance of emotion in football, Meyer once commented that "there was a lot of emotion at the Alamo, and nobody survived.") The Patriots went 8–8 in 1983, and the discontent turned louder. Midway through the 1984 season, Sullivan held a players-only meeting and listened to their complaints about the head coach. Twenty-four hours after Meyer fired defensive coordinator Rod Rust, Sullivan decided to fire Meyer. He was just the

second coach in the history of the franchise to be let go despite having a winning regular-season record.

"I'm proud of what I'm leaving this team," Meyer said. "I'm sure disruptions and decisiveness of some of the actions may have ruffled some feathers in the wrong areas. Ron Meyer is not a lap dog."

(Meyer later revealed that he knew what might be coming. In an interview with Will McDonough, he said he had a feeling something was up the night before he got fired. "I had a feeling it might happen, so when I went in my clothes closet that morning, I picked up this brown suit I hated and never wore," he told McDonough. "I figured it might be that kind of day. Oh, by the way, on the way out the door they told me to make sure I returned my [team-leased] car to Rodman Ford as soon as possible.")

Sullivan put a positive spin on the change in the coaching leadership. "We have a good football team that has every capability and possibility of being in the playoffs this year," he told reporters after the move was announced. "We felt the distractions and turmoil of the type that seemed to be developing were not in the best interests of the Patriots. So we went out and hired a very stable man who has tremendous football knowledge and experience."

BERRY BEGINS ERA OF GOOD FEELING

That man was Raymond Berry, who proved to be just the tonic the team needed. While Meyer was all fire and brimstone, Berry was a laid-back coach who knew how to get the most out of his team. By the time he arrived in New England, his resume as a player was unmatched—a six-time Pro Bowler, he was elected to the Pro Football Hall of Fame in 1973. His 12 catches for 178 yards and a touchdown in the 1958 NFL Championship Game made him a legend. The players knew his background, and they respected his body of work on the field. "Raymond Berry earned more respect in one day than Ron Meyer earned in three years," running back Tony Collins later told reporters.

"This whole word 'control' to me is a word that is not important," Berry said. "Control speaks of having a lot of power, like you're king or something. My ego is not in that area.

"You start talking about Raymond Berry's New England Patriots, you've got the wrong definition," he said. "I'm very privileged to be the coach of this

In 1983, running back Tony Collins ran for 1,049 yards to become just the third player in team history to gain more than 1,000 yards rushing in a season, following Sam Cunningham (1977) and Jim Nance (1966 and 1967). *Ronald C. Modra/Sports Imagery/Getty Images*

STANLEY MORGAN

Nicknamed the "Stanley Steamer," this wideout was one of Steve Grogan's primary targets throughout the late 1970s and 1980s. The Tennessee product, who played for the Patriots from 1977 until 1989, could stretch the field like no other—entering the 2009 season, Stanley Morgan's career average of 19.2 yards per catch was the best in NFL history among the 98 players with 500 or more receptions.

"It means that we were able to connect quite a bit on the long football," said Morgan when he was asked what the record meant to him. "I think a lot of times people tend to forget that, even though as small as I was, I did play running back at [the University of] Tennessee. [So as a receiver] catching the football, I was able to run with it; I was able to avoid being hit. I think when you put those together, that shows that I was able to make big plays to get downfield.

"I don't know if it would be easier to do today because a lot of the passes now are the short ball. [They're] just like a running play, just to pick up four or five yards, as good as running the football. I think you have more of that today than you did when I played. When I played, when we threw the football, we were basically going downfield with it.

Morgan leaps to make a catch against a Seahawks defender during a game at Foxboro Stadium in 1986. *John Sandhaus/NFL/Getty Images*

If we needed four or five yards, we gave it to Sam 'Bam' [Cunningham]."

A four-time Pro Bowler, he was happiest when he was playing for the Foxboro faithful.

"The fondest memories that I have will always be playing there in Foxboro, playing there in front of the fans there," Morgan said. "They treated me very, very well. I don't remember too many negative things that were said about me. They loved me and I loved them. So any time I had an opportunity to play in Foxboro, I loved it."

Stanley Morgan, 1979. *Bill Smith/ NFL/Getty Images*

football team. That's my role. I fit into this just like everybody else. It's a team operation."

The Patriots went 4–4 in the second half of 1984 under Berry's guidance, but the mood in the locker room was much improved, and there was great optimism heading into the upcoming season.

As the 1970s gave way to the 1980s, it was clear that the financial playing field in pro football had changed dramatically from what Billy Sullivan bought into when "The Foolish Club" decided to launch the new league two decades previous. The NFL was becoming a multibillion-dollar industry, and while the Sullivan family continued to have unabashed passion for the Patriots franchise, it was soon clear that they didn't have the financial wherewithal to compete with many of the other teams. Things got even worse when the family decided to get into the concert promotion business. They won the rights to bankroll and promote the Jackson family's Victory Tour, a cross-country tour with Michael and his brothers that many believed would be a cash cow for the franchise. Chuck Sullivan put up the team and the stadium as collateral.

The tour was a colossal failure for the Sullivan family. The size of the stage limited the number of concert-viewable seats in each of the venues by 25 to 33 percent. The Foxborough town fathers refused to allow a show to be played at Foxboro Stadium, an embarrassment for Sullivan and his family. Chuck Sullivan reportedly bickered with the Jacksons over the cost of hotels, concessions, and other amenities. As a result, midway through the 55-stop tour, the Jacksons had had enough of Chuck Sullivan, and promoter Don King took over the job as primary promoter.

Reports differ about how much money Sullivan lost for his trouble, but most agree that it was just over $20 million. The financial hit would deeply impact the future of the franchise.

Tony Eason, New England's first-round pick in the 1983 draft, stepped into the starting quarterback role for most of the 1984 season and posted the best passer rating of his career (93.4). *Jerry Wachter/Sports Illustrated/Getty Images*

CHAPTER 5

AN UNLIKELY RIDE

1985–1986

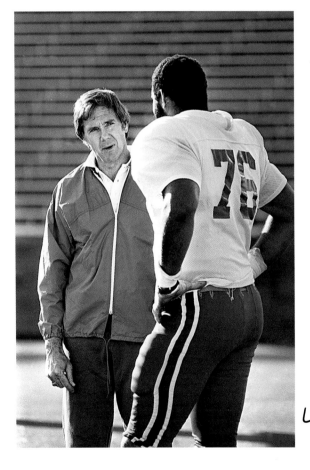

Shown here chatting with Pro Bowl offensive lineman Brian Holloway in 1984, Coach Ray Berry brought an easygoing attitude into the Patriots locker room during the mid-1980s.
Ted Gartland/AP Images

Over the years, Patriots fans had gotten used to riding a roller coaster of emotions. There was the optimism of the early 1960s, which ended soon after their unexpected trip to the 1963 AFC Championship and gave way to the doltish front office and questionable personnel moves of the late 1960s and early 1970s. With the arrival of Chuck Fairbanks and Bucko Kilroy, another wave of good feeling came in the 1970s, as the talented young squad seemed on the verge of a breakthrough, only to see it end with squabbling between Fairbanks and Billy Sullivan in the latter years of the decade.

But nothing could have prepared the Patriots and their followers for the stretch of 1985 and 1986. This two-year period saw the franchise enjoy the greatest season in its history to that point, only to watch it unravel just as quickly. A superior special teams effort and an opportunistic defense helped New England roll through the AFC in 1985 and land its first Super Bowl appearance. The Patriots had real stars on the roster, including future Hall of Famers John Hannah and Andre Tippett and Pro Bowlers like Raymond Clayborn, Craig James, and Steve Nelson. Quarterback Tony Eason had a firm grip on the starter's role. For the first time in 10 years, the franchise mattered again.

But, being the Patriots, their greatest moments were also tinged with disgrace. Multiple off-field incidents marred the celebration, including several

1985 NEW ENGLAND PATRIOTS

OFFICIAL TEAM PICTURE

Color Photo by Frank O'Brien

SEATED: (L to R) — Rich Camarillo, Fred Marion, Roland James, Ronnie Lippett, Raymond Clayborn, Tony Franklin, Rod McSwain, Ernest Gibson, Jim Bowman. FIRST ROW: (L to R) — Derrick Ramsey, Bo Robinson, Lin Dawson, Tony Eason, Steve Grogan, Tom Ramsey, Eric Jordan, Paul Lewis, Robert Weathers, Craig James, Tony Collins, Mosi Tatupu. SECOND ROW: (L to R) — George Luongo (Equipment Manager), Eddie Jackson, Ben Thomas, Ed Williams, Brian Ingram, William H. Sullivan, Jr. (President), Stanley Morgan, Greg Hawthorne, Cedric Jones, Derwin Williams, Stephen Starring, Irving Fryar. THIRD ROW: (L to R) — Garin Veris, Toby Williams, Dennis Owens, Andre Tippett, Don Blackmon, Larry McGrew, Steve Nelson, Julius Adams, Johnny Rembert, Ed Reynolds, Doug Rogers, Jon Norris, Lester Williams. FOURTH ROW: (L to R) — Ken Holland (Asst. Trainer), John Hannah, Tom Toth, Trevor Matich, Paul Fairchild, Brian Holloway, Ron Wooten, Peter Brock, Steve Moore, Darryl Haley, Guy Morriss, Kenneth Sims, Don Brocher (Asst. Equipment Manager). FIFTH ROW: (L to R) — Jim Pluemer (Asst. Trainer), Ron O'Neil (Head Trainer), Dante Scarnecchia (Asst. Coach-Special Teams/Tight Ends), Les Steckel (Asst. Coach-Receivers/Quarterbacks), Harold Jackson (Asst. Receivers Coach), John Polonchek (Special Asst. to Head Coach), Dean Brittenham (Asst. Coach-Strength/Conditioning), Rod Rust (Asst. Coach-Defensive Coordinator), Raymond Berry (Head Coach), Rod Humenuik (Asst. Head Coach-Offense/Offensive Line), Bobby Grier (Asst. Coach-Offensive Backs), Ray Hamilton (Asst. Defensive Line Coach), Eddie Khayat (Asst. Coach-Defensive Line), Jim Carr (Asst. Coach-Secondary), Don Shinnick (Asst. Coach-Linebackers), Mike Swiecicki (Visiting Clubhouse Attendant).

The Boston Globe

The 1985 New England Patriots

bizarre incidents involving talented wide receiver Irving Fryar. There was a fight after a playoff game between one of the Los Angeles Raiders and general manager Pat Sullivan. And, finally, a drug scandal helped send the team careening off the rails and back to mediocrity.

A RARE TASTE OF POSTSEASON GLORY

Heading into his first full season as head coach, Raymond Berry was already turning the Patriots around. He was ushering in an era of good feeling in the locker room, loosening the reins on the veterans who had been pulled tight by Meyer, a noted disciplinarian.

"Patriotism is running high in Boston," wrote *Playboy* magazine in its 1985 NFL preview. "The days of rancor and vicious infighting are over. New coach Raymond Berry has brought a sense of stability to the franchise. He has several super assets, such as runners Craig James and Tony Collins and a passing attack that includes quarterback Tony Eason and receivers Irving Fryar, Stanley Morgan, and Stephen Starring."

Even with all the optimism, the Patriots still appeared to be in the middle of the AFC pack, overshadowed by teams like the high-powered Dolphins (the defending conference champions led by Dan Marino and a wide-open passing attack), as well as the

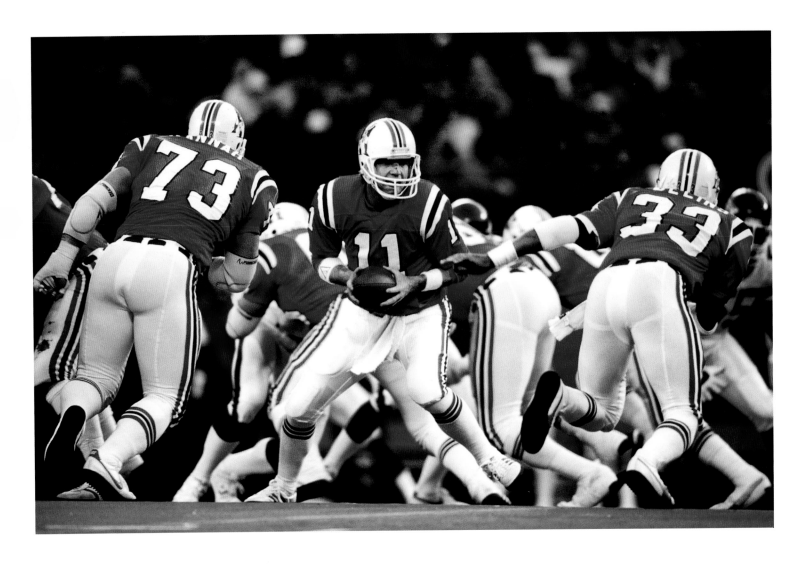

After taking over for Steve Grogan, quarterback Tony Eason (11) helped lead the Patriots to their first Super Bowl appearance in franchise history. Guard John Hannah (73), playing his final season, and running back Tony Collins (33) were other cornerstones of the offense. *Ronald C. Modra/ Sports Imagery/ Getty Images*

Broncos, Seahawks, and Raiders, all of whom had won 11 games in 1984 and appeared primed to do so again.

The enigmatic Eason had unseated Steve Grogan for the starting quarterback job in New England. For a team and a region that had grown accustomed to the grittiness and guts of Grogan, Eason was a distinct change. He was a prototypical pocket quarterback, part of the great 1983 quarterback class that included Dan Marino and Jim Kelly. But teammates always sensed an air of entitlement with Eason, a contrast to Grogan's workingman roots. (Eason was a first-round pick out of powerhouse Illinois, while Grogan was taken in the fifth round out of lesser-known Kansas State.) The fans sensed it too, and when the team started 2–3 with Eason at the helm, there was clamoring for Berry to turn the team back over to Grogan.

And as he had done for so many years, Grogan rallied the troops. With the veteran back at the helm, New England reeled off for six straight wins—until he broke his leg in a Week 12 overtime loss to the Jets. That bruising contest left some wondering if the Patriots had the character to stand toe-to-toe with New York, who gutted out the OT win and led esteemed *Sports Illustrated* writer Paul Zimmerman to say of the Jets, "Maybe, just maybe, this is the year."

But this time under Eason, the Patriots responded, winning three of their last four regular-season games and making the playoffs as a wild-card entry. By this time, they had gained an identity as a team that could run you into the ground—behind James (1,227 yards) and Collins (657 yards), the Patriots gained 2,331 rushing yards as a team, a

Craig James heads for the end zone on a 2-yard touchdown run to give New England a 17–14 lead over the Raiders in the second quarter of the 1985 AFC Divisional Playoff Game. *NFL/Getty Images*

mark that hasn't been matched by any New England team since. In addition, they had an exceptional special teams unit, as well as an opportunistic defense that forced plenty of turnovers. Their knack for getting after the ball had its roots in a drill that Berry had them practice—hiding one ball under stacks of tackling dummies, Berry would let two players at a time roll around in the pads until one of them came up with it.

The team's 11–5 regular-season mark set the stage for a dramatic run through the postseason. First up, the Patriots took on the Jets at the Meadowlands and shocked them with a 26–14 win. The secret to New England's success against the division rival was clear: turn turnovers into points and get a great effort from special teams. The Patriots forced four turnovers on the day—two fumbles, including one

on a kick return, and a pair of interceptions. In addition, Tony Franklin kicked four field goals, and the defense notched five sacks in the unlikely victory.

Next, they surprised the Raiders with a 27–20 win at the Los Angeles Coliseum. It was more of the same—the Patriots forced six turnovers, four of which led to 20 points. A third-quarter fumble in the end zone on a Sam Seale kick return proved to be the game-winner when Jim Bowman fell on the ball for the touchdown. James (104 yards) became the first running back all season to gain 100 yards on the Los Angeles defense. Franklin kicked a pair of field goals, and New England was on its way to the AFC Championship Game against Miami in the Orange Bowl.

During the Los Angeles game, Pat Sullivan spent most of the game on the sidelines taunting the

Raiders players and defensive end Howie Long in particular. "Where are you, Howie? We're coming to get you!" Sullivan hollered at the future Hall of Famer. Although Hannah told Long to "just ignore" Sullivan and play, the two kept at it.

After the game, things really got interesting. "I went up to him after the game to tell him I didn't appreciate some things he'd said about our organization," Sullivan told reporters. "We have pride, too."

"I didn't know him," Long said after the game. "He said, 'Let me tell you who I am.' I said, 'Wait a sec, big guy. You might have thirty million in the bank, but you ain't telling me nothing.' I faked like I was going to hit him, just to see him jump."

While Long faked, his teammate Matt Millen didn't, swinging his helmet at Sullivan and starting a fight between the 5-foot-10, 175-pound general manager and the 6-foot-2, 250-pound Millen and Long, who stood 6-foot-5 and 270 pounds. Millen used his helmet to split open Sullivan's head. The whole thing devolved into an embarrassing skirmish for both sides and ultimately drew a mild apology from Sullivan. "I guess I said things," Sullivan told *Sports Illustrated* a little sheepishly after the

Several Patriots defensive players signal that they have recovered a fumble—one of six Dolphin turnovers in the game—during the AFC Championship Game at the Orange Bowl in Miami on January 12, 1986. *Alan Schwartz/NFL Photos/Getty Images*

confrontation. "But we're a better team, and it feels good to say that. You bet, baby."

"I'm not going to let a classless, silver-spooned, nonworking sob like that tell me anything," Long said. "For me, it's God, [Raiders owner] Al Davis, and my wife, not necessarily in that order. [Sullivan] doesn't sign my checks. He's the jellyfish of Foxboro. Anytime he wants to lock it up in a closet and waive all legal rules, he can give me a ring. I'm listed."

"We put silver-and-black gift-wrapping on the Patriots for Don Shula," said Raiders cornerback Lester Hayes. "Miami has the greatest home-field advantage in the NFL. I give the Patriots two chances: slim and none."

Hayes wasn't the only one who saw it that way. Miami was riding a 9-game home winning streak and had won 18 of its last 19 games in the Orange Bowl. In addition, the Dolphins were 9–3 in home playoff games under Shula. Compounding matters was the fact that the Patriots had an 18-game losing streak in the Orange Bowl, including a withering 30–27 loss that was decided in the final minutes by a Fuad Reveiz field goal. The losing skid dated all the way back to 1966, when New England was able to come out of Miami with a 20–14 win—in the Dolphins' first year of existence. The Orange Bowl jinx weighed heavily on the Patriots' critics, but not in the New England locker room.

"I don't think there's any such thing as a jinx, and neither does the rest of the team," safety Fred Marion told reporters in the days leading up to the game. "If we play up to our capability, we can beat the Dolphins [in the Orange Bowl] or anywhere."

But just days before the conference championship, Fryar made headlines when he missed the Wednesday flight to Miami, saying he had cut his pinkie in a household accident. Later that week, however, he revealed that the injury came during a domestic dispute—reportedly, Fryar struck his pregnant wife, causing her to lash back at him with a knife.

Despite the theatrics, the jinx, and the critics, the Patriots showed up in the Orange Bowl on the afternoon of January 12, 1986, and were in control pretty much from start to finish. New England took the lead for good midway through the second quarter when Collins hauled in a 4-yard pass from

Head coach Raymond Berry gets a ride from his players after New England defeated the Miami Dolphins, 31–14, in the conference championship, sending the Patriots to their first Super Bowl. It was also the Patriots' first win in Miami since 1969. *Dave Cross/NFL/Getty Images*

Eason to make it 10–7. The Patriots pushed it to a 24–7 lead midway through the third when Robert Weathers added a touchdown reception of his own. New England gashed the Miami run defense for 255 yards on the day and forced an astonishing six Dolphin turnovers on the way to a 31–14 win.

After the game, Berry was carried off the field in celebration of perhaps the greatest win in the franchise's first quarter century.

"They did carry me off the field, didn't they?" Berry said with a smile. "I was floating already anyway."

"I feel like *Alice in Wonderland* was a true story, like I'm inside a wonderful fantasy," Pat Sullivan told reporters in the wake of the Miami win.

Wide receiver Stanley Morgan called it his best memory as a member of the Patriots. "That was unbelievable. The love that was shown in that locker room after the game, you can't even put that into words. It was just magnificent."

The win vaulted New England to the franchise's first Super Bowl, where they would face the formidable Chicago Bears in Super Bowl XX.

As for the Super Bowl itself, well, it *started* on a good note. The Patriots took a very early lead when linebacker Lawrence McGrew recovered a Walter Payton fumble on the second play of the game, and New England parlayed it into a 36-yard field goal and a 3–0 lead just 1:19 into the game—the quickest score in Super Bowl history at the time.

"I looked up at the message board," said Chicago linebacker Mike Singletary, "and it said that fifteen of the nineteen teams that scored first won the game.

"I thought, 'Yeah, but none of those fifteen had ever played the Bears.'"

The rest of the afternoon played out like a horror show for New England and its fans. The Chicago defense limited the Pats to 1 rushing first down and just 13 overall, 123 total net yards for the game, and 1-for-10 on third-down conversions. The Patriots

One of the rare opportunities for celebration by New England during Super Bowl XX came on Irving Fryar's 8-yard touchdown reception early in the fourth quarter, which cut Chicago's lead to 44–10. The Bears added a safety later in the quarter. *AP Images*

were able to bottle up Payton (he had just 61 yards on the day), but they were powerless to stop the rest of the Bears' offense. After the initial field goal, Chicago scored the next 46 points, setting a record for most points scored in a Super Bowl.

"It will be many years before we see anything approaching the vision of hell that Chicago inflicted on the poor New England Patriots Sunday in Super Bowl XX," wrote Paul Zimmerman in *Sports Illustrated*. "Don't laugh at the Patriots for their day of futility. You would have to laugh at too many other good teams, the Giants and Rams and Cowboys, who went down 44–0."

FROM BAD TO WORSE

The salt-in-the-wound moment came in the days following the historic loss when the *Boston Globe* published a series of stories that detailed massive drug use and abuse up and down the roster. The stories pointed the finger at Fryar, Raymond Clayborn, and five other players. (Only one, Clayborn, denied the story.) A team doctor was quoted as saying that

ANDRE TIPPETT

The 1980s were the era of great pass-rushing linebackers, and few were better than Andre Tippett. Taken in the second round of the 1982 draft out of Iowa, Tippett started slowly, serving as a special teams contributor and spot starter throughout his first few years in New England. He truly arrived in the middle of the decade, setting a Patriots franchise record with 18 1/2 sacks in 1984 and another 16 1/2 sacks the following season—he is still the only linebacker in the history of the NFL to ever record a total of 35 sacks in back-to-back seasons.

"I just remember seeing Andre as a guy that was dominant," said Patriots coach Bill Belichick, who faced him as an assistant for several years in the 1980s and 1990s. "Tight ends couldn't block him, couldn't run outside to his side, and couldn't run off tackle to his side. He was a very powerful pass rusher, but he was fast and athletic. He used great technique and used his hands well. He was able to get blockers off him well. He had a

Tippett levels Jets quarterback Ken O'Brien during the Wild Card Playoff Game in December 1985. *Ray Stubblebine/AP Images*

couple of years where he had thirty-five sacks over that span—that is unheard of."

He was named to the NFL's 1980s All-Decade Team and was named the NFL Linebacker of the Year by the NFL Players Association three straight seasons from 1985 to 1987; his 100 career sacks are still a New England franchise record.

In 2008, he was inducted into the Pro Football Hall of Fame, joining John Hannah as the only two players to earn induction after spending their entire careers with the Patriots.

"Andre possessed the perfect combination of strength, speed, and athleticism," said Patriots owner Robert Kraft of Tippett at his induction into the Hall of Fame.

Andre Tippett, 1992. *Ken Levine/Getty Images*

"In his prime, Andre was probably the most intimidating player in the game—I can't think of a higher compliment for a linebacker."

Tippett has worked in the Patriots front office since his 1994 retirement, and he currently serves as the team's executive director of community affairs.

"I came here in 2000, and he has been part of this organization in a number of different capacities since then," said Belichick. "He has been a great friend, a great asset to bounce things off of and talk to, and a great ambassador for the organization and football in this area. He talks to our rookies every year. He is always in the halls of the locker room and around the team. He is a very positive influence and example for all of us. He carries himself with great nature, as he should."

none of the seven had tested positive since early January, and several had been clean since the start of the season.

In the wake of the report, the Sullivan family canceled a planned parade for the team. Billy Sullivan later blamed the NFL Players Association for failing to take the drug problem seriously. (Players association chief Gene Upshaw fired back, saying, "I can't think of anything that the Sullivans haven't screwed up yet.")

Asked about the legacy of that team, Fryar sounded as if he was speaking for the long-suffering Patriots fans. "Everything we did for this organization this year is shot," Fryar told reporters after the drug scandal came to light. "This is our one time to the Super Bowl, and now we're right back in the basement. We might never get out."

Instead of an optimistic outlook for the team's chances to get back to the Super Bowl the next season, the drug scandal fostered the opposite environment. The leaking of the test results—which were supposed to remain confidential, according to the league's collective bargaining agreement with the players association—fostered a mood of distrust and created schisms between some players. Who leaked the news? Was it another player with a grudge? Was it management trying to make a player look bad? "This has been the toughest offseason I could ever imagine," offensive guard Ron Wooten told *Sports Illustrated* when the Patriots reported to camp in late July 1986. "And if there is a lack of trust, then I think that could stop us this year."

Beyond the drug controversy, a variety of other questions were dogging the Patriots. In the same *Sports Illustrated* story, charges of gambling were alleged against Fryar. (When the gambling questions were raised, Fryar took a polygraph test and passed it.) The team had lost Hannah and Julius Adams to retirement, two veterans who had done a lot to police the locker room and their teammates. Based on his performance in the Super Bowl, there were doubts about the future of Eason, who looked overwhelmed in the face of a savage rush from the Chicago Bears. And with the continued financial struggles of the Sullivan family, the sale of the franchise became a real possibility.

IRVING FRYAR

The occasionally mercurial Irving Fryar was the first wide receiver taken No. 1 overall in the draft when the Patriots took him out of Nebraska as the top pick in 1984. A supreme talent who was part of one of the greatest Cornhusker teams in history (his teammates included Mike Rozier and Turner Gill), he struggled in New England for several reasons, not the least of which he rarely had a quarterback who could get him the ball on a regular basis. In his nine seasons with the Patriots, Fryar went through nine quarterbacks. There were bright spots—he made the Pro Bowl in 1985, scored the Patriots' lone touchdown in Super Bowl XX, and had 1,014 receiving yards in 1991.

But more often than not, events away from the field overshadowed his playing career with the Patriots. There was a domestic disturbance in 1985 that ended up with him reportedly the victim of a knife attack. There were accusations of drugs and guns, and a bizarre car accident that happened miles from Sullivan Stadium during a game (Fryar had been injured and told the team he was driving home). And he was arrested in 1990 with a gun after a fight outside a Rhode Island nightclub.

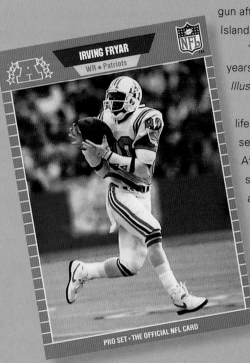

"I have a name for those years," he later told *Sports Illustrated*. "The Mess."

Fryar ended up getting his life together and had a wonderful second act on the NFL stage. After leaving the Patriots after the 1992 season, he played for Miami, Philadelphia, and Washington to close out his career. He made the Pro Bowl four times after leaving Foxborough, and he retired after the 2000 season, having spent 17 seasons in the NFL and coming away with 851 receptions, 12,785 receiving yards, and 84 touchdowns, along with 1 rushing and 3 punt return touchdowns. After his playing career ended, he moved back to his home state of New Jersey, where he opened up a church.

Irving Fryar, 1988. *Rick Stewart/ Allsport/Getty Images*

"It's going to be an interesting year," Pat Sullivan said in July 1986. He certainly wasn't wrong.

The Patriots raised the 1985 AFC champions banner prior to their regular-season opener on September 7 against Indianapolis, and then they proceeded to beat the Colts 33–3. New England started the season red hot, rolling to a 10–3 record that included victories over division rivals Miami, Buffalo, and the New York Jets. The Pats sent five players to the Pro Bowl: Clayborn, Franklin, Morgan (who broke the franchise single-season record for catches with 84), Tippett, and special teams standout Mosi Tatupu.

But it was Eason who was having perhaps his finest year in New England. After leading the team to victory in the season's first two games, Eason went off in Week 3 against Seattle, going 26-for-45 for three touchdowns and a then-team-record 414 yards, although the Patriots lost, 38–31, at home. The team then ran off a seven-game winning streak that included back-to-back comeback wins in November—first a 30–28 victory over the Rams in Los Angeles on November 16, when Eason connected on a 25-yard touchdown pass to Fryar in the final moments of the game, and then 22–19 at home against Buffalo on November 23. He went on to finish the season with 19 touchdown passes and 3,328 passing yards

"I can't say what it's done for his confidence, but it's done a whole lot for mine," Berry said of his quarterback late in November.

But even as they were winning games, the Patriots were not without weird incident. In the first half of the game against Buffalo at home, Fryar was hit hard and suffered a separated shoulder. At halftime, the team doctors decided that Fryar should be sidelined for the rest of the afternoon. According to reports, the receiver changed into street clothes and then left the stadium, climbing into his car for the ride home. About an hour later, Fryar crashed into a tree a few blocks from the stadium. When emergency services reached Fryar, his lip and nose were bleeding, his chest was bruised, and he was lying across the front seat with one foot outside of the car. He was taken to Norwood Hospital in Foxborough and then transferred to Massachusetts General Hospital

Raymond Clayborn earned a second straight Pro Bowl selection in 1986 while adding to his franchise-record 36 career interceptions with New England, but it was the off-field allegations that followed Clayborn and others during the season. *Otto Greule Jr./ Getty Images*

Seen here showing off his support for the New York Mets—who had just defeated the local club, the Boston Red Sox, in the World Series—Irving Fryar generated plenty of controversy in 1986. *Jeff Breland/AP Images*

in Boston, where he was held overnight for testing and X-rays.

Fryar was all right, but the team was beset by numerous injuries, and the Patriots hit the skids late in the season. Back-to-back losses to Cincinnati and San Francisco put them in a must-win situation entering the final game of the season against the Dolphins in Miami. With their backs to the wall, the Patriots came away with a 34–27 victory, setting up a first-round playoff matchup against the Broncos in Denver.

Things looked good for the Patriots, as they hung in against John Elway and the powerful Denver offense. New England took a 17–13 lead midway through the third quarter when Eason (who threw for 194 yards and two touchdowns in the game) hit Morgan on a 45-yard scoring strike that silenced the Denver crowd. The Broncos struck back later in the third with a 48-yard touchdown pass from Elway to Vance Johnson to make it 20–17, Denver's lead.

With just under two minutes to go in the fourth and holding precariously to that three-point lead, the Broncos punted. Mike Horan delivered an impressive kick to Fryar. Rather than let the ball bounce into the end zone so that the Patriots would start

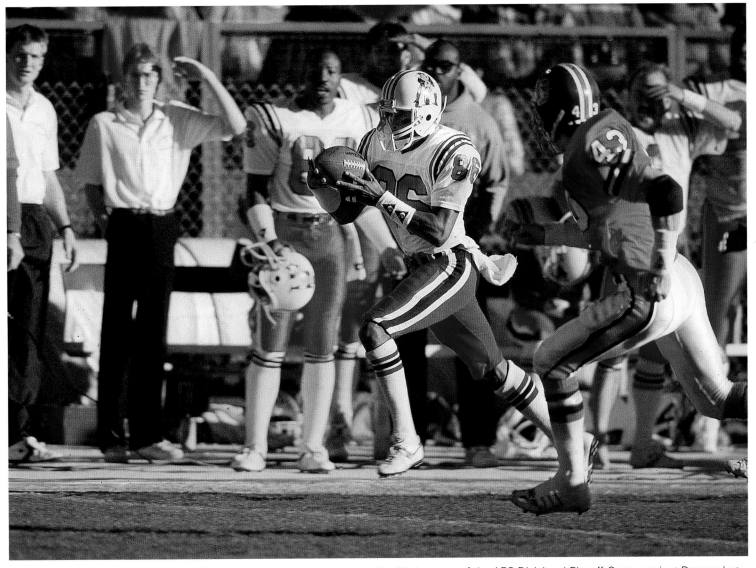

Stanley Morgan races toward the end zone with the go-ahead score in the third quarter of the AFC Divisional Playoff Game against Denver, but the lead didn't hold and the Patriots' season came to an end. *Richard Mackson/Sports Illustrated/Getty Images*

with the ball on the 20-yard line, Fryar fielded it at the 1-yard line and ran it 9 yards upfield before being pushed out of bounds.

With New England starting on the 10, Denver's Rulon Jones sacked Eason in the end zone for a safety on the first play of the series, effectively ending the game and New England's season. While the Broncos went on to the Super Bowl, the Patriots and Fryar were left trying to explain how a playoff game that had started so optimistically could end in such a bizarre fashion.

"There was a lot of room when I fielded the punt," Fryar said. "I thought I could break it. I always do.

"It was almost like a kickoff," he added. "Horan got off a great kick, and I just fielded it and did what my instincts told me to do."

"It's OK to field a punt in that situation," said Berry. "We needed a big play, and he knows what to do with the football. If he would have scored on that play, everyone would have called it a great play."

It was the end of a remarkable two-year run for the Patriots, who would now wait nearly a decade for their next taste of the postseason. In the meantime, they would enter one of the darkest periods in the history of the franchise.

SQUABBLING IN THE RUINS

1987–1992

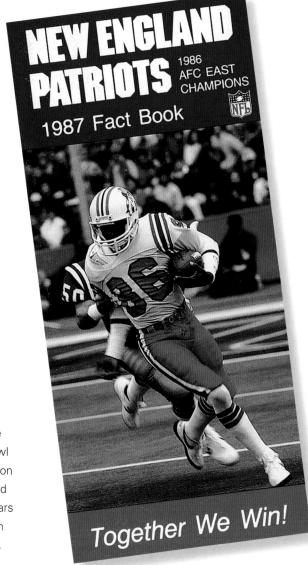

The Patriots' media guide for 1987 featured Pro Bowl receiver Stanley Morgan on the cover, but Morgan and most of the team's regulars sat out part of the season due to the players' strike.

NEW ENGLAND PATRIOTS 1986 AFC EAST CHAMPIONS
1987 Fact Book
Together We Win!

Plagued by economic woes and still reeling from the decision to serve as promoters for the Jackson family's Victory Tour, the Sullivan family was in major financial trouble by the late 1980s. The Sullivans had always struggled to keep pace financially with the rest of the pro football world, but there was never a question about the Sullivans' love of the game and of the franchise. While optimism and good cheer marked the start of Billy Sullivan's reign, it ended sadly for the Sullivan family. By the end of the 1980s, the on-field product had slid backward into mediocrity.

There were still great players—Andre Tippett and Stanley Morgan were Pro Bowl constants throughout the latter part of the 1980s—but there were just far fewer good players than in years past. After helping stock the AFC Pro Bowl roster with players throughout the late 1970s and into the 1980s, the Patriots saw their talent gradually dry up. In 1985, the Patriots sent eight players to the Pro Bowl; by 1989, they would send only one.

The Patriots finished with an 8–7 record in 1987, a season that was dogged by a players' strike. New England fared better with their replacement players than most teams did, as former Boston College star Doug Flutie, acquired from the Bears in a trade at the start of the season, crossed the picket line to play for the Patriots. The team went 9–7 in 1988—with Flutie taking more snaps than Steve Grogan. Both

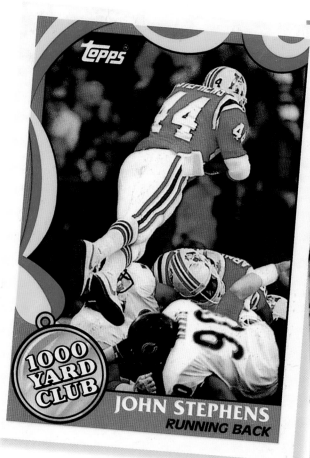

seasons saw New England finish in second place in the division, but 1988 marked the franchise's last plus-.500 season until 1994.

With the continued financial struggles of the Sullivan family, it soon became clear that they would be forced to sell sooner rather than later. With the team on the block, a parade of well-known names—including New York real estate developer Donald Trump, former U.S. postmaster Preston Tisch, and Denver oilman Marvin Davis—were rumored to have looked into the possibility of buying the Patriots. But in March 1988, Paul Fireman, chairman of Reebok, reached an agreement with the Sullivans to buy the team for $82 million, provided he could also purchase Foxboro Stadium. However, a court-appointed bankruptcy trustee overseeing the stadium sale said he would not agree to Fireman's $26-million bid for the stadium unless the deal to buy the team from the Sullivans was complete. The deal wasn't complete by the deadline, and Fireman lost out.

Running back John Stephens (44) ran for 1,168 yards—including a career-high 134 yards against Buffalo on October 23—and earned a Pro Bowl invitation in his debut season of 1988. Although he led the Pats in rushing in each of the next two seasons, he never quite matched his rookie production. *Rick Stewart/ Getty Images*

Former Boston College hero Doug Flutie joined the Patriots in 1987 and became the primary starting quarterback the following year.
Rick Stewart/Getty Images

THE KIAM ERA BEGINS

In the end, the team was sold to Victor Kiam. Many people believed that Kiam, the man who had made Remington shavers a household name, could inject new life into the Patriots. When the announcement was made, Kiam boasted of his New England roots—he graduated from Yale and held a graduate degree from Harvard Business School—and said he was "very excited with the opportunity of association with one of the NFL's premier franchises."

"My business is in New England, I live in New England, and I have received my education in New England schools," Kiam announced at the press conference. "I look forward to continuing the tradition of fielding a team of which all New England, and

particularly our football fans, can be very proud. . . . I especially look forward to working hand-in-hand with the Sullivan family in achieving the ultimate success—bringing the Super Bowl trophy to New England."

Under the terms of the sale, Billy Sullivan would remain as club president and a minority shareholder, while Patrick Sullivan retained his position as general manager. Billy Sullivan said in a statement, "On behalf of our fans, coaches, players, and front-office staff, I wish to extend our warmest welcome to Victor Kiam. Victor combines great personal achievement with a personal commitment to winning, which will substantially enhance our organization. I very much look forward to working with Victor in the years ahead."

Victor Kiam took over the Patriots in 1988, and after a 9–7 finish that year, the team went a combined 6–26 over the next two seasons—accompanied by several off-field headaches. *Damian Strohmeyer/Sports Illustrated/Getty Images*

Things didn't end up so neat and tidy, however. Kiam had leaned on other local businessmen for help in purchasing the team, namely Fran Murray, who put up $25 million to help purchase the team and had an option to exit in three years at a guaranteed profit of $13 million. Three years later, Murray wanted out, and Kiam needed to come up with $38 million for Murray's share—money Kiam didn't have. Murray extended the deadline, but only after Kiam agreed to give the NFL partial ownership. Murray also announced he would begin searching for a buyer, and the league, in effect, took control of the team.

A deal was eventually worked out in 1991, but by that time, the franchise had slid even further down the NFL food chain. Kiam was losing money

on the team, partly because he was saddled with a terrible stadium contract—he didn't see a penny of revenues from concessions, parking, or luxury suites at Foxboro Stadium.

On the field, things weren't any better. In 1989, the Patriots led the NFL in number of players on the injured-reserve list with 19; the next-closest club had 11 and the league average was 5. In his final year as a starter, Steve Grogan led New England to wins over division foes the Jets, Bills, and Colts, but the Patriots won only two other games. Five of their 11 losses were by fewer than seven points, and while they weren't going to be headed to the Super Bowl any time soon, there appeared to be enough talent around which to build for the future.

Pro Bowl linebacker Johnny Rembert (52) tried to hold the defense together through an injury-plagued 1989 season. Rembert, who played in all 16 games, is seen here trying to tackle the Raiders' Bo Jackson during a November loss. *Vic Milton/NFL/ Getty Images*

But in the wake of that 5–11 season—the only sub-.500 season of Berry's coaching career with the Patriots—Kiam and Patrick Sullivan demanded that Berry relinquish control over personnel decisions and that he reorganize his staff. The head coach wanted to fill the offensive and defensive coordinator jobs with men from his current staff, but Kiam and Sullivan wanted him to go outside the organization. Berry refused—his contract gave him control over the football operation—and on February 27, 1990, he was fired. He left the Patriots after five and a half seasons with a better record (48–39) than any of the nine coaches in the history of the franchise.

In his own press conference at a Cambridge hotel, Berry took a philosophical view of his firing.

"It boils down to a real simple formula, actually," said Berry. "I was hired to coach the team and make coaching decisions. Per our agreement, that was my area and that's what I have done. In Pat's job as general manager, Pat has to make general manager's decisions, and one of those is that if he doesn't agree with my coaching decisions, he can fire me. And he's done that. . . . It's about as simple as that. He's doing his job and I'm doing mine. And we both have the right to do that because this is America."

The next day, the team announced that former defensive coordinator Rod Rust would return to the franchise as head coach. Rust had led the Patriots defense from 1983 to 1987, the last three and a half years under Berry. At the time of his hiring, the 61-year-old Rust was the second-oldest coach in the NFL.

Refuting any concerns about his age, Rust said in his introductory press conference, "Energy level and enthusiasm and commitment to what you want to do are the critical factors." He added that he had never harbored a burning ambition to be a head coach. "It's not like this is some profoundly deep event in my life. I'm very happy about it."

HITTING ROCK BOTTOM

But things got worse under Rust, with the franchise hitting its unquestioned low point. On the field, the team finished a disastrous 1–15 in 1990, its only year under Rust.

Things had started positively enough under Rust—there was a narrow loss to the Dolphins in Miami and an impressive win over the Colts in Indianapolis. They then lost 14 straight—badly. Only three of the losses were less than double-digit defeats. The capper came in the season finale against the New York Giants, a 13–10 loss at Foxboro Stadium. While the Patriots submitted their best defensive effort of the season (they held New York to just 111 passing yards), it was, in effect, a road game. With most of the 60,410 in attendance composed of Giants fans who had followed their team north from the tri-state area for the afternoon, the Patriots were hooted out of their own stadium by an army of New York football fans. The few New England fans in attendance left no doubt as to what they thought about the future of the franchise, with one dissatisfied customer holding a sign that read: "Patriots 1990–1991: Rust in Peace."

The 1–15 Patriots scored only 181 points in 1990—the fewest total in the NFL since the 16-game schedule was adopted in 1978. They never held the lead in any of the season's last seven games. They broke the previous team mark for worst record, set by the 1981 club that was 2–14. For the first time in the team's 31-year history, New England was winless at home. Small wonder that a *USA Today* readers' poll found the 1990 Patriots to be the worst pro football team of the Super Bowl era, beating out even the winless Tampa Bay Buccaneers of 1976.

Indeed, this was a lousy football team. Between 1990 and 1992, the Patriots won a total of nine regular-season games.

"The toughest year probably was 1990," recalled Tippett. "I know Rod Rust took on the responsibility of being the head coach that year, and I think that that was tough on him. We all tried to help as much as we could by working hard in practice and giving him one hundred percent and not trying to take advantage of the fact that it's my defensive coordinator and so I am going to take some days off. I think a lot of us were dedicated to working hard and trying to help him help this organization, but as you look back now, there were so many holes in the boat that you just did not have enough fingers to stop the leaking and the hemorrhaging that was going on. You have to take your hat off to a guy like that who

Rod Rust had seen success as the team's defensive coordinator in the 1980s, but his tenure as head coach in 1990 was nothing short of a disaster. *NFL/Getty Images*

agreed to take on that responsibility. It was almost a sinking ship before it got going."

Remarkably, things were even worse off the field. On September 17, 1990, *Boston Herald* reporter Lisa Olson was working on an off-day story when she was verbally assaulted in the locker room by a collection of players, including Zeke Mowatt, Robert Perryman, and Michael Timpson.

The NFL's investigation into the incident, which resulted in a 108-page report, said Mowatt was seen fondling himself near Olson and asking her: "Is this what you want?" The reporter told the NFL how the players "positioned themselves inches away from my face and dared me to touch their private parts." Owner Kiam made things even worse, calling Olson a "classic bitch" and wondering aloud why female reporters couldn't do their interviews on the field instead of in the locker room.

"I'm sure [the incident] looms large in Lisa's life, but I can't get excited about it," Kiam said.

The sportswriter fled the country and later settled a civil suit with the franchise for a reported $250,000. Meanwhile, the losses kept piling up. The team was run on the cheap by inept management. With the sex scandal, they were horrifically unlikable. Any charm that came with playing or watching a game at what was now known as Foxboro Stadium had long since worn off. Fueled by alcohol and emboldened by a lack of security, the crowds had become unruly and occasionally dangerous. With plenty of other

DICK MACPHERSON

It never seemed like Dick MacPherson was ever having a bad day. The man they called "Coach Mac" was always ebullient, always upbeat, and always smiling. A longtime New Englander, MacPherson—who was born in Old Town, Maine—came to the Patriots from Syracuse, where he coached the Orangemen from 1981 to 1991. (Prior to that, he was also a head coach at the University of Massachusetts.) His overall record at Syracuse was 66–46–4 and included an undefeated season in 1987, when his team finished 11–0–1 and tied Auburn in the 1988 Sugar Bowl.

He never enjoyed the same level of success with the Patriots, but he did turn a 1–15 team into a 6–10 one in his first year in New England; he received serious consideration for NFL Coach of the Year honors because of it. Things turned sour for him in his second season. MacPherson missed

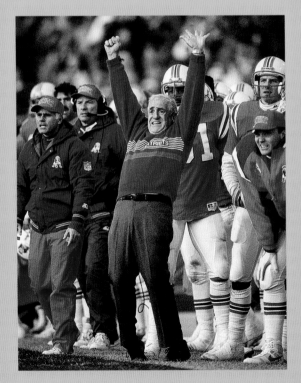

seven games with acute diverticulitis, which required surgery. In addition, philosophical differences between him and CEO Sam Jankovich started badly and got worse. After MacPherson's second season ended 2–14, he reportedly resisted Jankovich's idea that some of the 12 assistant coaches be dropped. So the head coach was fired.

The day he was let go—two years and a day after he had been handed the position—he talked about the day he took the job and how it was a dream come true for a lifelong New Englander.

"I dreamed of coming here and putting this thing together," he said at a news conference the day he was fired. "I didn't stop dreaming until right now."

Dick MacPherson celebrates on the sideline during a game against the Jets in 1991. *Damian Strohmeyer/ Sports Illustrated/Getty Images*

Victor Kiam is looking none too pleased while answering reporters' questions in the wake of the Lisa Olson incident. *Richard Howard/Time Life Pictures/Getty Images*

talented teams to watch—the Red Sox, Bruins, and Celtics, all of whom enjoyed great success in the late 1980s and early 1990s—fans stayed away in droves. When it appeared that team management was going to move the Patriots, few raised opposition.

"It was frustrating at times. You know, it was what it was, and it was nothing that I had any control over. All I had control over was how I prepared, how I contributed to the team," Tippett recalled. "And like I said, it was kind of frustrating because you become the laughingstock a little bit, and I kind of grew up in the league where you saw things like that happen. You know, I can remember back in the early eighties, you were always threatened to get traded to Green Bay at the time; Green Bay was awful in the early eighties, and then look what happened to those guys."

A BRIEF REBOUND UNDER COACH MAC

In an attempt to add some luster to the organization, Kiam appointed Sam Jankovich as the team's chief executive officer and owner's representative in December 1990. Promising a "new era" in Patriots football, the former athletic director at the University of Miami did not promise widespread change within the organization.

"There are not going to be massive changes," Jankovich told reporters at his introductory press conference. "I don't think they are necessary. There are good people here. We're not coming in with a broom and sweeping it. If there are changes to be made, I'll make them."

But things were so miserable during the season that, shortly before Rust was fired after the end of the year, Jankovich confessed, "We just have to get this year over with, and when January comes, start putting all the pieces together."

One of the final links to the old days was broken in January 1991 when Pat Sullivan, upset with his diminished role under Jankovich, resigned.

"I recognized that things are not permanent, and I felt very strongly that I wanted to have a role within the organization that was a responsible role," Sullivan told reporters. "When I recognized that I

New head coach Dick MacPherson addresses his team at training camp in Smithfield, Rhode Island, prior to the 1991 season. *Damian Strohmeyer/Sports Illustrated/ Getty Images*

really wouldn't have the responsible role that was important, it was time to move on."

On January 7, 1991, Maine native Dick MacPherson was named the third Patriots head coach in as many years. The team had tried to keep the hiring a secret, but the news went public when MacPherson's brother, a parish priest, announced it to his flock. MacPherson was able to energize the franchise, however briefly. He wasn't the best X-and-O guy, but his zest for the game was infectious, and it rubbed off on his team.

"What the hell is wrong with a sixty-year-old man being excited?" he asked with a smile at his introductory press conference. "It's easy to be a young coach. The secret is to be an old coach. I read where President [George H. W.] Bush is proud that he was the youngest pilot in the U.S. Navy during World War II. But that's not an accomplishment. The guy I like is the oldest pilot in the Navy!"

The 1991 Patriots finished with a 6–10 record, but the team won three of its last five games. On paper, the team wasn't all that good. New England had just two Pro Bowlers—tackle Bruce Armstrong and tight end Marv Cook—and precious little else. But they were a fun club. They kick-started the season by breaking a 14-game losing skid with a 16–7 win over the Colts in Indianapolis. They also won a pair of overtime games at home and came away with wins over Houston, Buffalo, and the New York Jets. They went out on a high note. Playing in front of just 20,131 fans (the smallest non-strike stadium crowd in franchise history) in the regular-season finale, the Patriots pulled out a dramatic, come-from-behind 23–17 overtime win over the Colts. A touchdown pass from Hugh Millen to rookie tight end Ben Coates with seven seconds left tied the game, and Millen added to his burgeoning legend with a touchdown throw to Michael Timpson in overtime that put the Colts away and sparked a celebration that included an ebullient MacPherson tackling Millen. The rest of the team celebrated too—19 players had clauses that paid out after five wins, and the victory cost Kiam as much as a quarter of a million dollars.

Toward the end of the season, Jankovich engaged in a little back-patting. In an editorial in the *Boston Herald*, he wrote about the exciting progress that was being made in Foxborough. "A year ago Friday, I joined the New England Patriots organization," Jankovich wrote. "Three days after taking the position of chief executive officer, our team traveled to the Meadowlands in New Jersey, where we lost to the Jets, 42–7. As many of you know, a great deal has happened since that game a year ago, including a victorious return to New Jersey last Sunday when we defeated the Jets, 6–3, in a tough, physical, hard-fought football game. Sunday's victory demonstrated the progress we have made in this organization."

MacPherson's feel-good approach won him coach of the year votes, but after hearing the news, he wasn't having any of it.

"Number one, the talent level [in 1990] was not 1–15," MacPherson told reporters. "Number two, I think that Sam Jankovich being hired by Victor Kiam to try and bring this whole thing around is there. The attitude of the players toward ownership that things are going to be done the right way to make sure they could perform to the best of their abilities is there. Thirdly, [there's] the emergence of Hugh Millen, which is a bonus."

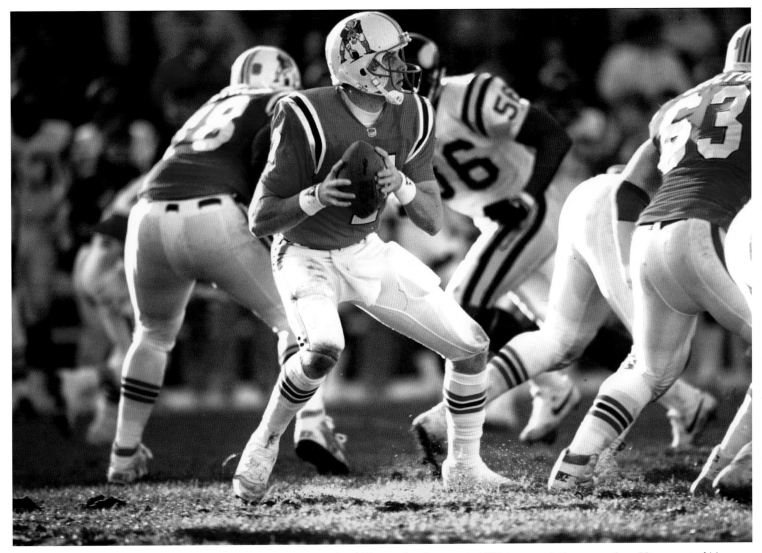

Hugh Millen helped the Patriots improve from a one-win team in 1990 to a six-win team in 1991 by completing more than 60 percent of his passes in his first year in New England. Millen also threw 18 interceptions against just 9 touchdowns. *Anthony Neste/Sports Illustrated/ Getty Images*

It all went south for MacPherson and Jankovich the following season. The Patriots lost their first nine games—the worst start in franchise history—and Millen and Armstrong, arguably their two best players, suffered season-ending injuries.

"You run out of words," Millen told *Sports Illustrated* in November 1992. "I try to give a good quote. I try to think of something, but I'm about used up. It hurts like being hit in the stomach with a sackful of nickels. I said that already. You reach a point where you literally drive home and wonder how you could feel any worse."

In addition, the coach was hospitalized with acute diverticulitis (an inflammation or infection of the intestines) in early November. Tight ends/ special teams coach Dante Scarnecchia took control of the team and was at the helm when New England won its only two games of the season, back-to-back victories in November.

"You've got to roll with the punches to play in New England," quarterback Tommy Hodson said shortly after MacPherson went down. "You feel sick for Coach Mac. He's been through a lot. He's a good man going through some tough times. We lost

BRUCE ARMSTRONG

The Patriots have had some great offensive linemen—
John Hannah, Leon Gray, and Jon Morris—but one of the best was
Bruce Armstrong, a durable tackle out of Louisville who had to be
dragged out of the starting lineup.

Of 220 possible non-strike games over the course of his
career, Armstrong started in 212 (including the last 118 of
his career consecutively), making him the single player with the
most starts of any Patriot. A six-time Pro Bowler, he only missed
games in the second half of the 1992 season, after tearing the
medial collateral ligament and both his anterior and posterior
cruciate ligaments in his right knee against Buffalo in a November
1 loss to the Bills.

"Bruce is the greatest left tackle in the history of
the franchise and one of the best players ever to wear a
Patriots uniform," owner Bob Kraft told reporters when
Armstrong announced his retirement in 2001. "His unique
accomplishments justify waiving
the rule for induction into our hall
of fame, where he will take his
proper place alongside the very
best who have played for
the Patriots."

**A battle of Bruces. New England's
Pro Bowl tackle Bruce Armstrong
takes on Buffalo's Pro Bowl
defensive end Bruce Smith in a
1997 game at Gillette Stadium.**
Mitchell Layton/Getty Images

New England
PATRIOTS

GAMEDAY

Tackle
BRUCE ARMSTRONG
Two-Time
Pro Bowl Selection

November 6, 1994
Cleveland Stadium
$3.00

the leader of our football team, but at least this isn't something strange or controversial."

ORTHWEIN SPARKS OPTIMISM

There was a ray of hope, however. James Busch Orthwein, the great-grandson of beer baron Adolphus Busch, mercifully took the team off Kiam's hands in May 1992 in a deal that totaled a little less than $110 million in payments and debts he assumed as part of the purchase. A St. Louis native, Orthwein reportedly had his eyes on moving the team to his hometown to replace the recently departed Cardinals. When word got out that the Patriots could be on the move—reportedly they were to be renamed the St. Louis Stallions—few people could muster even a shrug.

But the Patriots had a lease with local business-man Bob Kraft, who had quietly started to position himself to take over the franchise. Kraft started buying up the land around the stadium in the late 1980s and then bought Foxboro Stadium when it was put up for sale in 1988.

"For a while we thought we wanted to own the team," Kraft said in a 1992 interview with *Sports Illustrated*. "Now that we have the stadium, you realize you're much better off this way. You go to the game, and if the Patriots lose, you're disappointed for about forty-five minutes. Then you ask, 'How much popcorn did we sell?'"

Stymied in his attempts to move the team, Orthwein started the process of trying to overhaul the franchise. Just a few months after he assumed ownership of the Patriots, the team resorted to offering discount packages of tickets for $10 apiece—fans had to buy at least four—to boost advance sales for the home opener against Seattle. "Football is a consumer product," Orthwein, a former ad executive, told the *Boston Globe* after the ticket promotion boosted advance sales by 10,000. "Just as beverages and other products fall into certain slots, football appeals to a certain audience, too. I do think that many of the marketing practices used with other products apply to professional football as well."

Although the 1992 team went 2–14, the new owner knew he had to do something about the on-field product. That's when he went looking for a new coach, and his target was Bill Parcells.

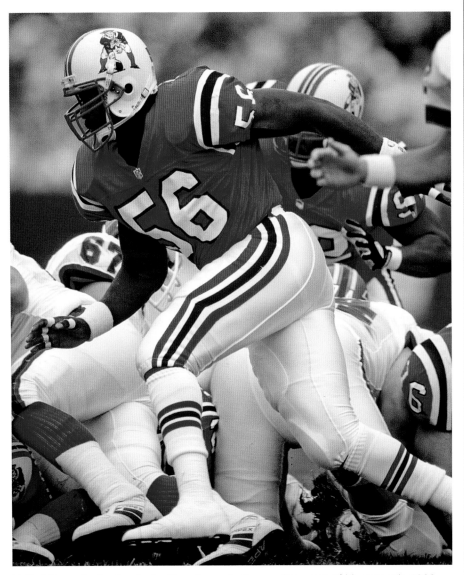

Hall of Fame linebacker Andre Tippett was in the waning years of his career in 1992, but he still led a weak Patriots defense with seven sacks. *Allen Dean Steele/NFL/ Getty Images*

BIG TIME

1993–1996

Heading into the 1993 season, James Busch Orthwein had his sights set on bigger and better things for his Patriots, hoping to break a string of losing seasons by hiring a big-time head coach. *Damian Strohmeyer/ Sports Illustrated/Getty Images*

When the nightmarish 1992 season came to a close, so did the reign of Dick MacPherson and Sam Jankovich. On January 8, 1993, owner James Busch Orthwein fired MacPherson. The next day, Jankovich resigned. The ever-upbeat MacPherson refused to say a bad word about the organization, despite the less-than-honorable treatment he received while he was the head coach.

"This one setback will not deter my optimistic feeling about this great game," MacPherson told reporters. "How much I treasure the memories. I thought I'd be here a little longer. . . . I loved being the head coach here. I hope the next guy will like it as much as I do. We've got some great people here. This is not a 2–14 football team, and I have to live with that. . . . Having a great organization that everybody could be proud of . . . that was my dream."

MacPherson's dream may not have come true, but Orthwein's was about to: Bill Parcells was available, and Orthwein was going to get him.

Bill Parcells had been out of work, at least as far as coaching was concerned, since announcing his retirement after leading the New York Giants to a second Super Bowl victory in 1991. Over the next two years, his name surfaced as a candidate pretty much any time a head coaching vacancy appeared. When the Patriots came calling, Parcells was lured by the promise of complete control—not just on the field, but also in personnel decisions and the front office.

Other candidates did interview for the job, leaving some to wonder what might have been: Mike Ditka, Buddy Ryan, and Packers defensive coordinator Ray Rhodes also met with Orthwein about the job. Ditka as head coach of the New England Patriots certainly would have been entertaining, but when you consider his post-Bears career, he was by no means the man to lead a franchise out of the wilderness. (He would go on to spend three seasons with New Orleans, compiling a 15–33 record, with his most notable moment coming when he traded away all of the Saints' 1999 draft picks, plus their first-round selection in 2000, for running back Ricky Williams.)

Ryan was coming off a fairly successful stint with the Eagles in Philadelphia, but he was still considered enough of a loose cannon that the Patriots opted to stay away. Instead, Ryan went to Houston and served as the defensive coordinator of the Oilers for one season. His main claim to fame that year was a sideline fistfight with offensive coordinator Kevin Gilbride. Ryan also later served as the head coach in Arizona for two seasons, finishing with a 12–20 record. Among those who fell short, Ryan probably had the best chance at the Patriots job because of his connection with Patrick Forte, the Patriots' vice president of administration, who had worked for Philadelphia when Ryan was coach there.

Rhodes would have been an interesting choice—an excellent defensive coordinator in Green Bay and San Francisco, he would have been the first African-American coach in the history of the franchise. But he would ultimately prove to be overwhelmed as a head coach; he coached Philadelphia for four seasons and Green Bay for a single season and had a 37–42–1 mark with zero postseason wins.

None of them had the Hall of Fame resume that Parcells had. So, in the end, it was Parcells. On January 21, 1993, Orthwein introduced him as the new head coach, complete with a five-year, $5.5 million contract. Forte was the general manager and James Hausmann the business boss, but it was Parcells who was running the show.

"Bill is going to tell us what he wants," said Orthwein. "Patrick is going to work hard at finding what he wants, and Jim is going to find out how to afford it and get it done."

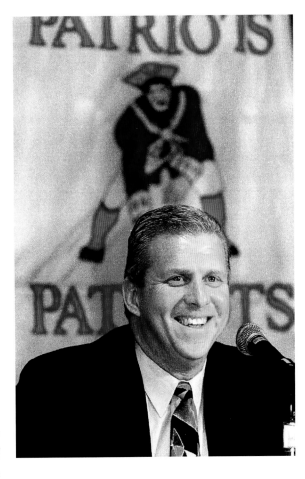

Bill Parcells' arrival in New England was greeted with great enthusiasm by fans and the media. At his introductory press conference, Parcells pledged to improve the team to championship-caliber status. *John Mottern/AFP/Getty Images*

Parcells' introductory press conference was such an event that Massachusetts Governor William Weld made an appearance. "I want to improve the Patriots to the point where we can compete for a championship," Parcells said after being introduced as the twelfth head coach in the history of the franchise. "I pledge to the fans and the players that I won't rest until we approach that goal."

SUDDEN IMPACT

The change was instantaneous. January 21, 1993, marked the dawn of a new age in New England. Fans and media alike were giddy at the prospect of Parcells at the helm of the Patriots—the team took a then-record 979 season-ticket orders the same day the announcement was made. Foxboro Stadium was considered one of the worst venues in the league, the entire roster needed to be turned over, and there was still the threat that the entire team was going to pack up and move to St. Louis. But they had Parcells.

BILL PARCELLS

On the surface, the marriage between Bill Parcells and the New England Patriots was as unlikely a union as you could find. Lauded as one of the finest coaches of his generation, Parcells had many parallels with the great Vince Lombardi: Both were gritty, East Coast guys from Jersey who believed that football was not just a game but also a test of character. As coaches, they endorsed a tough, physical game. Neither shied away form expressing their opinions, often in colorful language. In addition, Parcells played high school basketball at River Dell High School in New Jersey in the mid-1950s for Coach Mickey Corcoran, who played high school ball under Lombardi two decades before that.

Corcoran later told reporters that he saw more than a little bit of Lombardi in Parcells. "The thing about Lombardi," Corcoran told *Sports Illustrated* in 1995, "is that he didn't know a great deal about basketball, but he was a great basketball coach. I think Bill possesses many of the traits Vince had. They're disciplinarians. They're committed to excellence and totally dedicated to coaching. And they both placed a priority on the coach–player relationship, which I think is the most overlooked aspect of coaching. Whether it's the thirties, the sixties, or the nineties, human nature doesn't change. Players look for help, look for direction, look for a way to win, and they'll follow the coaches like Lombardi and Parcells who can lead them."

The legend of Parcells was born in the 1980s in New York. He took over as head coach of the Giants in 1983 at the end of one of the woeful stretches in that team's history. One of the NFL's flagship franchises with a proud tradition, the Giants had

Bill Parcells, 1994. *Scott Halleran/Allsport/Getty Images*

posted just one winning season in the previous 10 years and were only 5 years removed from one of the most ignominious moments in NFL history, the "Miracle in the Meadowlands." (Needing to just kneel down and kill the clock at the end of a game against Philadelphia, the Giants instead chose to call a running play. Quarterback Joe Pisarcik fumbled the football on the exchange with the running back, and the Eagles recovered the football and scored the game-winning touchdown.)

In Parcells' first season in New York, things weren't looking any better. He made waves when he benched starting quarterback and first-round pick Phil Simms in favor of Scott Brunner. That resulted in a 3–12–1 season after which management came close to ditching Parcells in favor of University of Miami head coach Howard Schnellenberger. But the following year, he made Simms the starter again, and slowly but surely, things started to turn around. There were 9–7 and 10–6 finishes in 1984 and 1985, and a 14–2 finish in 1986 that led to a win in Super Bowl XXI. Four years later, Parcells and the Giants secured a second title with a victory over Buffalo in Super Bowl XXV.

Then Parcells announced his retirement in the months following the second Super Bowl victory; he later divulged that he had health problems. (While working as a TV analyst in 1991, he had an angioplasty, the first of many corrective procedures on his heart.)

However, as was the case with Lombardi—who, after leaving the Packers, came out of retirement to coach the Redskins—the lure of coaching was too great for Parcells, and the thought of reviving a franchise was perhaps an even greater temptation. In 1992, he came oh-so-close to returning, committing to become the Tampa Bay Buccaneers' new head coach. But at the last minute, he turned his back on Tampa, leaving Bucs owner Hugh Culverhouse to tell reporters, "I feel like I've been jilted at the altar." (Afterward, Culverhouse rushed into what could only be described as a shotgun wedding with Sam Wyche. The Bucs won just 35 percent of their games over the next four seasons before Wyche was shown the door.)

As promised, Parcells took the Patriots back to championship contention, solidified with their defeat of the Jacksonville Jaguars in the 1996 AFC Championship Game. Unfortunately, New England came up short in the Super Bowl, and then the coach walked away, to a job with the division-rival New York Jets. *Winslow Townson/AP Images*

From that point forward, Parcells became the go-to name for every vacant coaching job—"Uh-oh, coach *fill-in-the-blank* looks like he could be on the hot seat. Is Parcells interested in returning to football?" He interviewed with Green Bay, but that didn't work out. Then came James Busch Orthwein, offering up complete control of one of the most god-awful franchises in all of football. *A latter-day Vince Lombardi? Coming to Foxborough?*

Parcells was particularly intrigued by the Patriots job for two reasons. First, he did have a history in New England. He had been the linebackers coach there in 1980, and it was as an assistant under Ron Erhardt that he was tagged with the nickname "The Tuna." There are two schools of thought as to where the nickname came from. The story told by Parcells is that one of the other assistants tried to fool him with a prank involving a free turkey giveaway, only to hear him respond, "Who do you think I am? Charlie the Tuna?" The second comes from veteran linebacker Steve Nelson, who said the players called him "Tuna" because he looked like one. Whichever story is true, the nickname took hold quickly.

Parcells was also interested in the New England job because he was promised free rein by Orthwein. He would have complete control over football operations, an appealing prospect for a coach who was used to getting the players he wanted. No GMs or personnel guys gumming up the works. He was going to be in charge. Nothing was put in writing between the coach and owner, but no matter—the on-field decisions were going to be made by him or, barring that, guys who answered to him.

As the team worked its way up the standings, including winning a division title in Parcells' second season on the job, tensions emerged after Orthwein sold the team. The new owner, Robert Kraft, didn't share Orthwein's belief in giving total control to the head coach on personnel decisions. Soon, Parcells was butting heads with Bobby Grier (newly promoted as director of player personnel) and other front office executives. After the coach made good on his promise to return the Patriots to championship-caliber status by leading them to Super Bowl XXXI, Parcells walked away.

The new era in Foxborough came complete with its own brand-new logo. *Jed Jacobsohn/Getty Images*

The Patriots had a new coach and, later that year, a new look. On March 31, it was announced that the old Pat Patriot logo that had adorned the side of the team's helmets for years was gone, replaced with a newer, sleeker-looking minuteman. (The new mascot was tagged with the nickname the "Flying Elvis.") In addition, the primary colors of the uniform changed from red to blue. Now, all they needed were some new *players* to wear those fancy new uniforms.

To that end, the roster started turning over pretty quickly. Every successful coach has his guys, players he loves who will follow him from team to team like disciples, and Parcells was no different. Many of the new faces were actually old faces, players who had been a part of his Giants teams of the late 1980s and early 1990s and helped him win a pair of Super Bowl titles: Myron Guyton, Dave Meggett, Steve DeOssie, Adrian White, Reyna Thompson, and Matt Bahr were just a few of the old New York players who followed Parcells from the swamps of Jersey to New England during his first few seasons with the Patriots. In addition, Parcells brought with him eight former assistants who helped build two Super Bowl champions in eight years, a group of coaches that included Romeo Crennel, Charlie Weis, Al Groh, and Johnny Parker, most of whom jumped at the chance to reunite with their old boss. "He called me to see if I wanted to come with him," Parker told *Sports Illustrated* shortly after the old gang reunited in Foxborough. "I asked him one question: 'Do you really want to do this thing?' He said, 'As much as I ever wanted to do anything in my life.'

"That was enough for me."

Not joining the rest of Parcells' lieutenants in New England was former New York defensive assistant Bill Belichick. Belichick had been the defensive coordinator for the Giants from 1985 through 1990 and was widely credited with being the true power behind the throne. While Parcells received tremendous credit, Belichick was seen as a young mastermind—Belichick's defensive game plan that helped the Giants defeat Buffalo, 20–19, in Super Bowl XXV is on display at the Pro Football Hall of Fame. Instead of New England, Belichick would head to Cleveland to become the new head coach of the Browns.

No matter—the rest of the crew was in place. Now, the real work began.

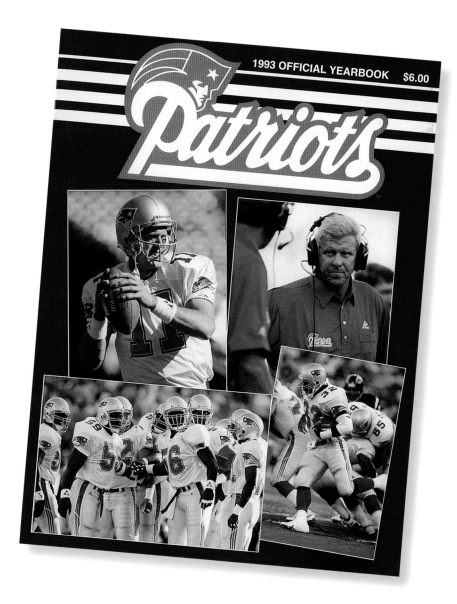

BLEDSOE OR MIRER?

In the spring of 1993, the task was simple: The Patriots had the first pick in the draft, and if you were a New England football fan, you were either a Drew Bledsoe guy or a Rick Mirer guy. Bledsoe was a tall, strong-armed pocket passer out of Washington State. At 6-foot-5 and 230 pounds, he *looked* like a pro-style quarterback, the kind of player you could slap on a brochure to tease possible season-ticket buyers into shelling out hard-earned money to support the team. Then, there was Mirer, a star at Notre Dame who was more athletic and had better wheels. At 6-foot-3 and 210 pounds, he had the size, but he was also considered

Even as a rookie, Drew Bledsoe was ready to lead his team on the field for the 1993 opener. He struggled in his debut (14 of 30 with one interception), but the young quarterback proved to be the first major step toward building a winning squad in New England. *Rick Stewart/Allsport/ Getty Images*

to be a classic leader, even more so than Bledsoe. He didn't have the pro-style background of Bledsoe, but that Notre Dame pedigree could go a long way. If you squinted real hard when you looked at Mirer, you might be able to see a little Joe Montana in him.

The pick turned out to be Bledsoe, much to the relief of the pass-catchers on the team.

"What really helped out more than anything was drafting [Drew] Bledsoe," recalled tight end Ben Coates. "When we drafted Bledsoe in '93, me and him clicked together and the chemistry and everything was there. The coaching staff went with it and rolled with it, and it carried us quite a way."

The quarterback and the coach eventually fell into something of a love-hate relationship. Parcells was East Coast grit, while Bledsoe was more West

Coast cool. Parcells was an old-school guy in the mold of Lombardi. As the son of a coach, Bledsoe had an appreciation for the history of the game. It was just hard to think about that when you're 21 years old and the first pick in the NFL Draft. "Just remember one thing: I don't want a celebrity quarterback on my team," Parcells barked at Bledsoe during training camp in 1994. "I hate celebrity quarterbacks. You understand?"

"You know exactly where you stand with him," Bledsoe told reporters shortly after signing. "His rules are simple. Do what he says. The things he asks aren't simple—he might want you to be at a certain weight, or he might want you to learn a certain number of things in a short period of time—but you had better do them. Because he will check."

Shots of a red-faced Parcells unleashing his sideline wrath on the young quarterback were commonplace on TV and in the newspapers, so much so that Bledsoe's mother, Barbara, once complained to reporters, "I don't like it. That's not going to help Drew perform better." (Parcells' response? "Tell her not to watch the games.") But together, Parcells and Bledsoe would deliver a jolt of respectability to the beleaguered franchise. The changes weren't immediately evident in the win column—New England went 1–11 out of the gate in 1993, including a Week 4 blowout loss to the Jets at the Meadowlands that saw them get hooted off the field. But all the while, there was a gradual sense of improvement. The deficits became smaller and smaller as the season went on, finally breaking through on December 12 with a 7–2 win over the Bengals at home, a victory that put them at 2–11 on the year. In the end, the Patriots won the last four games of the 1993 season, including a dramatic overtime win over the Dolphins in the season finale at Foxboro Stadium that kept Miami out of the playoffs. The optimism helped deliver hope to a team that hadn't seen the postseason since 1986.

Off the field, things were also getting interesting. Orthwein was making it known he would sell the team for the right price, and there was no shortage of suitors. Bob Kraft, along with noted author Tom Clancy and local businessman Jeffrey Lurie, were all potential buyers for the team. But it was clear that Kraft held the upper hand: A season-ticket holder since 1972 and native of Brookline, he had always aspired to own a local sports franchise, but the timing was never right. In the case of the Patriots, Kraft took a roundabout approach in buying the team, taking almost 10 years from when he first set out to finally acquiring the entire franchise and stadium, as well as all the land that surrounded it.

He started in the mid-1980s by gradually acquiring pieces of real estate around the stadium—the Sullivans owned the team and the stadium, but they didn't own the surrounding land—and eventually locked up the purchase rights to 300 surrounding acres. In 1985, Kraft bought a 10-year option on the property, paying a group of Boston businessmen $1 million a year for first dibs to buy the land someday for $18 million.

Ben Coates' diving touchdown catch against Seattle on September 19 wasn't enough to prevent the Patriots from dropping their third straight game to start the 1993 season. The tight end led New England with eight TDs on the year. *Damian Strohmeyer/Sports Illustrated/Getty Images*

Leonard Russell's 116 yards rushing against the Arizona Cardinals in Week 5 helped secure the Patriots' first win of 1993. The 24-year-old running back rushed for a total of 1,088 yards for the season, only the seventh 1,000-yard season in team history. *Bernstein Associates/Getty Images*

An enthusiastic Bob Kraft greets fans before the start of a game against the Colts at Foxboro Stadium in December 1994. The new owner's passion for the team was infectious in New England. *Susan Walsh/AP Images*

Kraft had a chance to buy the team when the Sullivans put it up for sale in 1986, but he continued to bide his time, and Victor Kiam stepped forward and bought the team for $87 million. But Kraft kept moving forward. In 1988, he purchased the stadium, putting up $25 million with a partner to buy it from the Sullivan family, easily outbidding a $16 million offer from Kiam. He now owned the stadium and the land around it, and with Kiam thinking about dumping the team after a couple of miserable seasons, it finally appeared to be his time.

But Kiam ended up selling to Orthwein. After Orthwein found he wouldn't be able to move the team to St. Louis, he offered Kraft $75 million to buy out the remainder of the lease at Foxboro Stadium, which, if Kraft agreed, would free Orthwein to move the Patriots to St. Louis. Kraft counter-offered. Instead, Kraft said he'd buy the whole thing for $172 million, a record price for an NFL franchise at that point. With Kraft holding the stadium lease, Orthwein had no choice but to accept the deal. The two agreed on the deal on January 21, 1994, and officially signed the paperwork on February 25, making Kraft the fourth owner in the history of the franchise.

KRAFT TAKES CONTROL

Fans responded quickly to the sale. A day after the deal became official, the franchise sold 5,958 season-ticket packages, a staggering display of faith in a team that had given fans very little to cheer about the last few seasons.

"My objective is to bring a championship to New England," Kraft told reporters after the deal became final. "We didn't do this to be a doormat for other teams. We want quick NFL approval to take advantage of the unique window of opportunity in the free agent market and work very closely with Coach Parcells to take advantage of it and give us a very special team coming into this season."

Orthwein was perhaps the least memorable owner in the history of the franchise. He didn't have the flair of either Sullivan or Kiam or the local roots of Kraft, but the part he played in Patriots history is a positive one. He was a stopover, the right man for the transitional period during which they went from middle-class franchise to the penthouse. He guided the team through a rocky period, and in many ways, he accomplished more in his 20 months as owner of the Patriots than most owners do in a lifetime. He spent the money needed to pull a legend out of retirement and stood back while Parcells put a top-flight personnel team in place. He boosted the financial worth of the team and did whatever he could to re-establish it as a relevant player on the NFL landscape. Ultimately, he left the team in far greater shape than when he took control.

Oh, and he made himself a tidy profit in the process.

Back on the field, the 1994 season brought the big splash: New England won its last seven games, rolling into the postseason with a 10–6 record and a division title. In that stretch, Bledsoe truly arrived as an elite NFL quarterback. Against Minnesota on a cold November afternoon at Foxboro Stadium, the Pats dug themselves a 20–0 halftime hole, but behind their young quarterback, they answered the bell in the second half, eventually tying the game late. New England won the coin toss at the start of overtime and started on its own 33-yard line. Then Bledsoe started them marching downfield. He completed five passes to bring his team to the Vikings' 25 and eventually

worked the Patriots down to the 14-yard line, where it looked like they were going to settle for a field goal. But fullback Kevin Turner slipped quietly out of the backfield, and the quarterback—who ended up going 45-for-70 for 426 yards and three touchdowns in the game—found him in the end zone to complete the 26–20 comeback win.

The increased reliance on the passing game was something out of the ordinary for Parcells, who built a run-first, pass-second team in his days with the Giants. Those New York offenses were all about imposing their will through a brutally tough ground game, controlling the clock, and beating the tar out of their opponents. But behind Bledsoe, the Patriots were airing it out on a regular basis. In 1994, Bledsoe led the league in attempts, completions, passing

yards, and interceptions. While the running game stumbled (only one player, the unfortunately named Marion Butts, ran for more than 400 yards that season), there were no such worries about the passing game; five players finished the season with at least 400 receiving yards, topped by tight end Ben Coates, who had 1,174.

"Drew felt, for one, that I was going to catch every play that he threw to me," Coates said about the chemistry he developed with Bledsoe. "Even if you were in the flat, he would throw it one hundred miles an hour, and he knew I was going to catch it. He knew I was somebody that he could depend on when the game is on the line, a crunch situation . . . he knew where I was going to be at all times. If something broke down or didn't go the way it was supposed

Kevin Turner's fourth-quarter touchdown reception against the Vikings on November 13 sealed a dramatic come-from-behind victory for the Patriots—and kick-started a seven-game winning streak to end the 1994 season.
Damian Strohmeyer/Sports Illustrated/Getty Images

On New Year's Day 1995, the Patriots faced the Cleveland Browns and Parcells' old coaching assistant, Bill Belichick, in New England's first postseason appearance since 1986. *David Liam Kyle/Sports Illustrated/ Getty Images*

to go, he knew exactly where I was going to be, so it worked out for him and also for me."

Parcells made no bones about the style of play he preferred, but in this situation, you work with what you have.

"You have to use what you have available to you and try to use it the best you can," Parcells told reporters that fall. "Eventually, you'd like to construct a system that plays along the lines of the way you'd like to play. I'd rather be playing a slightly different way. But hopefully, we'll get around to doing that someday."

Parcells and the Patriots earned a wild-card berth and were due to play old friend Belichick and his Browns in Cleveland. The game was tied 10–10

at halftime, but the Browns pulled out a 20–13 win to end New England's season.

Despite the quick playoff exit, an era of good feeling started to bloom around the franchise. Locally, they had made tremendous inroads—their success that fall coincided with a players' strike in Major League Baseball (and the Celtics were coming off their worst season in 15 years), meaning a sports-starved region that fall only had the Pats to focus on. They made the most of it, as TV ratings and attendance skyrocketed. They had changed their uniforms and added a new, sleeker logo. In addition, they signed a radio deal with WBCN, one of the pre-eminent rock stations in the country. The Patriots were now *cool*. On April 29, 1995, for

BOBBY GRIER

While Bobby Grier wasn't the last straw in the Bill Parcells–Robert Kraft relationship, his escalating status in the Patriots front office throughout the mid-1990s certainly laid the groundwork for Parcells' journey out of town.

A former assistant coach and scout for the Patriots in the 1980s and early 1990s, Grier was named the Patriots' director of pro scouting after Parcells took over as head coach in 1993. In the beginning, the two had a warm, cordial relationship. In 1995, Grier was promoted to director of player personnel by Kraft, who believed his team should have a consortium of decision-makers. Parcells, who had been wooed to New England by the previous ownership with the promise of final say on all personnel matters, was upset. As his new title suggested, Grier took control of many of the personnel decisions—much to the consternation of Parcells. Their relationship began to cool, and in 1996, when the Patriots went with Grier's decision to draft a wide receiver over Parcells' desire for a defensive lineman, according to Grier, that sealed it for Parcells.

"Any time before the draft, Bill and I would talk five or six times a day,"

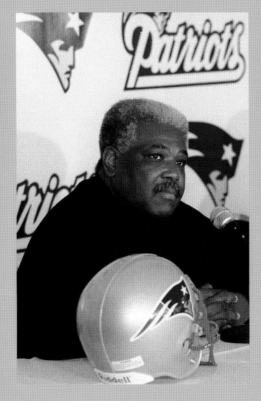

Bobby Grier, 1999. *David Kamerman/AP Images*

Grier told reporters in 1997. "We would have lunch together. We would talk at football practice. Bill is a great storyteller, and I would enjoy those talks. Then, after the [1996] draft, we might have talked a couple of times a day and most of it on the phone. It was never like it was before. I had to deal with some things, some attitude from him. Let's just leave it at that."

When Pete Carroll was hired as head coach in 1997, Grier was again promoted, this time to vice president of player personnel. But a weak link in the overall chain of command was detected—if players had a problem with something, they simply went over Carroll's head to Grier with their complaint. As a result, the players saw Carroll as weak and ineffectual. He quickly lost control of the locker room, and he was fired after three seasons.

Instead of the move paying off for Grier, however, things soon backfired: In 2000, Bill Belichick took command of the franchise and put an end to the dysfunctional front office hijinks. Grier was fired shortly after the 2000 NFL Draft, and assistant director of player personnel Scott Pioli took over Grier's responsibilities.

the first time in franchise history, every home game for the upcoming season sold out before the season began. On a national level, the Pats had become a force to be reckoned with, a talented young team on the rise that had a peerless coaching staff and strong ownership.

But just as things were looking up, the relationship between Kraft and Parcells started to sour. The things Parcells had agreed to when he signed his contract with Orthwein were being taken away

from him under the new ownership. When it came to personnel decisions, Kraft decided to give new director of player personnel, Bobby Grier, more and more control, much to the consternation of the head coach. Parcells asked Kraft to void the final year of his contract, and the owner obliged.

The team struggled in 1995, losing five of the first six games and finishing with a 6–10 mark. Bledsoe's completion percentage dropped to just over 50 percent, and the Patriots ranked 23rd out

Linebacker Willie McGinest led the Patriots with 11 sacks in 1995 for a defensive squad that was ranked near the bottom of the league. He moved to defensive end in 1996 and played in the Pro Bowl. *J. D. Cuban/Getty Images*

of 30 teams on offense. The defense was no better, allowing more yards than all but two other teams.

The tensions between the head coach and the rest of the organization bubbled over at the 1996 draft, where there was a major clash over who to select with the seventh overall pick. Parcells preferred to build his team from the inside out and wanted a defensive lineman; Grier and others in the organization were enamored with the breakaway speed and big-play capability of Ohio State wide receiver Terry Glenn. Ultimately, the Patriots selected Glenn, sending Parcells into a rage.

"For about twenty-four hours, I made up my mind that I was finished here," Parcells later told *Boston Globe* columnist Will McDonough. "I didn't want any more to do with this guy [Kraft]. But you know, here's what I'm going to do. I'm going to get in the greatest shape of my life. I've already started to lose weight. I'm not leaving here 6–10. I'm going to come back here and prove I'm better than that. I did a lousy job. I know that. But next year we've got a chance to be pretty good. I'm just going to have as little to do with this guy as I can and just focus on coaching the team. Then when it's over, I'm out of here. I'm going to retire. This will be my last year coaching."

Parcells did get some good news when it was announced that his longtime defensive coordinator Bill Belichick would be able to rejoin him for the 1996 season. Fired after five seasons as a head coach in Cleveland, Belichick would become an assistant head coach in New England, as well as run the secondary.

A TRIP TO THE SUPER BOWL

As the drama between Kraft and Parcells continued to play out behind the scenes, the 1996 Patriots soon were recognized as one of the best young teams in the AFC. Six Pro Bowlers—including Bledsoe, running back Curtis Martin, and electric kick returner Dave Meggett—formed the nucleus of a team that won 7 of its first 10 games to vault to the top of the AFC East. The only thorn in their side was the Denver Broncos, who came into Foxboro Stadium on November 17 for a clash between the two premier young teams in the AFC—New England was 7–3, while Denver was 10–1. With a cavalcade of stars, the Broncos were seen as a true measuring stick for the Patriots, a way to

TERRY GLENN

While the ascension of Bobby Grier drove a schism between Bill Parcells and Robert Kraft, things went from bad to worse with the appearance of Terry Glenn in 1996.

The Patriots held the seventh overall pick in the 1996 NFL Draft, and New England was looking at going one of two ways. There was Terry Glenn, an All-American wide receiver at Ohio State who was sought after by some members of the Patriots offense for his soft hands and game-breaking speed. Only problem was that Parcells didn't want anything to do with Glenn, instead craving a big defensive lineman, such as Cedric Jones, Duane Clemons, or Tony Brackens, to help build his defense from the inside out. Kraft and director of player personnel Bobby Grier wanted Glenn, and they made it clear in no uncertain terms who New England should take—the choice would be Glenn.

"I didn't know what was happening," Parcells later recounted in his autobiography. "They said that Glenn was going to be the pick. I said we had agreed it was going to be a defensive player and that was it. I was mad as hell. I said, 'OK, if that's the way you want it, you got it.'"

Parcells made up his mind to quit over the decision, but then he reconsidered. However, the die had been cast. Parcells was furious that he was not allowed to make the final call on personnel decisions, a key factor in what drew him to New England in the first place. And even though Glenn ended up recording 90 receptions for 1,132 yards and 6 touchdowns in his rookie season, he came to embody the growing tension between Kraft and Parcells.

Parcells left after the 1996 season, but Glenn spent six seasons in New England and caught 329 passes for 4,669 yards and 22 touchdowns while in a Patriots uniform. After a stormy split with New England and Coach Bill Belichick in 2001, Glenn was reunited with Parcells in Dallas; Parcells later confessed to being wrong about the receiver.

Terry Glenn, 1999. *Brian Bahr/Allsport/Getty Images*

Curtis Martin runs through the fog and the Steelers defense during the divisional playoffs in Pittsburgh on January 5, 1997. Coming off his second-straight 1,000-yard season, Martin gained 166 yards and scored three touchdowns in the contest. *Rick Stewart/Getty Images*

gauge their status against one of the traditional powerhouses of the conference. But New England came up way short, suffering an embarrassing 34–8 loss, punctuated by Broncos tight end Shannon Sharpe. When the outcome of the game was no longer in doubt, the veteran was caught by NFL Films on the sidelines placing a mock phone call to the president, imploring him to call out the national guard because they were "killing the Patriots."

But New England was able to shake off that loss and win four of its final five regular-season games on the way to an 11–5 record. It was the most regular-season victories for the franchise since it posted an identical mark back in 1986.

In the playoffs, the Patriots beat Pittsburgh in a divisional contest at Foxboro Stadium that was swathed in fog, pulling out an easy 28–3 win thanks to three touchdowns and 166 yards rushing by Martin. It was expected that they would be heading to Mile High Stadium to meet the Broncos in Denver. But thanks to Jacksonville's 30–27 upset win

behind quarterback Mark Brunell, the Patriots hosted the AFC Championship Game for the first time in franchise history. In a freezing cold Foxboro Stadium, the Patriots smothered the Jaguars, 20–6, to advance to the second Super Bowl in franchise history.

Despite their best attempts to downplay the matter, Kraft and Parcells were the big story all week at the Super Bowl. The "will-he-stay-or-will-he-go" drama angered the Packers, who were in a lather that all the attention was on the New England soap opera and not on what they were about to accomplish—namely, restore the proud name of Green Bay to its rightful spot atop the football world.

In Super Bowl XXXI at the Louisiana Superdome, the Packers jumped out to a 10–0 lead before two short touchdown passes on play-action fakes by Bledsoe—first to tight end Keith Byars from 1 yard out and then a 4-yard toss to Coates—gave New England the lead after one quarter. Then Green Bay scored 17 unanswered points in the second quarter and headed into halftime with a 27–14 lead.

The Patriots were in striking distance in the third quarter when Martin rumbled for an 18-yard touchdown run to cut the Packers' lead to 27–21. But things blew up in their faces when Green Bay kick returner Desmond Howard put a charge into the game on the following play with a 99-yard return for a touchdown, paving the way for a 35–21 Packers win. The final nail in the coffin came late in the contest when Green Bay defensive lineman Reggie White—foolishly left one-on-one against young New England lineman Max Lane—picked up back-to-back sacks late to seal the contest.

After the game, the writing was on the wall. Parcells did not fly home with the team, instead leaving with his agent. It was later revealed that in the weeks leading up to the Super Bowl, Parcells made over 50 calls to Hempstead, New York—the headquarters of the New York Jets. Belichick would later say the whole circus involving Parcells was a distraction at the Super Bowl. "Yeah, I'd say it was a little bit

Keith Byars (41) and Ben Coates (87) both scored first-quarter touchdowns in Super Bowl XXXI, but the Pats were only able to score one more touchdown in the game, while the Packers racked up 35 points en route to a 14-point victory. *Charles Krupa/ AP Images*

of a distraction all the way around," he told author Michael Holley in the book *Patriot Reign*. "I can tell you firsthand, there was a lot of stuff going on prior to the game. I mean, him talking to other teams. He was trying to make up his mind about what he was going to do. Which, honestly, I felt [was] totally inappropriate. How many chances do you get to play for the Super Bowl? Tell them to get back to you in a couple of days. I'm not saying it was disrespectful to me, but it was in terms of the overall commitment to the team."

No one was really all that shocked when Parcells officially stepped down as head coach of the Patriots on January 31, 1997, just five days after the Super Bowl. During his farewell press conference, he was asked about having control over personnel. It was a

DANTE SCARNECCHIA

In the transitory world of the National Football League, few coaches can boast a record of longevity like Dante Scarnecchia. Even fewer can say they've gone as long as he has with one team. With the exception of two seasons, Scarnecchia has been a part of the New England Patriots family since 1982. He's worked under six different head coaches during his time in New England, been to five Super Bowls, and held a wide variety of jobs—special teams coach, offensive line coach, defensive assistant, offensive line coach, and interim head coach.

"To think I've been here this long, and have had this kind of run, is extraordinary," Scarnecchia said in early 2008. "Plenty of coaches have come and gone since I've been here, a lot of them much better coaches than I am.

"It's been a really fortunate, unbelievable set of circumstances. I can't explain it."

He joined the Patriots in 1982 as a special teams and tight ends coach. After a brief two-year stint (1989–1990) with the Indianapolis Colts, he returned to the Patriots in 1991, where he spent two years under Dick MacPherson as a special teams and offensive line coach, even taking over head coaching duties on an interim basis in 1992 when MacPherson was ill for the final eight games of the season. From 1993 through 1996 under Bill Parcells, Scarnecchia was initially a special assistant, but he later became a defensive assistant for linebackers, the first time he had coached defense in the NFL.

When Parcells left the team after the 1996 season and Pete Carroll was hired as the new head coach, Scarnecchia returned to his role of special teams coach. In Carroll's final season with the Patriots, Scarnecchia was reassigned to be offensive line coach, a position he holds to this day. Bill Belichick additionally appointed Scarnecchia as the team's assistant head coach in 2000.

Dante Scarnecchia, 2004. *Rick Stewart/Getty Images*

"A smart football coach," Belichick said of Scarnecchia in 2008. "A detailed guy who works hard and who gets his players to work hard, too, and who isn't worried about where the credit goes. Which is about all you can ask of a guy."

Much of the attention at Super Bowl XXXI was focused on Coach Bill Parcells and questions about his future in New England. As it turned out, less than a week after the game, Parcells announced that he was stepping down as head coach. *Brian Bahr/Allsport/Getty Images*

deal he had agreed to in principle under Orthwein, but never got in writing. Consequently, it was a point that ultimately finished him in New England. He responded with one of the most memorable sound bytes in the history of New England sports: "If they want you to cook the dinner, at least they ought to let you shop for some of the groceries."

He didn't leave without a fight—New England was able to wrest four draft picks from the Jets in exchange for the head coach. But Parcells and New York won the day in the court of public opinion. Kraft was seen as the guy who forced Parcells out of town.

As they had done in the mid-1970s and mid-1980s, the Patriots came close to achieving real, sustained success, only to slide back down toward NFL mediocrity. But this time, things would ultimately turn out differently.

8

TRANSITION

1997–2000

New Jets head coach Bill Parcells and new Patriots head coach Pete Carroll share a laugh before the game at Foxboro Stadium on September 14, 1997. Carroll had big shoes to fill in New England, but he came out on top in this first meeting with the ex–Patriots coach, with a 27–24 overtime win. *Winslow Townson/AP Images*

Bill Parcells had departed for New Jersey, signing a six-year, $14.2 million contract with the Jets. In his place, Kraft and the Patriots decided to hire Pete Carroll, a younger coach with an impressive resume as a defensive coordinator. He had been the Jets' defensive coordinator from 1990 to 1993 and took over as head coach for the 1994 season, leading New York to a 6–10 record. He then spent two years as defensive coordinator with the 49ers before New England gave him another shot at a head-coaching job. On February 3, 1997, the 45-year-old Carroll became the thirteenth head coach in franchise history, signing a five-year contract with New England.

It was very clear from the start that Carroll was going to be far different from Parcells. His ebullient nature and West Coast cool were a far cry from the Lombardi-like approach of Parcells. Carroll could play piano and harmonica, as well as juggle. His earnestness and genuine enthusiasm for the task that lay ahead shone through in his first press conference.

"We're following a heck of a coach. We're following a heck of a season," Carroll told reporters. "It couldn't get any tougher. I like it. It'll be fun."

Acknowledging that people would compare every move he made to his predecessor, Carroll had a quick response: "As great as Johnny Carson was, Jay Leno wasn't going to try and be Johnny Carson. He was going to be himself. And I'm going to be myself. I'm going to be me. What will really be compared is how we win."

Asked who was going to "shop for the groceries"—a not-so-veiled reference to Parcells' shot at Kraft on his way out of town—Carroll had another quick reply: "What's all this about groceries? All I know is when I go shopping with my wife, she makes me push the cart."

Kraft assured the media that Carroll was not an interim coach by any means. "I want everyone in the organization to know he's not on trial and that the club won't panic if it suffers a setback next season," he said in explaining the deal.

Around New England, reaction was mixed. While no one was sure what to expect with Carroll, the players were happy to be liberated from Parcells' gulag and out from under his shadow. Several of

them, including Drew Bledsoe, lined up to take shots at the old coach. "He didn't say anything to any of the players," Bledsoe told reporters. "You'd like to think that, when you go through some of the things we all went through with the guy, he'd at least say goodbye. But from the get-go, Bill has been about Bill. That's the way it is. That's the way he is."

Bledsoe also spoke optimistically about the new field boss. "It's exciting to come in here to a positive atmosphere, where the coaches are excited about working with you and where you're excited about being here," he said. "It's not like before, when you came in every day wondering if you were going to get beat down. . . . Now, you don't feel like somebody is waiting to cut you down when you came to work."

"Bill's yelling and screaming had worn itself out," Ben Coates told reporters. "I don't think his leaving will affect us. Once we're on the field, things will be the same, just quieter."

TEDY BRUSCHI

While other players received more accolades, went to more Pro Bowls, and churned out better numbers than Tedy Bruschi, no player was more readily identifiable as the heart of the great New England teams of the early days of the twenty-first century than Tedy Bruschi.

Bruschi was a third-round draft pick out of Arizona in 1996 who was an undersized defensive lineman with a big motor. He quickly distinguished himself as part of a new generation of linebackers in New England, a group that included players like Willie McGinest and Ted Johnson who started their careers under Bill Parcells but came of age under Bill Belichick.

"We [didn't] really know what to do with him," said Belichick, who also joined the Patriots in 1996 as assistant head coach to Bill Parcells. "All along the way he heard, 'too small,' 'too slow,' 'too this,' 'too that,' and [he] just kept getting better and better and working harder and outworking and out-competing pretty much everybody he faced."

Bruschi was the emotional centerpiece of the Patriots, a fiery leader who—even though he grew up in California and attended the University of Arizona—became an adopted son of New England. He ended up going to five Super Bowls and was on the winning side three times. But 10 days after winning his third Super Bowl ring, Bruschi was admitted to the hospital because of a stroke. A long rehab process followed, but the linebacker returned to the game and played another three-plus years, finally calling it a career days before the start of the 2009 season.

"There isn't one moment and I'll never have just one moment," Bruschi said, looking back on the amazing arc of his professional career. "I'm very fortunate to have so many."

Tedy Bruschi was the emotional leader on the Patriots defense for 13 seasons. *Jim McIsaac/ Getty Images*

Bruschi capped off the lone Pro Bowl season of his career with a sack and an interception in the 24–21 win over Philadelphia in Super Bowl XXXIX, on February 6, 2005. *Jed Jacobsohn/Getty Images*

NEW COACH, NEW ATTITUDE

After a few months under Carroll, it was clear the team was pleased with the change. No one was walking on eggshells anymore, and the loose vibe was certainly more pleasing to the veteran players. The head coach even started a pickup basketball league among the players.

"Pete Carroll has turned the team over to the players," veteran defensive back Willie Clay told reporters. "It's different this year. This is the New England Patriots, coached by Pete Carroll. It's our team. Last year, we were just players on Bill's team."

Even without Parcells, there was still more than enough left for another trip to the Super Bowl. "There's enough talent here for a Super Bowl repeat, only this time it'll be quieter," wrote *Sports Illustrated*'s Paul Zimmerman of the 1997 Patriots. With Parcells in New York and Carroll running the show in New England, things started nicely for Patriots fans—New England started 2–0, winning back-to-back games by a combined score of 72–13 and making Carroll the first coach in the history of the franchise to start 2–0. Meanwhile, Parcells' Jets were 1–1 after the first two weeks.

Then came the apocalyptic showdown that was Tuna Bowl I. It marked Parcells' return to Foxborough for the first time as head coach of the Jets and Carroll's first chance to coach against the team that had fired him a few years before. The rivalry between the two teams had never really cooled, and now, it was on par with the Red Sox and Yankees.

The two head coaches at the center of the drama were taking their own unique view of the pre-game hype. Parcells: "I think you're making too much of this. All that hype evens up after the first punch in the mouth." Carroll: "It's a wonderful buildup for the fans. I love it. It's great."

Patriots cornerback Ty Law also reflected on the meaning of the game. "This is not the AFC Championship Game. This is not the Super Bowl," he told reporters. "But there is no way you can escape that this game means a lot to a lot of people's egos."

As it turned out, the game did live up to the hype. In front of a national TV audience—and signs directed at Parcells that read "BILL PAR SELL OUT" and "CAN THE TUNA"—Bledsoe threw

Drew Bledsoe came out firing in the 1997 season opener, throwing for 340 yards and four touchdowns in a 41–7 thrashing of San Diego. Bledsoe and company won their first four games under the new coach. *David Stluka/AP Images*

In 1997, Curtis Martin posted his third straight season with more than 1,000 yards rushing, while also chipping in another 296 receiving yards, all despite missing three games to injury. *Al Messerschmidt/ Getty Images*

his ninth touchdown pass of the season on the fifth play of the game to give the Patriots an early edge, sending the Foxboro Stadium crowd into a frenzy. Running back Curtis Martin was, in the words of teammate Chris Slade, "a beast," finishing with 40 carries for 199 yards. But the Jets hung in and eventually tied the game at 24 with 31 seconds left in regulation on Neil O'Donnell's 24-yard touchdown pass to Keyshawn Johnson. New York then forced a fumble on the ensuing kickoff, but the Patriots' Mike Jones blocked Jets kicker John Hall's 30-yard field-goal attempt. New England eventually won it in over-time on a 34-yard field goal from Adam Vinatieri.

The Patriots went 5–1 to start the season, but in many ways, that win over Parcells and the Jets

was the highlight for a 1997 Patriots team that could be labeled as underachievers. They finished with a 10–6 record and clinched another division title—their second straight—with a 14–12 win over Miami in the regular-season finale. But they did not make it back to the Super Bowl. In fact, they didn't even return to the AFC Championship. In the postseason, they beat the Dolphins, but fell to the Steelers in a dramatic divisional playoff game in Pittsburgh. That one ended when, with the Patriots driving for what would have been a go-ahead score, future New England linebacker Mike Vrabel sacked Bledsoe and forced a fumble with less than two minutes remaining in the game to ensure a 7–6 win for Pittsburgh.

TUNA KEEPS TWEAKING THE PATS

That offseason was a difficult one for New England. In March, Parcells and the Jets signed Martin to an offer sheet he knew the Patriots wouldn't be able to match. A third-round pick out of Pittsburgh in 1995, Martin had developed into one of the premier running backs in the AFC. He was the NFL's Offensive Rookie of the Year when he rushed for 1,487 yards and 14 touchdowns and caught 30 passes for 261 yards and 1 TD. In 1996, he rushed 316 times for 1,152 yards and 14 touchdowns, while catching 46 passes for 333 yards and 3 touchdowns. In 1997, Martin missed three games with injuries but still gained 1,160 yards on 274 carries and scored 4 TDs, along with 41 receptions for 296 yards and a touchdown.

With their number-one ground threat gone to a division rival, the Patriots turned to the draft to try to replace him. With their first overall selection, they chose Robert Edwards, a bright young star out of Georgia. Edwards had an immediate impact in New England, rushing for 1,115 yards in his rookie season. Buoyed by receiver Terry Glenn (team-high 67 catches) and tight end Ben Coates (team-high 792 receiving yards), the Patriots offense was in fine form for much of the 1998 season, and they went through high-octane stretches during which they were among the best units in the league. In four of their first five games, the Patriots scored at least 27 points, with the high-water mark coming in a 40–10 blowout of the Kansas City Chiefs in Week 6.

Patriots fans may not have expected Robert Edwards to be Superman, but he was being asked to fill some pretty big shoes at running back with the departure of Curtis Martin. Edwards came through with 1,115 rushing yards and a team-high 12 total touchdowns. *Mike Powell/ Allsport/Getty Images*

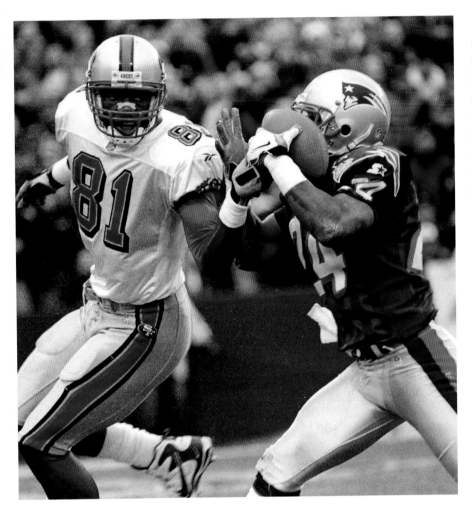

All-Pro cornerback Ty Law led the league with nine interceptions in 1998, including this one in a 24–21 win over San Francisco in December. *Stuart Cahill/AFP/Getty Images*

The quarterback was able to play through the pain for much of the season, but he struggled down the stretch before giving way to backup Scott Zolak for the two final regular-season games. (Zolak, a popular and likeable backup, was one of the few players left on the roster from the bad old days of the early 1990s; he predated Bledsoe. He was always on the bubble when the final cut-downs came but always managed to survive.) Zolak guided the team to one win and one loss in the last two games. With a 9–7 final record, New England was good enough to secure a wild-card spot in the playoffs, but the team was not good enough to beat the Jaguars in Jacksonville in the postseason opener. With Zolak at the controls, the Patriots lost, 25–10, ending their season.

The season was by no means a failure. The Patriots had made the postseason despite suffering some serious injuries; in all, 16 starters—including Bledsoe, Coates, Johnson, and linebacker Chris Slade—missed a total of 58 games due to injury. And New England made the playoffs while playing in the toughest division in football. (Four of the five AFC East teams finished above .500 in 1998—no other division had more than two plus-.500 teams that season.)

Silver linings notwithstanding, the season was certainly unsatisfying for the people in Foxborough, who had to suffer as Parcells and the Jets, featuring an aggressive young squad that looked an awful lot like the one he left behind in New England, made it all the way to the AFC Championship Game before losing to Denver. Meanwhile, it was clear that the Patriots had started to backslide ever so slowly under Carroll, going from an AFC title under Parcells to one postseason win under Carroll to zero playoff victories in 1998. Shortly after the end of the season, the fates added to New England's misery: Edwards, the man drafted to replace Curtis Martin, suffered a horrific knee injury while playing a game of *beach football*, of all things, in an exhibition game in Hawaii as part of the Pro Bowl festivities. No one knew how long he would be out, but the first indications were that his professional football career could be over.

"I'm trying to be optimistic about Robert and have to remain so until we get the facts and see the MRIs," Carroll told reporters. "They will take a

New England struggled within the division, however, losing both games to the Jets in addition to defeats in Miami and Buffalo. The Patriots also suffered a fair share of injuries, including to the team's leading tackler, Ted Johnson, who tore his right biceps tendon while trying to tackle Pittsburgh's Jerome Bettis in a December win over the Steelers.

Bledsoe played through a gruesome injury to his right index finger, suffered when he hit his hand on the helmet of a pass rusher, necessitating a pin to be placed inside the finger to stabilize two fractures. Despite the injury, Bledsoe led the team to a pair of dramatic November wins, first rallying the Patriots past Miami, 26–23, on November 23 and then leading a 25–21 comeback victory the following week over Buffalo, which ended when Bledsoe connected with Coates in the end zone on a 1-yard pass with no time remaining.

Filling in for the injured Bledsoe, backup quarterback Scott Zolak couldn't get the Patriots past Jacksonville in the AFC Wild Card Game on January 3, 1999. *John Mottern/AFP/Getty Images*

An artist's rendering shows the proposed new stadium for the Patriots in downtown Hartford, Connecticut, unveiled during a press conference in November 1998. *AFP/Getty Images*

couple of days to evaluate. This type of injury, though, can be tough on making a quick recovery. We have to set our sights ahead, get moving, and take the necessary steps."

Carroll was asked by a reporter if he felt the Patriots were snakebit.

"The road sure has been bumpy, which has made things difficult for us," Carroll replied. "We just have to take it one situation at a time. Robert's injury just starts the process all over. It ain't easy."

Ultimately, Edwards barely escaped without having his leg amputated below the knee. However, he was never the same player again.

A ROUGH ROAD

In addition to the Edwards injury, another disturbing run of off-field events caused some to wonder who exactly was running the show in Foxborough. Bledsoe and teammate Max Lane were involved in a stage-diving incident at the Paradise Rock Club in Boston that left one woman injured. Glenn was part of an embarrassing series of incidents that left him with a rap sheet that included offensive touching, civil battery, and infliction of emotional distress, as well as driving to endanger and speeding.

(Teammates Lawyer Milloy and Vincent Brisby were also part of a 1999 fight with Glenn.)

The 1998 offseason was the culmination of a miserable stretch for New England sports fans, who saw more and more defections of star coaches and players, as well as a mounting series of losses on the field. Parcells had left the Patriots for their archrivals, the Jets. Roger Clemens had departed the Red Sox for Toronto. Under Rick Pitino, the 1997–1998 Celtics finished below .500, in sixth place in the NBA's Atlantic Division. And in 1997, the Bruins missed the playoffs for the first time in 30 years.

Compounding the misery for the Patriots were two things: First, the hated Jets were coming off a successful season of their own under Parcells. Just two seasons after New York went 1–15, the former Patriots coach guided the Jets to the AFC Championship Game, and his new team had clearly passed Kraft, Carroll, and the suddenly flagging Pats for AFC East supremacy. Public sentiment, which had been in Kraft's corner for such a long time, started to turn against the owner, who was seen as the man who drove Bill Parcells out of town.

Second, it appeared that Kraft's plans for a new stadium on the South Boston waterfront had gone up in smoke when the club ran into neighborhood opposition, as well as a roadblock on Beacon Hill, which made it clear state legislators were not going to approve the use of tax dollars for a new stadium. The owner came off looking foolish and greedy, and he started searching for a new location. Eventually, in November 1998, he settled on Hartford, accepting a deal that would move the team to Connecticut in 2001.

The site of the proposed new stadium was polluted and clearly not usable, however, which allowed Kraft to back out of the deal at the last minute and return to Foxborough when a deal was struck with lawmakers that would allow the team to build a new stadium with some public money for infrastructure, most of which went to improvements for Route 1.

Carroll, meanwhile, was heading into a pivotal season, one that could go a long way in determining his future as a coach in the NFL. For his part, he brushed off any talk that he could be on the hot seat. "I feel like I'm at a crossroads before every season,"

Carroll said. "I do mercenary work, fighting wars of paramount significance, and I always feel the utmost urgency to win. How can I feel more?"

In the midst of all this, the Patriots kicked off the 1999 season with a stunning 30–28 win over the Jets at the Meadowlands, shocking the pundits who had New York as a Super Bowl favorite. Early in the contest, Jets quarterback Vinny Testaverde went down with a ruptured Achilles tendon. ("When Vinny went out of the game, it lifted the black clouds over our heads," Terry Glenn told reporters.) Drew Bledsoe threw for 340 yards and Adam Vinatieri connected on a 23-yard field goal late to pick up the Patriots. The win kick-started a run of four straight victories and six in their first eight games to allow them to take control of the AFC East race.

But then, the offense completely disappeared. The Patriots scored just 108 points in the last eight games, and coordinator Ernie Zampese was criticized heavily by fans. The low point came when New England lost at Philadelphia 24–9 and at home to Buffalo 13–10, a game in which the Patriots had 225 yards and Bledsoe threw for just 101 yards. The Pats ended the season with a 20–3 win over Baltimore (151 yards as a team, with 108 passing yards by Bledsoe), leaving New England with an 8–8 record.

The writing was on the wall. Carroll was fired on January 3, 2000.

"This is a business of accountability, and two years ago we won the division. Last year we barely made the playoffs, and this year we're 8–8," Kraft said. "We need a momentum change."

"I'm proud of being 27–21 and making the play-offs the first two years I was here," Carroll said. "I'll forever be disappointed that we didn't win more."

The Carroll regime was not a failure. He was well liked and provided a welcome change for many of the veterans who had chafed under the stern direction of Parcells. The only problem was that the pendulum swung too far in the other direction—under Carroll, the Patriots resembled a mostly rudderless ship, lacking a real focus or direction. The talent was there, but there was none of the sense of urgency in the locker room that the players felt under Parcells. The diminishing returns the team underwent with Carroll at the helm—a 10–6 mark in 1997 gave way to a 9–7 record

Terry Glenn made 69 catches for a career-best 1,147 yards in 1999 and earned his one and only trip to the Pro Bowl, but the New England offense as a whole appeared to be sliding backward. *Joseph Patronite/NFL Photos/Getty Images*

the following season and an 8–8 mark in 1999—left the franchise looking for some new direction. Ultimately, Carroll will be remembered as a coach who did many great things with the Patriots, but also as someone who was merely keeping the seat warm for the next great coach to take over in Foxborough. It was up to Kraft to find that guy.

ALL EYES ON BELICHICK

It was clear who the Patriots were interested in. The fans, the players, and the rest of the NFL knew it. Kraft wanted Bill Belichick to take over his football team. Kraft had grown close to Belichick when he had been an assistant with Parcells; the longtime Parcells lieutenant spent a year with the Patriots as an assistant after he was fired from Cleveland, his only other head-coaching situation. He had followed Parcells to New York to become a Jets assistant. Kraft and the Patriots contacted the Jets the day Carroll was let go, asking for permission to speak with Belichick about their new head coach vacancy.

However, it was a complicated situation. A day after the Patriots fired Carroll, Parcells held

a press conference announcing that he was resigning as head coach. ("Bill's not coming back," Parcells said. "You can write that on your chalkboard.") He then named Belichick the new head coach of the Jets. Even though Parcells claimed that his decision had no connection to the fact that the Patriots were clearly pursuing Belichick, the whole thing appeared to be a ruse, a convenient way for Parcells to get back at the owner whom he still abhorred.

Things ratcheted up to a whole new level the following day when Belichick strolled into the press conference, which was initially set up to hail his arrival as the new head coach of the Jets, to resign after a day on the job. His announcement caught everyone—the media, the Jets front office, even Parcells—by surprise.

"Due to the various uncertainties surrounding my position as it relates to the team's new ownership, I've decided to resign as head coach of the New York Jets," said Belichick in a hastily handwritten letter of resignation presented to Parcells and team president Steve Gutman just minutes before he repeated it to a shocked media gathering.

Belichick explained that the uncertain owner-ship situation surrounding the Jets had given him pause when it came to accepting the head coach job. (His previous experience with shaky ownership in Cleveland gave him unique perspective in this area.) In addition, there was the question as to when he would be able to get out from under Parcells' long shadow—by his estimation, he had been hearing the same thing from Parcells for almost 15 years. Enough was enough.

"Bill and I have conversed about this for months and even years," Belichick said. "Another thing that has been brought out repeatedly is, 'Belichick has known about this transition for a year. He's had plenty of time to get ready for it.' Well, I remember back in 1987 with the Giants, that was a strike year. We were coming off the Super Bowl and we had a terrible team. We couldn't beat anyone. We were not very good. Bill told me in 1987, 'I can't keep doing this. One more year and you can have it.' I heard it at New England, too. I've heard it since 1987 for an extended period of time.

"We all know how Bill is. He sometimes reacts emotionally to a loss or a bad season or a series of bad performances. Every time Bill says that, I take it with a little bit of a grain of salt. Because that's what it's been for the last twelve, thirteen years, whatever it is."

In New England, football fans celebrated—the Jets were in disarray, and it appeared the Patriots were going to get the coach they had hoped for. However, some observers wondered aloud why a head coach with a 37–45 record would be so sought after by the Patriots.

After much behind-the-scenes drama and negotiations, Patriots owner Bob Kraft finally got his guy in late January 2000, announcing the hiring of Bill Belichick as the team's new head coach. *Steven Senne/AP Images*

BILL BELICHICK

Coaching football was in Bill Belichick's blood—his father, Steve, was a former coach and scout at Navy who was well respected in his profession as a peerless talent-evaluator and game-planner. As a youngster, Belichick often trailed after him, and the two spent plenty of time together in the film room. And so when the time came for a career decision, it was a no-brainer for the younger Belichick: Shortly after graduating from Wesleyan, he took a $25-per-week job as an assistant to Baltimore Colts head coach Ted Marchibroda, driving coaches and players to the airport and breaking down film.

He quickly rose through the ranks, moving from Baltimore to Detroit to Denver and gaining more experience throughout the late 1970s before landing with the New York Giants in 1979 as a defensive assistant and special-teams coach. That started a 12-year run with the Giants during which he came to be recognized as one of the premier defensive assistants of his generation. He was named Parcells' defensive coordinator in 1985, and blessed with great talent, he utilized stars like Lawrence Taylor to help lead New York to victories in Super Bowl XXI (over Denver) and XXV (over Buffalo).

The win over Buffalo was perhaps Belichick's signature game as New York's defensive coordinator. The heavily favored Bills entered the contest looking like an unstoppable force, having rolled through the league with a high-octane passing attack. In the Super Bowl, the Giants employed a series of exotic looks in the secondary that included multiple defensive backs to slow down the Bills' passing game. While Buffalo running back Thurman Thomas ran for 135 yards, the team was unable to generate its usual big numbers in the passing game, and it ended up losing 20–19. Belichick's game plan from that contest is now on display at the Pro Football Hall of Fame.

Even before the win over the Bills, the strength of his resume as a defensive coordinator made Belichick a perennial head-coaching candidate. He took several interviews over the years, and in 1991, he accepted the head-coaching job with the Cleveland Browns. He managed to turn the team around, going from 6–10 his first season to 11–5 and a playoff berth in 1994. He wasn't always the best coach when it came to PR—he made several missteps in dealing with the media and, occasionally, the fan base, especially when it came to benching local legend Bernie Kosar—but the results were tough to argue with.

But the Browns were not long for Cleveland. Owner Art Modell, unhappy with his stadium situation, decided to move the team to Baltimore. The tsunami of negativity that followed swept the entire franchise up in its path, including Belichick, who was charged with keeping his team focused and prepared through what one player later described as an eight-week nightmare.

"It was terrible," Belichick told *Sports Illustrated* 10 years later. "To walk into that building every day and have everyone in the entire organization wondering what are we going to do."

"There's no situation I've been in, before or since, that even would remotely approach that one for negativity and affecting the overall focus of the team," Belichick said. "Not within one hundred miles. It touched every single person in the building, every secretary, every ball boy. I felt badly for everyone involved."

With all that jewelry, Bill Belichick's winning legacy can never be questioned. *Mark Mainz/Getty Images*

Belichick has been an innovator and a leader on the sidelines for a full decade in New England, teaming with quarterback Tom Brady to produce three Super Bowl champions. *Andy Lyons/Getty Images*

Belichick was fired by Modell—over the phone—before the team packed up and moved to Baltimore. With a 37–45 record as head coach, Belichick decided to return to the Bill Parcells coaching family. He spent a year in New England with his old boss as an assistant head coach/secondary coach and struck up a friendship with owner Robert Kraft. The two became close away from the field, forming the basis for what would later become a model owner-coach relationship, and when the time came for Kraft to pick a successor to follow Pete Carroll, he knew exactly who he wanted.

After the protracted legal fight that allowed Belichick to escape from the Jets, he was named the head coach in New England in January 2000. With the Patriots, he has reached unparalleled heights, becoming the first coach in NFL history to win three Super Bowls in four seasons. His unique team-building approach relies on the concept, "It's not about collecting talent, it's about assembling a team." His management style has drawn the eyes of people outside of the game of football—in 2004, he was named one of the 100 most powerful and influential people in the world by *Time* magazine. His entry was penned by former Giants quarterback Phil Simms, who was with Belichick in New York when Belichick was defensive coordinator and their Giants won two Super Bowls.

"He has learned from his early mistakes," Simms wrote. "Bill is innovative because he has a fine-tuned plan and doesn't vary from it. Now teams are starting to copy the Belichick model: Don't just go after the big-time free agents; find players who really complement your team. Rings spawn imitation."

For his part, Belichick has viewed the whole "coach-as-genius" thing warily. In the wake of being named to a list that included Oprah Winfrey, Bill Gates, and Condoleezza Rice, he was suitably chagrined. "It was flattering to be on that list when I can't even get my dog to come when I call him," he said. "I'm not able to influence things in my own household, like what show we're going to watch on TV. I take out the trash like everybody else."

"Why any team would want to hire this man as a head coach is baffling," argued *The Sporting News* in its January 17, 2000, issue. "Why Patriots owner Bob Kraft apparently is willing to give Belichick more power than he was willing to give Bill Parcells is beyond all reason. Belichick is a coaching testament to Laurence J. Peter's theory. Known as the Peter Principle, it states that in any hierarchy, a person tends to rise to the level of his incompetence. Just because Belichick is a great defensive coordinator doesn't mean he can be an effective head coach. In fact, he already has been an awful head coach in a

five-year run with the Browns. It is possible that he has learned from his mistakes and would be a different head coach, but it's also possible that a pig will learn to use silverware."

Kraft and Parcells finally agreed to détente, and the deal was done. Parcells initially called the Patriots owner—who thought it was a prank at first—to jumpstart the process to free Belichick from his Jets contract. ("I told him it was Darth Vader calling, and he said he knew who that was," Parcells later told reporters with a smile.) On January 27, 2000, twenty-four days after the Patriots fired Carroll, Parcells and Kraft brokered a deal that allowed Belichick to become the fourteenth head coach in the history of the franchise.

"We mended a lot of fences," Parcells proclaimed. "We came to an agreement that regardless of what happened with Bill Belichick, this border war with the Jets and Patriots needed to come to a halt. I was anxious that we make an attempt to repair the relationship."

In the end, the Patriots gave New York their No. 1 draft pick for 2000 and a fourth- and seventh-rounder in 2001. The Jets gave the Patriots a No. 5 pick in 2001 and a No. 7 in 2002.

Commenting on the deal to reporters, Bledsoe said that, while giving up a first-round draft pick was not something any team wants to do, "to get a coach of the caliber of Bill Belichick, it's probably a worthwhile thing to do."

At his introductory press conference, Belichick said with a smile, "Hopefully, this press conference will go a little better than the last one I had," referencing his farewell press conference with the Jets. "The opportunity to be in coaching was something I wasn't sure I would have as late as twenty-four hours ago, and I'm extremely grateful for the opportunity to coach in the 2000 season. It was quite an ordeal, but it's behind me."

Belichick was asked about the opportunity to get out from under Parcells' shadow.

"If I wanted to get out of Bill's shadow, I wouldn't have come to New England. There's a shadow up here, too."

It was a bold move, but Kraft based much of his decision on the single season the two spent together.

Although their time together in New England as quarterback and head coach would be relatively short, Drew Bledsoe (right) spoke highly of his new coach after Belichick's hiring was announced. *Elise Amendola/AP Images*

In that time, it was clear that Belichick appealed to Kraft as more than just a coach.

"When I was thinking of hiring Bill, I know a lot of people thought that I was making an error, and they based it on how he dealt with the media and they sent me tapes from his experience in Cleveland," Kraft said. "But in the end, I am into substance; I am not into lipstick and powder. When I spent time with Bill in 1996 when he was on our staff, I found him to be someone I could relate to, who I felt good about. Maybe part of it was his training in college in economics, but to be good in the business of football today—and good to me is not being good one year but try to sustain it year in and year out—you have to understand economics and you have to understand value and you have to understand the salary cap and how it works and know that if you make bad decisions, you will be penalized for many [years], not just quarters."

Kraft explained how he was putting his decision in "Wall Street terms," adding, "You know how management is thrown out when they don't do well; you have the same thing here. What you have to guard against is [that] if you have a management team with a short-term focus, they'll do whatever they have to do to win in the short term and maybe cripple your cap in the long term. If they leave or get fired, you are in deep trouble. I think every discussion I had with Bill he understood value and players and how they fit under the cap. And if we've had any success, I think a great part of it is his judgment in knowing players and how they fit in a system in the salary cap era."

THE NUCLEUS OF A DYNASTY

The hiring of Belichick started a transformative four-month stretch that saw New England add two more key pieces: general manager Scott Pioli and quarterback Tom Brady. That trio, along with Kraft, ultimately formed the nucleus of the New England dynasty in the 2000s.

The relationship between Belichick and Pioli stretched back to the mid-1980s, when Pioli was an undergrad student at Central Connecticut and made the trek every summer to Giants training camp, where Belichick was defensive coordinator. The two were introduced by a mutual friend and struck up a

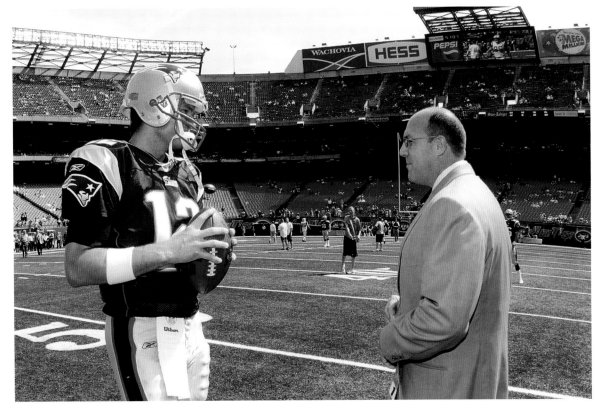

Tom Brady and Scott Pioli—shown here in 2007—both joined the Patriots in 2000 and were integral to the team's emergence as an NFL powerhouse in the decade ahead. *David Drapkin/Getty Images*

The signing of safety Lawyer Milloy, who was coming off of an All-Pro season in 1999, was a key step to bolstering the New England defense in the new century. *Ezra Shaw/Getty Images*

friendship. They remained close after Pioli graduated, and Belichick eventually hired him as a pro personnel assistant in 1992 in Cleveland—despite the fact that Pioli had what sounded like a better job offer with the 49ers. In Cleveland, Pioli was responsible for evaluating both college prospects and veteran free agents, as well as negotiating various player contracts. His stature as a personnel man started to grow within the organization, as well as around the league. After Belichick was fired by the Browns at the close of the 1995 season, Pioli remained with the franchise for one more season until the two were reunited in New York, where, in 1997, Pioli was hired as the New York Jets' director of pro personnel.

And so, when Belichick made Pioli the GM of the Patriots on February 11, 2000, it was hardly a surprise. The hiring was largely ignored—the team earned bigger headlines that week when they announced a flurry of personnel moves, including the release of Coates and Armstrong, as well as the renegotiation of a seven-year, $35 million deal for veteran safety Lawyer Milloy.

But the decision to bring Pioli on board would be the second major step in assembling the pieces for New England's championship run.

"I have come to respect Scott Pioli as a fine evaluator of talent with a keen eye for stocking a team relative to its specific needs and system," said Belichick in a written statement issued by the franchise. "I have seen the positive results of Scott's very progressive player personnel system and am particularly impressed with his record of consistently integrating capable second- and third-tier players, as well as front-line starters. Scott Pioli is a fine addition to the New England Patriots, and I look forward to his contributions for years to come."

It was clear that the two were on the same page when it came to personnel—they would later confess to disagreeing on only a handful of football decisions in their time together. In addition, Belichick and Pioli were of like mind when it came to their team-building approach. All their decisions were governed by a simple yet direct mission statement: "We are building a big, strong, fast, smart, tough, and disciplined football team that consistently competes for championships."

DICK REHBEIN

Dick Rehbein is one of the great unsung heroes of New England sports. The former Patriots quarterbacks coach, who passed away in August 2001, was the member of the organization who first laid eyes on Tom Brady as a collegian at Michigan and made sure the Patriots went after him in the 2000 draft. "Someday, this is going to be a Joe Montana or Brett Favre," Rehbein told his wife.

A longtime Green Bay fan growing up, he ended up working for the Packers and remembered the story of legendary Green Bay scout Red Cochrane. Cochrane told Packers head coach Bart Starr about a quarterback out of Notre Dame named Joe Montana, but the Packers passed on Montana (who ended up going in the third round to San Francisco), and Cochrane stormed out of the draft room. Rehbein wanted to make sure that this time there would be no mistake.

Of course, Brady wasn't a first-rounder, so the draft had some anxious moments for Rehbein. New England didn't have a first-round pick—it was awarded to the Jets as compensation for the Belichick deal—but the team went after tackles Adrian Klemm (in the second round) and Greg Robinson-Randall (in the fourth). The team also picked up running back J. R. Redmond in the third round and followed that with tight end Dave Stachelski, defensive tackle Jeff Marriott, and cornerback Antwan Harris in the fifth round. Then—finally—came Brady. The Patriots took him in the sixth round, 199th overall. The coach celebrated with a gleeful phone call to his wife when the pick was official. "We got him," he said happily.

Rehbein did not live to see Brady achieve all the things the coach believed he could—he died of a heart problem the summer before that magical 2001 season. Almost five years after his death, Rehbein's widow found some of his old journals that cemented the fact that Rehbein was right about the sort of player Brady would become: "He's coming along," wrote Rehbein of the young quarterback. "He's going to be a great player . . . OUTSTANDING."

"[Pioli] and Bill make such a good match," said Ravens GM Ozzie Newsome. "But the biggest thing is the unbelievable trust between them."

Roughly three months after the Patriots decided to make Belichick their head coach, they made an even bigger move. In the sixth round of the 2000 draft, they selected quarterback Tom Brady. Of course, on draft day, Brady wasn't seen as a future star. He was thought to be smart, but lacking in many physical areas, including arm strength. He was on the skinny side and looked a bit slow. Plus, the Patriots already had a star quarterback in Bledsoe, someone so firmly entrenched in the job he had been given a nine-figure contract by the owner, who referred to him as part of his extended family. Small wonder that the selection did not spark a single question from the media in Belichick's post-draft press conference.

"The value board at that point really just clearly put him as the top value. Brady is a guy who has obviously played at a high level of competition in front of a lot of people," Belichick told the media shortly after the selection was made. "He's been in a lot of pressure situations. We felt that this year his decision-making was improved from his junior year after he took over for [Brian] Griese and cut his interceptions down. [He's] a good, tough, competitive, smart quarterback that is a good value, and how he does and what he'll be able to do . . . we'll just put him out there with everybody else and let him compete and see what happens."

The 2000 season came and went with little fanfare. New England finished with a 5–11 record as Belichick and Pioli began installing their program. On paper, there really wasn't much that was memorable about that year—no memorable wins, no gut-wrenching losses. The Patriots opened the season with consecutive losses to Tampa Bay, the Jets, Minnesota, and Miami before Belichick won his first game as head coach of the Patriots with a 28–19 victory over the Broncos in Denver on October 1, 2000. Belichick and Bledsoe were awarded game balls. Belichick was asked where he was going to put his. "If my kids don't get a hold of it, it'll probably go on my mantel," he said.

There were occasional blips on the radar screen—a training camp fight raised some eyebrows. In addition, Law was caught at the Canadian border in possession of the drug ecstasy. (The cornerback pleaded ignorance, claiming it wasn't his bag. "I had no idea that it was in the bag," he said, offering to take a drug test to prove he was clean. "I know this sounds stupid and maybe a little bit unbelievable, but that's the truth, the honest-to-God truth.")

Receiver Troy Brown celebrates one of his two touchdowns scored against Denver on October 1, 2000, to give Bill Belichick his first win as head coach. Brown went on to lead the team in receptions that year. *David Zalubowski/AP Images*

A closer look at the 2000 Patriots team, however, reveals that the seeds of future greatness were being planted. Game by game, the deficits grew smaller, and it was clear to the more proficient eye that the team was becoming more and more competitive. In addition, on the practice field, Brady was showing signs of his future greatness.

That offseason was key for the franchise. Brady was making strides in all areas—between the end of the 2000 season and the start of training camp in 2001, the team held 60 offseason workouts. Brady was there for every one of them, something that wasn't lost on his veteran teammates. From outside the organization, no one could see it coming. But Brady's bid to become the starting quarterback of the Patriots had begun in earnest. He was there almost all the time, getting stronger and faster, watching film, and building a consensus in the locker room among his teammates. Veteran wide receiver David Patten spent some time with Brady between the 2000 and 2001 seasons, and he remembered a session where Brady was advising him on how to change a route on the fly. Patten recalls thinking that this wasn't coming from some phony, know-nothing kid, but someone who really knew what he was talking about.

"You just don't hear that coming from a backup," Patten thought of Brady's comment at the time. "What if he were starting?"

"Tom carried himself like this was his team," added Patten later.

At the same time, Belichick and Pioli continued their radical overhaul of the organization, making small moves that would have sizable impact down the road. The phrase "it's not about collecting talent, it's about building a team" was at the heart of New England's team-building approach. No matter how much money you made, no matter how you were being used previously, if Belichick and Pioli thought you'd fit the Patriots' system, you found a home in Foxborough.

To that end, the acquisition of veteran linebackers Mike Vrabel and Roman Phifer were relatively quiet transactions, but those players would help form the nucleus of the New England defense through the early days of the twenty-first century. The two epitomized a new spirit, one that depended almost as

Heading into the 2001 season, Tom Brady (12) was looking to challenge Drew Bledsoe (11) for the quarterback job in Foxborough. *Damian Strohmeyer/Sports Illustrated/Getty Images*

much on brains as it did on brawn. Both were heady players, but both had reputations for being good spare parts. Vrabel was a part-time linebacker who was plucked off the scrap heap in Pittsburgh, while the well-traveled Phifer was a Belichick favorite. (Phifer played in New York when Belichick was an assistant under Parcells with the Jets.) Belichick added more of his favorites, signing Anthony Pleasant and Otis Smith, two players who had been a part of his defenses for several years.

That year in the draft, they selected a pair of players who would become cornerstones of the franchise for the better part of the next decade. Defensive lineman Richard Seymour was taken in the first round with the sixth overall selection, and left tackle Matt Light was tapped by the Patriots in the second round, 48th overall. Belichick and Pioli also combed the waiver wire for players who would be a good fit for the team. Sixty-five of the eighty-eight players on the roster in the summer of 2001 were brought in by Belichick and Pioli for relatively little money, a stunning turnover that took place in a relatively short amount of time. It was a notion that some football insiders scoffed at, but which would pay off in surprisingly quick fashion. It became known as "The Patriot Way."

9

DYNASTY

2001–2005

The ball sailed through the air of the Superdome, carrying with it 42 years of bad mojo. There had been sexual harassment suits, inept coaches, and bad ownership; comically inept drafts, poor officiating, and flat-out bad luck; drug scandals, lack of money, and out-of-date facilities.

But when Adam Vinatieri's kick split the uprights that fateful Sunday night in New Orleans, the Patriots were reborn. They had moved from a late-night punch line to Super Bowl champions.

How did they get there? Even from the start of the season, it had been a long journey to the top of the football world. In 2001 training camp, they looked like almost any other team—coming off a 5–11 season, they certainly didn't appear to be title contenders. On offense, quarterback Drew Bledsoe had been awarded a nine-figure contract and appeared to be solidly entrenched as the franchise quarterback. However, he had precious few options. The New England offense had a handful of quality skill position players, including overachieving veteran Troy Brown (a team-high 83 receptions in 2000) and mercurial wide receiver Terry Glenn (a team-high 963 receiving yards that same season), but it wasn't exactly a group of world beaters. The moves the Patriots made in the offseason—acquiring middle-of-the-road veterans like running back Antowain Smith and wide receiver David Patten—didn't convince people that the team was going to be

any better than the one that had lost three of the last five games of the 2000 campaign. On defense, there were a few familiar faces, including Pro Bowl defensive backs Ty Law and Lawyer Milloy, but not much else. The season-opening loss to the lowly Bengals in September 2001 confirmed the worst fears for many fans—the Patriots were strictly a middle-class team.

BRADY'S ARRIVAL

Everything changed for the franchise in Week 2 of the 2001 season. The game, which was initially postponed because of the September 11 tragedy, took place on September 23 at Foxboro Stadium. The Patriots came out flat, and they were trailing the Jets 10–3 with 4:43 left in the game when Bledsoe fled the pocket, rolling away from defensive lineman John Abraham toward the New England sideline in an attempt to stop the clock. Before he

could get to the first-down marker, he took a savage hit from linebacker Mo Lewis. Despite the severity of the hit, Bledsoe initially appeared to be all right. He was sidelined for a play before being reinserted, and then he was removed for backup quarterback Tom Brady.

It turned out that Bledsoe was hurt far worse than anyone realized. The quarterback suffered a sheared blood vessel and had lost a ton of blood. At the end of the game (a 10–3 loss for New England), he was taken to Massachusetts General Hospital for tests.

Enter Brady. A sixth-round pick out of Michigan the year before, he had progressed steadily up the depth chart, moving from No. 4 quarterback in 2000 to the backup job at the start of the 2001 season. The 24-year-old's willingness to learn and desire to improve were evident from the start. Veterans

The Patriots–Jets game at Foxboro Stadium on September 23, 2001, was an opportunity for the league and fans to honor those who had died in the September 11 terrorist attacks. The game proved to be a turning point for New England on the field as well. *Ezra Shaw/Allsport/ Getty Images*

TOM BRADY

On September 26, 2001, Tom Brady walked into his first press conference as a starter, carrying a confidence that belied his age. It had been a long time coming for Brady, who had managed to overcome obstacles throughout his life as a young quarterback to reach the NFL.

Out of high school, he wasn't even considered good enough to become a quality college quarterback. After two seasons as a starter at Serra High in San Mateo, California, where he completed 219 passes for 3,514 yards and 33 touchdowns, his father had to send out tapes of the young Brady to colleges in an attempt to get him noticed.

He signed with Michigan and entered college as the seventh-string quarterback. He made some headway his first two seasons, but he kept getting passed on the depth chart by quarterbacks like Scott Dreisbach and Brian Griese. He even considered transferring to Cal because of a lack of playing time. But Brady finally won the starting job as a junior, and he won the support of head coach Lloyd Carr, who told reporters at the beginning of the season, "I'm excited about Brady. I think he is talented enough to be an NFL quarterback at some point."

In truth, in the eyes of Carr, he wasn't even talented enough to be the full-time quarterback at Michigan. Brady ended up splitting time with in-state hero Drew Henson for large parts of Brady's junior and senior seasons. Regardless of the platoon, Brady went 443-for-711 for 5,351 yards, 35 touchdowns, and 19 interceptions in his college career.

But when it came to evaluating Brady, the numbers that really mattered were wins and losses. As a college starter, he went 20–5, and he finished his career at Michigan with a performance that was a taste of things to come: Brady rallied the Wolverines from fourth-quarter deficits to win three times during the regular season.

The season concluded with another stirring comeback, this one in the FedEx Orange Bowl against future NFL star Shaun Alexander and Alabama on January 1, 2000. Brady and the Wolverines trailed Alabama by 14 in the second half, but then he led Michigan to three touchdowns in a 12-minute span in the third quarter and rallied the Wolverines to a 35–34 overtime win. In the end, Brady was 34-for-46 for 369 yards and four touchdowns, setting numerous Orange Bowl passing records, including touchdown passes, passing yards, passing attempts, and completions.

"Tom Brady has everything you want in a quarterback," Carr gushed to reporters after the game. "The guys around him love him and believe in him, and if you knew him, you'd believe in him too."

Tom Brady, 2007. Rob Tringali/ Sportschrome/Getty Images

"This kid has a future in the NFL," Carr added. "Those guys who have doubted him, like they doubted Brian Griese, will be proved wrong. Twenty wins as a starter speaks volumes about who he is."

"Ten and two, Orange Bowl champions, beating the SEC champions" Brady said after the game. "It's a great way to end your career."

But the numbers didn't make the scouts take notice. Come draft day, Brady waited and waited, while other quarterbacks came off the board before him. Chad Pennington was the only quarterback taken in the first two rounds, and then Gio Carmazzi, Tee Martin, and Marc Bulger were all taken before Brady on draft day in 2000. The Patriots eventually called his name with the 199th overall pick, a sixth-rounder so innocuous that no one asked about him in Belichick's post-draft press conference. The young man who would eventually become an NFL legend was taken one round after Dave Stachelski, a tight end out of Boise State.

"If we thought he was going to be this good, I don't think we would have waited for the 199th pick to take him," Patriots GM Scott Pioli said years later. "We definitely don't have things figured out. Trust me."

With the arrival of Brady, the franchise that had suffered year after year of bad luck was finally able to turn things around. In his second season, Brady was thrust into the starting lineup after an injury to Drew Bledsoe, and he managed to keep the starting job even after the veteran quarterback was deemed healthy enough to play.

Since then, Brady has led the Patriots to three Super Bowl titles, while capturing two Super Bowl MVP awards for himself—all before he turned 30 years old. He was also named regular-season MVP in 2007.

That season, he helped rewrite the franchise record book with several new NFL team records, including most points scored in a season (589), largest point differential in a season (+315), and most touchdowns in a season (75). The Patriots became the first team in league history to go 16–0 in the regular season, and they tied the single-season mark with 18 overall victories. In addition, Brady and receiver Randy Moss set an NFL single-season record in 2007 for most touchdown passes between a passer and a receiver (23), with Moss' 23 touchdown catches also a league record for a receiver.

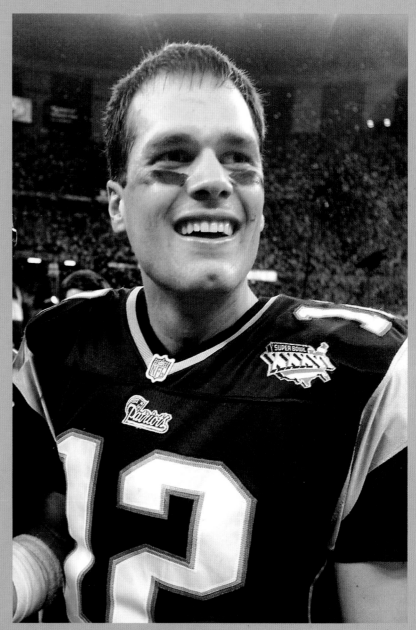

The wide-eyed Brady showed incredible poise and leadership in leading the Patriots to a championship in just his first season as a starting quarterback in the NFL. He was selected to the Pro Bowl and named Super Bowl MVP that year.
Jeff Haynes/AFP/Getty Images

In his first NFL start, Tom Brady led the Patriots to a convincing 44–13 win over Indianapolis. Brady completed only 13 passes, but a solid running game and tough defense carried the day. *Damian Strohmeyer/Sports Illustrated/Getty Images*

were impressed at how often he stayed after practice and worked, while his younger teammates marveled at the hours he spent in the film and weight rooms. But the general public didn't know much about him—he had thrown just one pass in his NFL career, during a blowout game as a rookie. But he was now the man in charge of the New England offense. With the benefit of hindsight, it's safe to say he grew into the role of starter.

"Who wants to shoot?" Brady asked with a smile at the beginning of his first press conference as a starter in the National Football League. The youngster was quizzed on a variety of topics, including whether or not he anticipated being nervous ("Not a bit, man. Not a bit," he said, reminding people he played in front of 112,000 as a collegian at Michigan), his thoughts about Bledsoe ("It's hard to be overly excited from my standpoint, just because he's a friend that's in the hospital. You don't get excited about something like that."), and whether he was preparing the same way he had been when he was a backup. ("I am preparing," Brady said. "This is the way it's been with me as

the backup. The difference is I know I'm playing this week. I think everyone is giving me a lot of support around here.")

His first start wouldn't be easy. It came against a rapidly improving Indianapolis team, one that featured future NFL MVP Peyton Manning. The Colts had won their first two games, putting up a combined 87 points in the process. The New England defense set the tone early against Indianapolis when veteran linebacker Bryan Cox—who had spent the entire week boasting about their defense—delivered a crushing hit on receiver Jerome Pathon. The Patriots forced four turnovers in the game. On the other side of the ball, Brady didn't exactly have a dream start—in his first play from scrimmage as an NFL starter, he was sacked by Colts defensive end Brad Scioli for a 9-yard loss. But he rebounded nicely and finished 13-for-23 for 168 yards in the 44–13 win.

"I was lying in bed [Saturday night] and kind of envisioning the things that were going to happen in the game," Brady said after the win. "The outcomes and the possibilities, and never did I think it would be a runaway victory like this was. It was our day. A lot of things bounced our way. You need that in football."

"He did a real solid job," Belichick said of Brady, who received a game ball for his effort.

Offensive lineman Mike Compton said, "I wouldn't have known by one second in there that it was Brady's first start. He ran the show."

Brady credited Bledsoe for helping him get through the game. He told reporters that Bledsoe gave him the following advice before the game: "Tom, the most important thing for you . . . is to go out there and smile and have fun. You're as prepared as you can be. I have a ton of confidence in you. . . . Let everything else take care of itself."

It was the sort of performance Brady would come to be known for as a rookie: poised, calm, accurate. The Patriots tried not to put too much on his plate. They didn't want to have to put Brady in a position to win the game for them; they just wanted to make sure he wouldn't lose any games for them.

THE LEGEND IS BORN

While the Patriots didn't lose the following week's game because of Brady, his performance certainly didn't help matters. In a blowout loss to the Dolphins in Miami, he had what is still considered one of the worst games of his career, going 12-for-24 for 86 yards and four sacks. The performance was bad across the board, so much so that in the days after the game, Belichick took his team out behind the stadium together, and they ceremonially buried the game ball, putting the bad loss behind them.

They did just that the next week against the Chargers. In a game that was perhaps the first sign of the Brady legend, the Patriots got off to a slow start. Although the quarterback threw the first touchdown pass of his career in the first half—a 21-yard connection to wide receiver Terry Glenn, who was making his first start of the season after being benched the first four games of the season and who fired the ball into the stands in celebration—New England was facing a 26–16 deficit with just over eight minutes remaining in the contest. A loss would send Brady and the Patriots to a 1–4 start and have people wondering about the future of the quarterback as well as the head coach in New England.

And that's where it all started. The quarterback engineered a field goal drive and then hit tight end Jermaine Wiggins with a game-tying touchdown pass in the final minute of regulation. A late San Diego field goal attempt fell short, and Adam Vinatieri made them pay for it in overtime, hitting a 44-yard field goal in the extra session to lift the Patriots to a 29–26 win.

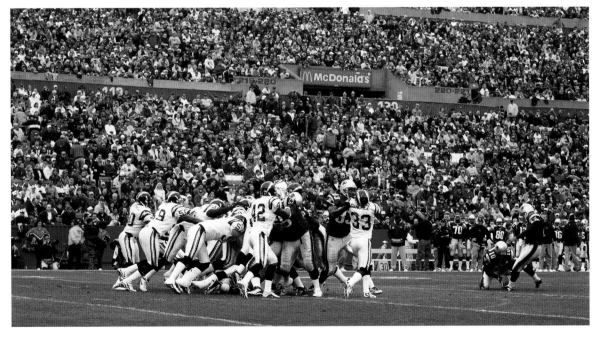

Kicking game-winning field goals would become a theme for Adam Vinatieri in 2001. His first came against San Diego at Foxboro Stadium on October 14; his last would be the biggest kick in franchise history, in Super Bowl XXXVI. *Al Bello/ Allsport/Getty Images*

David Patten celebrates his 29-yard touchdown run in the first quarter of the game at Indianapolis on October 21, 2001. He would add a touchdown pass and a touchdown reception in the Patriots' 38–17 victory. *John Harrell/AP Images*

"Never a doubt, huh?" Brady said with a smile in his postgame press conference.

The comeback win jumpstarted New England. They followed it with their second blowout victory in four weeks against the Colts, this time in Indianapolis by a 38–17 score. Wide receiver David Patten became just the sixth player in NFL history to rush, catch, and throw for a touchdown in the same game. This was followed by a loss at Denver, but then came another pair of wins that brought New England to a 5–4 record heading into a nationally televised game with the high-powered St. Louis Rams. The Patriots hung with the Rams for three-plus quarters, before a late miscue cost them the game.

Meanwhile, a quarterback controversy was brewing. In the days following the loss to St. Louis, Bledsoe received a clean bill of health and expressed his desire to return to the field as soon as possible. Brady, meanwhile, appeared to have a hammerlock on the job and had no interest in giving it up, not to anyone. In his weekly radio show, Belichick said that Brady would be the starting quarterback for the "foreseeable future."

"It is what it is," he told reporters the next day when asked about the decision to keep Bledsoe on the bench. "Nobody scripted it this way. It just worked out that way. My job . . . is to make the decisions for the football team, and that is what I am going to do. I am going to make the best decisions I can for the football team. That is what Mr. Kraft is paying me to do, and that's what I am going to do. I am going to make the decisions that I feel are best for the football team, T-E-A-M, as in team."

The coach added that it wasn't about Bledsoe losing a job. "This is strictly about the team," he continued. "It's about getting the team ready. I don't think you can get two quarterbacks ready. I feel that for us to get our starting quarterback ready, we need to give that player the majority of reps. When Drew was the quarterback, it was the same way."

Bledsoe clearly was not happy about the decision. When asked about it during an impromptu locker room press conference, he said quietly, "I looked forward to the chance to compete for my job, and I'll leave it at that." Nevertheless, the decision to go with Brady appeared to galvanize the team.

New England wouldn't lose the rest of the way. They finished the regular season with six straight victories in all sorts of forms and fashions. There were narrow wins (17–16 at the Jets and 12–9 at the Bills) and blowouts (38–6 at the Panthers).

Capping off the home portion of the regular season in style, they delivered a 20–13 win over the Dolphins on December 22 in the final regular-season game to be played at Foxboro Stadium. For the finale, the Patriots brought back a bunch of former players to pay tribute to a place that held so many memories for a generation of New England football fans. It was a sweet moment for the old place, and the players and coaches did their part in the salute, taking a final, 10-minute tour of the stands before they left the field.

Belichick joked that when it came to closing down stadiums, he was a "real veteran," having gone through the same thing when the Browns played their last game at Cleveland Municipal Stadium.

"Oh man, that was a great day today," Belichick recalled of the Foxboro farewell. "It was a great, emotional day with the crowd and the fans. It was a great atmosphere, and it was great to be a part of it.

"I was just thinking about the appreciation of our fans and how strongly they have supported us over the years," Belichick added. "And not just now, this season. It was even the case when I was here on the staff back in '96."

"It'll be ten minutes I won't ever forget for the rest of my life," linebacker Tedy Bruschi said.

Antowain Smith, who rushed for a career-high 156 yards and a touchdown in the victory, stood in one end zone and swayed back and forth to the cheers. He told reporters he took more punishment from the fans on his way around the field "trying not to get pulled into the stands."

"But it felt great to be out there," he added.

"WE ARE ALL PATRIOTS"

Foxboro Stadium still had one more great game left. The divisional playoffs against the Raiders came on a snowy Saturday night in January 2002. After a back-and-forth three quarters that saw Brady stumble through a snowdrift on the way to the first rushing touchdown of his career, Oakland carried a 13–3 lead

Antowain Smith, who led the Patriots with 1,157 yards rushing and 12 touchdowns in 2001, put up 156 yards and scored once against Miami in the final regular-season game at Foxboro Stadium. *Ezra Shaw/Getty Images*

Fumble or incomplete pass? Charles Woodson's hit on Tom Brady in the waning minutes of the 2001 Divisional Playoff Game caused the ball to come loose and led to a storm of controversy when referees declared it an incomplete pass and thus still New England's ball. *Matt Campbell/AFP/ Getty Images*

into the final quarter. The Patriots scored a touchdown to cut the deficit to three. With under two minutes remaining, Brady was leading a late drive when he was hit by his former Michigan teammate Charles Woodson as he was delivering a pass. The ball came loose, Oakland's Greg Biekert collected the fumble, and the rest of the Raiders started celebrating. New England's dream season had apparently come to a close.

Then referee Walt Coleman went under the hood to review the play, to determine whether Brady had actually fumbled or if he was in the process of attempting a pass when the ball came loose; if the latter, it would be ruled an incomplete pass, and the Patriots would get the ball back. When Coleman returned to the field, he announced, "After reviewing the play, the quarterback's arm was going forward . . ." The crowd drowned out the rest of the call. The ball went back to the Patriots, and the legend of the Tuck Rule was born. (League officials later pointed to Rule 3, Section 21, Article

2, which states that a passer who has begun to bring the ball forward can't be deemed to have fumbled if he hasn't tucked the ball into his body.)

Still, it would have all been for naught if not for Adam Vinatieri. In the final minute of regulation, the kicker delivered a 45-yard field goal—a low line drive that barely made it over the crossbar—to tie the game. The Patriots got the ball first in overtime and never gave it up; Vinatieri's 23-yard kick gave them an unlikely win. (Long snapper Lonie Paxton became a cult hero when he celebrated the winning field goal by making a snow angel in the end zone.) Overall, Brady was 32 of 52 for 312 yards, but the real hero was Vinatieri, whose two clutch field goals—and one that would come a couple of weeks later at Super Bowl XXXVI—would seal his status as the finest big-game kicker of his generation.

The Patriots followed the win over Oakland with a rather anticlimactic victory over the Steelers in the AFC Championship, a game highlighted by the return of Bledsoe, who came in after Brady went down

ADAM VINATIERI

Adam Vinatieri was never just a kicker. The South Dakota native, a former high school wrestler, was just as much of an athlete as any professional football player he shared a locker room with. Signed by the Patriots in 1996 as an undrafted free agent, he made a name for himself after he caught Dallas kick returner Herschel Walker from behind on a return attempt. It drew praise from Bill Parcells.

"That day he told everybody that I was a football player, more than just a kicker," recalled Vinatieri later of the blessing he got after the game from Parcells. "That meant the world to me."

Always considered one of the best kickers in the league, Vinatieri really established his legacy in the 2001 postseason, when he connected on a pair of big field goals in the middle of a New England snowstorm to beat the Raiders in the divisional playoffs, as well as making the game-winning field goal to beat the Rams in Super Bowl XXXVI. He delivered another game-winning kick two years later to help deliver a second Super Bowl title in three years to the Patriots.

"He is a pressure kicker," Belichick said of Vinatieri after Super Bowl XXXVIII. "If you have got to have one kick with everything on the line, he has got one in him."

"Adam is the most clutch kicker in the game," quarterback Tom Brady said.

Following the 2005 season, Vinatieri signed with Indianapolis as a free agent, finishing his 10 seasons with the Patriots as the team's all-time leading scorer with 1,158 points.

Mr. Clutch comes through again. Vinatieri delivers the game-winning kick in Super Bowl XXXVIII against the Panthers. *Bill Frakes/Sports Illustrated/Getty Images*

Adam Vinatieri secured his place in Patriots lore with a pair of clutch field goals in the snow against Oakland in the 2001 playoffs. *John Iacono/Sports Illustrated/Getty Images*

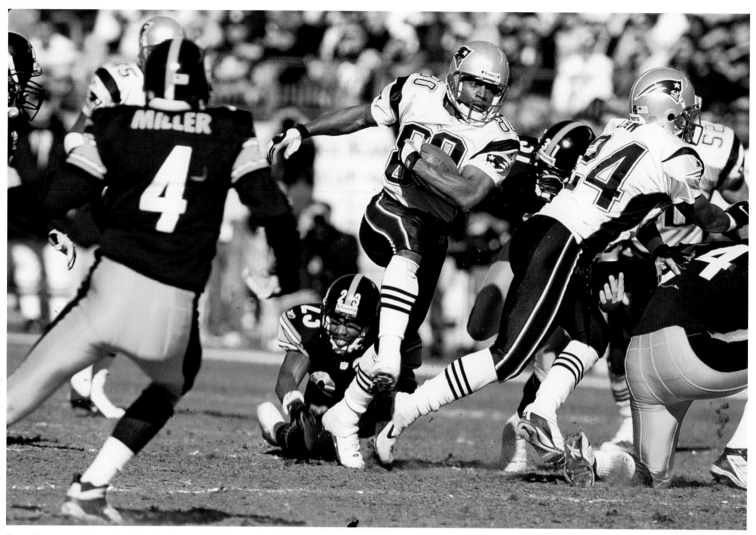

Troy Brown got New England going with his punt return for a touchdown against Pittsburgh in the first quarter of the 2001 AFC Championship Game. Brown also rushed for 121 yards from the backfield. *Al Messerschmidt/Getty Images*

with an ankle injury. "Guess who's back?" Bledsoe said with a smile when he entered the New England huddle for the first time since September. It would mark Bledsoe's final appearance in a New England uniform, but he went out with style and class, tossing a touchdown pass to Patten to help lift the Patriots to a win. New England also got some standout special-teams play in the game, with Troy Brown returning a punt for a touchdown and the Patriots returning a blocked field goal for another score.

The triumph brought them to the second Super Bowl appearance in franchise history: Super Bowl XXXVI in New Orleans against the mighty St. Louis Rams. Some early controversy brewed about

who would get start at quarterback—Exactly how bad was Brady's ankle? Had Bledsoe won his job back with his performance against the Steelers?—but Belichick quickly put that to rest by announcing that Brady would get the call against the Rams.

Just months after September 11, Super Bowl XXXVI was positioned as a nationwide celebration set against a red, white, and blue backdrop. And the Patriots were the perfect team for America to root for. New England was portrayed as the classic underdog, willingly embracing the concept of team and placing a higher, nobler goal over individual triumphs. That was never more the case than during the player introductions; while the Rams starters

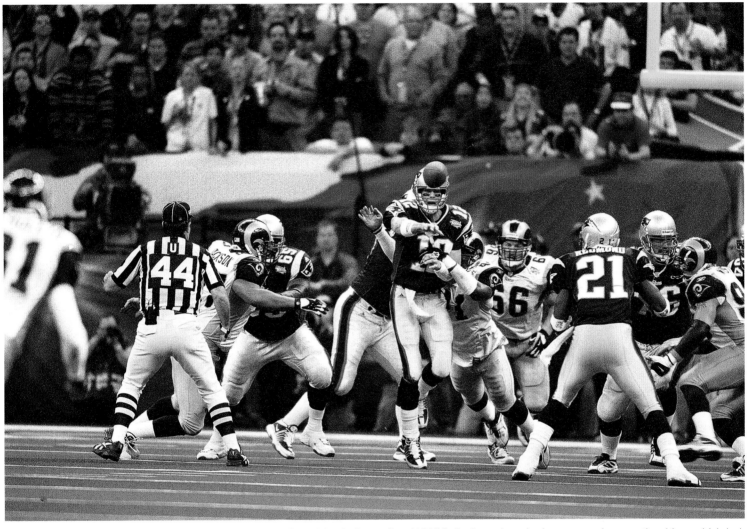

Tom Brady dishes off to J. R. Redmond (21) during the final drive in Super Bowl XXXVI. Redmond made three receptions on the drive, which led to Adam Vinatieri's game-winning field goal as time expired. *Al Tielemans/Sports Illustrated/Getty Images*

were introduced individually, the Patriots chose to come out as a team.

New England had lost to St. Louis earlier in the season in a game where they blitzed quarterback Kurt Warner all night long. This time, they hung back, running multiple defensive packages out there while focusing on slowing down the Rams' high-powered attack. The approach worked, and the Patriots took a 17–3 lead into the fourth quarter.

A pair of late St. Louis touchdowns tied the game, setting the stage for more Brady heroics. As broadcaster John Madden urged New England to take a knee and play for overtime, the quarter-back marched the Patriots into field goal range with

seven seconds left on the clock. Vinatieri came on to attempt a 48-yard field goal, which split the uprights as time ran out. New England was the unlikeliest champion in Super Bowl history.

As red, white, and blue confetti rained down from the ceiling of the Superdome, Belichick embraced defensive captain Lawyer Milloy, Brady held his head in disbelief, and Kraft gratefully accepted the Vince Lombardi Trophy. "We are all Patriots, and tonight the Patriots are world champions!" Kraft proclaimed from the podium in the wake of the historic victory.

The images that stick with people to this day are two different shots of Brady. In one, he is face-

Patriots players and coaches ride in Duck Boats through the streets of Boston for a victory parade following the team's victory in Super Bowl XXXVI. Hundreds of thousands of fans braved freezing temperatures to celebrate the city's first championship in 16 years. *Olivia Hanley/AP Images*

to-face with Bledsoe, moments after the game was over. While Bledsoe's face is a mask of emotion, Brady is as wide-eyed as a six-year-old on Christmas morning. Brady slaps him on the shoulder pad and exclaims, "We won!" The second image is of Brady on the podium after the game. He's holding his head and shaking it back and forth as confetti gently falls around him. The two images perfectly encapsulated the quarterback for the New England fans; in living rooms and sports bars around New England, many Patriots fans were doing the exact same thing. They had now completely embraced him as one of their own.

"Everybody got it done," said Brady, who completed 16 of 27 passes for 145 yards and a touchdown. "It was awesome. We were the true reflection of team out there today."

They were feted at the White House, and referencing their decision to come out as a team instead of individually, President George W. Bush said they were a great example of the can-do American spirit.

"It wasn't one of those things where the spotlight was on any individual," Bush said in a ceremony at the White House. "Everybody went out at the same time. I thought that was a pretty good signal to America that teamwork is important, that the individual matters to the team, but the team is bigger than the individual. I appreciated so very much that signal to the country."

Brady was riding a wave of success. He was dubbed "The New Prince of the NFL" in a *Sports Illustrated* cover story, served as a judge at a national beauty pageant, was in demand as a national pitchman, and was linked romantically with everyone from Mariah Carey to Tara Reid to Paris Hilton. The following spring, when he showed up for minicamp in Foxborough, he looked weary.

"You can age real quick in one year, believe me," he said. "It was quite a change. A lot of the things I used to do are a lot tougher now."

A SHINY NEW HOME

The Patriots were experiencing a sort of harmonic convergence. They were the world champions, and they were moving into a beautiful new stadium, completed during the offseason—making New England

the first team in NFL history to win a Super Bowl one year and move into a new home the next.

CMGI Field, which would later be renamed Gillette Stadium, was built adjacent to old Foxboro Stadium at a cost of $325 million. (After a battle with the legislature over funding, public money provided $70 million for infrastructure, including much-needed work on access roads.) The 68,000-seat venue had all the amenities that the old Foxboro Stadium lacked. There were chair backs for all the seats, and all were angled toward midfield—pleasant changes for fans who had braved the chilly metal bleachers at the old stadium. There was a full complement of luxury boxes; Kraft gained 46 luxury suites and two club lounges with the move. And there were deluxe locker rooms that dwarfed the accommodations at

the old place, as well as a guaranteed hot shower, something the players didn't always get after a practice or game at the old stadium.

"Getting a hot shower, that's one of the biggest things," veteran wide receiver Troy Brown said.

When the Patriots came out blazing at the start of the season, there was no reason to think they weren't going to assume their rightful place atop the AFC once again. They scored 115 points in their first three games, causing Brady to wonder aloud to teammate David Patten on at least one occasion whether they could go undefeated. They crushed the Steelers on opening night in their new place, 30–14, and followed that up with a 44–7 domination of the Jets in the Meadowlands and a dramatic 41–38 overtime victory over the Chiefs at Gillette Stadium.

The Patriots christened their new home, Gillette Stadium, with a 30–14 win over the Steelers on September 9, 2002, in front of a capacity crowd.
Al Bello/Getty Images

TROY BROWN

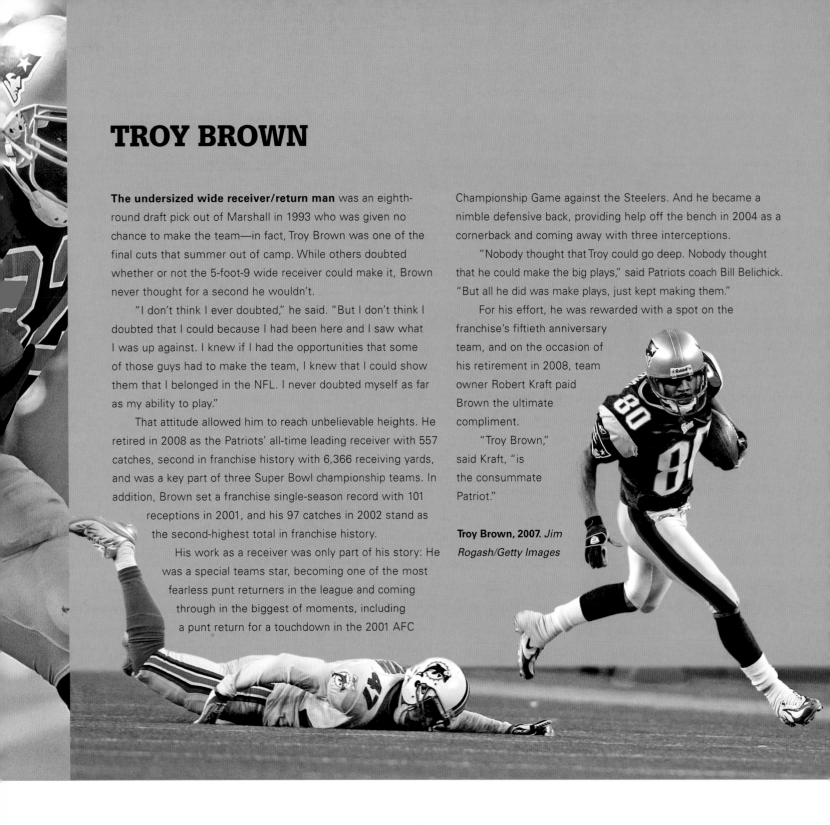

The undersized wide receiver/return man was an eighth-round draft pick out of Marshall in 1993 who was given no chance to make the team—in fact, Troy Brown was one of the final cuts that summer out of camp. While others doubted whether or not the 5-foot-9 wide receiver could make it, Brown never thought for a second he wouldn't.

"I don't think I ever doubted," he said. "But I don't think I doubted that I could because I had been here and I saw what I was up against. I knew if I had the opportunities that some of those guys had to make the team, I knew that I could show them that I belonged in the NFL. I never doubted myself as far as my ability to play."

That attitude allowed him to reach unbelievable heights. He retired in 2008 as the Patriots' all-time leading receiver with 557 catches, second in franchise history with 6,366 receiving yards, and was a key part of three Super Bowl championship teams. In addition, Brown set a franchise single-season record with 101 receptions in 2001, and his 97 catches in 2002 stand as the second-highest total in franchise history.

His work as a receiver was only part of his story: He was a special teams star, becoming one of the most fearless punt returners in the league and coming through in the biggest of moments, including a punt return for a touchdown in the 2001 AFC Championship Game against the Steelers. And he became a nimble defensive back, providing help off the bench in 2004 as a cornerback and coming away with three interceptions.

"Nobody thought that Troy could go deep. Nobody thought that he could make the big plays," said Patriots coach Bill Belichick. "But all he did was make plays, just kept making them."

For his effort, he was rewarded with a spot on the franchise's fiftieth anniversary team, and on the occasion of his retirement in 2008, team owner Robert Kraft paid Brown the ultimate compliment.

"Troy Brown," said Kraft, "is the consummate Patriot."

Troy Brown, 2007. *Jim Rogash/Getty Images*

At that point, a certain level of satisfaction set in. The Patriots allowed themselves to slip a little bit, losing the edge that had made them so great the previous season. According to some Chargers players, the Patriots talked a lot of trash during warmups before a September 29 game in San Diego—the Chargers responded with a 21–14 defeat of New England. It was the first of four straight losses and the beginning of the end for the 2002 team, which couldn't stop the run and paid for it with losses down the stretch to Oakland, Tennessee, and the Jets. At season's end, New England was on the outside of the playoffs looking in, a rude shock to the system for a team that, the year before, had become America's sweethearts.

In the days before Super Bowl XXXVII, Belichick wrote an editorial in *The New York Times*, a

semi-serious guide for the next coach to win the big game. Called, "OK Champ, Now Comes the Hard Part," he listed 37 pieces of advice for whichever coach ended up taking home the Lombardi Trophy. The list started as a way to prepare for all the good things that would come their way: "You might think back thirty years, when your gofer job entailed picking up Raiders or Oilers game film at the airport at one a.m., and then smile because you're at work and there's confetti stuck to your face," and "You'll hug your family. But this time, eight hundred million people will be watching you. Try to remember to fix your hair." Then, the list turns to the bad things, many of which seemed to encapsulate the 2002 Patriots. "You'll notice that all your opponents know your team a little better than they did this season: they'll hit you a little harder and play a little better

when you show up. Deal with it"; and "Remember, the Smart Coach/Moron Coach Meter, which is currently way off the charts in the right direction, can be very moody."

DYNASTY DELIVERED

Changes would have to be made during the 2003 offseason. The Patriots went out and signed premier outside linebacker Rosevelt Colvin as a free agent, bringing a premier pass rusher to a team that had trouble getting sustained pressure on quarterbacks the year before. Colvin had opened his career in Chicago and had been a longtime favorite of Belichick. The signing was one of the least surprising transactions of Belichick's tenure—in the days leading up to a 2002 game between the Patriots and Bears, Belichick spoke extensively about Colvin's

Tom Brady and the Patriots offense were looking for answers during their disappointing 9–7 season in 2002. Wearing throwback uniforms on Thanksgiving Day, New England pulled off a 20–12 win over the hapless Detroit Lions. *Al Messerschmidt/ Getty Images*

Ty Law greets Lawyer Milloy before the Patriots' game in Buffalo for the 2003 season opener. Former New Englanders Milloy and Drew Bledsoe helped the Bills stymie the Patriots, 31–0. *Damian Strohmeyer/Sports Illustrated/Getty Images*

greatness. (As it turned out, Colvin only played two games for New England in 2003 before missing the rest of the year due to injury.)

In addition, the Patriots added veteran safety Rodney Harrison, a big hitter who instantly made his mark with the team: In his first week of training camp, he went jaw-to-jaw with Brady, hit Troy Brown so hard the two nearly came to blows, and mixed it up with veteran running back Kevin Faulk. Harrison quickly became a fan favorite and a go-to guy for the younger defensive backs, who called him "Hot Rod" and frequently teased him about his age.

The biggest move came in the days leading up to the 2003 season, when New England cut loose Lawyer Milloy. The veteran was considered a key figure in the team's recent success, but he refused to take a pay cut, and the Patriots decided to release him.

"Today is a day that nobody is happy about," Belichick said, explaining the move to a shocked media corps in the workroom at Gillette Stadium. "This isn't the way we wanted this story to end. It was the hardest situation that I've had to go through like this, here or anywhere else."

The decision was made all the more difficult when Buffalo—New England's division rival—scooped Milloy up just days before the two teams were to play in the season opener. Buoyed by the re-energized Milloy and an absolutely flammable Drew Bledsoe, the Bills crushed the visiting Patriots, 31–0. The defeat—which remains one of the worst losses of the Belichick era—gave the critics ample opportunity to take their shots at Belichick and his approach. "Let me say this clearly—they hate their coach," analyst Tom Jackson famously proclaimed on ESPN.

But the Patriots, as they did so many times over the years under Belichick, responded to the adversity. They were able to split their first four games, going to Philadelphia and rebounding to beat the Eagles 31–10. They followed that with a 23–16 win at the expense of the Jets, before stumbling against Steve Spurrier and the Redskins, 20–17—a loss that came when tight end Daniel Graham was unable to come up with a key Brady pass in the final few moments.

Four weeks into the season, the Patriots were 2–2 and stuck squarely in the middle of the NFL pack. As a home game against powerful Tennessee loomed, no one was quite sure which direction the season was going to go.

The 38–30 win over the Titans on October 5, 2003, kicked off a two-year run unlike anything New England football fans had ever seen before. The 2003

Patriots, who collected 14 wins, didn't often overwhelm their opponents; only 6 of the victories were by double digits. Instead, they took their time, waiting for an opponent to make a mistake and then capitalizing on it with a big play at a key moment. They won shootouts (a 38–34 win over the Colts was highlighted by a last-second goal-line stop by Willie McGinest), low-scoring games (there were two 12–0 wins and a 9–3 victory), and the occasional laugher (New England would get revenge on Buffalo in the regular-season finale, taking a 31–0 blowout in exchange for the rout in the season opener). There were taut, well-contested affairs in which Belichick outsmarted the opposition—including a November win over Denver where the Patriots deliberately took a late safety, but ended up getting the ball back down the stretch and came away with a 30–26 victory in the final minute.

All-Pro defensive tackle Richard Seymour (93) celebrates after stopping Tennessee quarterback Steve McNair at Gillette Stadium on October 5, 2003. The Patriots' 38–30 win over the Titans started a 12-game winning streak to end the season. *Darren McCollester/Getty Images*

Safety Rodney Harrison (37) picks off a Peyton Manning pass in front of Indianapolis tight end Marcus Pollard during New England's 24–14 win in the AFC Championship Game on January 18, 2004, in Foxborough. *Ezra Shaw/Getty Images*

In the postseason opener, the Patriots beat the Titans in a chilly thriller at Gillette Stadium—temps dropped near zero as Adam Vinatieri's 46-yard field goal with 4:11 left gave the Patriots a 17–14 victory, their thirteenth straight win. In the AFC Championship Game, it was Peyton Manning and the Colts who got a dose of the nasty New England winter. Ty Law picked off three Manning passes, and Rodney Harrison added another as the Patriots rolled to a relatively easy 24–14 win, carrying New England to its second Super Bowl in three seasons.

"He went out and proved he's the best corner in the league," Harrison said of Law. "We were really ticked off because no one gave us credit. It was all about Peyton Manning. To go out and pick, pick, pick a guy that everybody was building up . . . it was huge for us."

This trip to the Super Bowl was far different for New England than the first one under Belichick. This time around, no one was calling the Patriots underdogs—that mantle was reserved for the NFC's Carolina Panthers, who had pulled off a surprising postseason run under quarterback Jake Delhomme to land themselves in the first Super Bowl in the history of the franchise.

As for the game itself, Super Bowl XXXVIII was initially a dud—neither team scored for almost the first 27 minutes of play—before it turned into one of the most dramatic finishes in Super Bowl history. As had been the case so often that season, New England was able to hang around and hang around, waiting for the opposition to make a mistake and then taking advantage. In the Super Bowl, that mistake came when Carolina kicker John Kasay booted a kickoff out of bounds late in the fourth quarter with the game tied at 29. That gave the Patriots the ball on their own 40-yard line with 1:08 left and all three timeouts.

As was to be expected, Brady maneuvered the Patriots into field goal range, finding Troy Brown for a 13-yard connection and Deion Branch for a 17-yard pass play, putting New England at the Carolina 23. And as he had two years previous, Adam Vinatieri delivered with the championship on the line, connecting on a 41-yard field goal to give the Patriots their second Super Bowl crown in three seasons and setting off another celebration complete with red, white, and blue confetti.

"It was a great team effort," Belichick said shortly after Vinatieri's kick went through the uprights. "We've done it fifteen weeks in a row. This team met all comers this year, fifteen straight. There's been some heart attacks, but they came out on top."

BACK TO BACK

The Patriots won their first three games of the 2004 season, including a road victory against division rival Buffalo. As September rolled into October, New England kept winning. A 24–10 victory over Miami at Gillette Stadium on October 10 marked their 19th consecutive victory dating back to the previous October, setting a new NFL record for consecutive wins. (They broke the previous record of 18 straight shared by the Chicago Bears of 1933–1934 and 1941–1942, the Miami Dolphins of 1972–1973, the San Francisco 49ers of 1989–1990, and the Denver Broncos of 1997–1998.)

"They're some great teams, and it's nice to be a part of that," linebacker Tedy Bruschi said of the record, but he added, "during the season the only milestone that teams want is the Super Bowl."

"I did tell the [players] that I felt they should be proud of what they accomplished and that no other team in pro football has done that," Belichick said.

"But that being said, that is not our only goal, to win four games. So, we are going to try to do a little more than that."

"He rarely celebrates anything," Harrison said of Belichick's postgame reaction, "and to lead a team to nineteen victories in a row is something to be proud of."

Commissioner Paul Tagliabue issued a statement saying, "The Patriots' achievement is not only unprecedented but also remarkable when you consider how competitive our league is today. Congratulations to the entire Patriots organization on this extraordinary milestone."

The streak wouldn't last much longer—the Steelers blew out the Patriots on Halloween at Heinz Field, 34–20. "It's not weird at all," Bruschi said of New England's first defeat since September 28, 2003. "We knew it was a possibility every week. That's why we played so hard and prepared so hard every week. But a couple of things happened, a couple of mistakes . . . and [the Steelers] were rolling." There was another regular-season loss to contend with when New England was shocked by the Dolphins in Miami.

Deion Branch celebrates the first points of Super Bowl XXXVIII, a 5-yard touchdown pass from Tom Brady in the second quarter. Branch caught 10 passes for 143 yards in the game, including the final play to set up the winning kick by Adam Vinatieri. *Mark J. Terrill/AP Images*

COREY DILLON

Corey Dillon. The name itself conjures images of the classic NFL malcontent, a talented but unhappy performer stuck in a culture of losing. The running back was the very best thing about some very bad Cincinnati Bengals teams throughout the late 1990s and into the early years of the twenty-first century. In the spring of 2004, he saw a way out. The Patriots came calling, hoping to swing a deal for Dillon.

Dillon and his agent met with Patriots management that spring in an attempt to convince New England he was a changed man. The Patriots believed him, and on Patriots' Day, they announced a deal for the occasionally combustible running back, sending a second-round pick to Cincinnati.

The move shocked people around the league. Dillon wasn't known as the sort of guy who would fit in with the Patriots. He was not known as a high-character guy. He publicly hammered his own team despite the fact that they were in playoff contention in 2003. At one point, he went on a national talk show wearing a Raiders jersey and called a teammate "a bum." In addition, he tossed his equipment into the stands at the end of the season and openly lobbied for a trade when it was clear that Rudi Johnson had passed him on the depth chart in Cincinnati.

"I think everybody pretty much broke even," Dillon said. "We're talking about the New England Patriots. They're the defending Super Bowl champs. They got exactly what they wanted. I guess Cincinnati got exactly what they wanted. Corey Dillon got exactly what he wanted. I'm happy. It's a good deal all around, I think."

Dillon added that he would always have love for Cincinnati and that fan base, "but today is a new day. I'm just going to finish what I started in Cincinnati in New England. It's the first time I've been this excited about a season since I've been in college."

True to his word, Dillon was a good soldier, and he propelled the Patriots offense to even greater heights than the previous season. Dillon rushed for at least 100 yards in 9 of his 15 regular-season starts in 2004 and ended the season with 1,635 rushing yards. He also ran for a game-high 75 yards

and scored a touchdown against the Eagles in the team's Super Bowl triumph.

Although Dillon continued to lead New England's running attack in 2005 and 2006, he couldn't match his earlier successes and retired after the 2006 season, having gained 3,180 yards rushing with 37 touchdowns in three seasons with the Patriots.

Corey Dillon, 2004. *Jeff Gross/Getty Images*

Fans cheer a Patriots touchdown during New England's 24–10 victory over Miami at Gillette Stadium on October 10, 2004. It was the team's 19th consecutive win dating back to October 5, 2003. *Stephan Savoia/AP Images*

Compared to the previous postseason wins against the Colts and Steelers, in which the Patriots dominated their AFC rivals, Super Bowl XXXIX was almost anticlimactic.

Against the Eagles, New England produced its least dramatic of the three Super Bowl victories, taking the lead for good early in the fourth quarter and going on to a 24–21 win that was only that close because Philadelphia scored a late touchdown. Receiver Deion Branch took home MVP honors for his 11 catches for 133 yards. Corey Dillon rushed for 75 yards and a touchdown, while Brady was 23-for-33 for 236 yards and two touchdown passes—for the first time in New England's three Super Bowl appearances, Brady did not walk away with the game's top individual award.

Corey Dillon reaches into the end zone for a touchdown early in the fourth quarter of Super Bowl XXXIX to give the Patriots a 21–14 lead over the Eagles. Dillon ran the ball 18 times during the game. *Al Tielemans/Sports Illustrated/Getty Images*

The only sense of Super Bowl drama came from the Philadelphia receiving corps. In the days leading up to the game, there was some question as to whether or not a hobbled Terrell Owens would play. The occasionally mouthy wide receiver did play, and he turned in a terrific performance, catching nine passes for 122 yards, a performance that would have been good enough for MVP honors if the Eagles had found a way to win. And speaking of occasionally mouthy wide receivers, Philadelphia's Freddy Mitchell—who had caused a bit of a flap in the week before the game by saying he didn't know the names of the players in New England's secondary—got his comeuppance at the end of the evening. After holding him to one catch for 11 yards, Belichick told *Sports Illustrated* exactly what he thought of Mitchell: "All he does is talk.

He's terrible, and you can print that. I was happy when he was in the game."

Belichick was far more complimentary of his own players after the game.

"These players have just played great all year," he said. "They've played their best in big games, and they deserve it. They really deserve it."

Super Bowl XXXIX marked the end of an era for the Patriots coaching staff. Romeo Crennel soon departed for Cleveland to become head coach of the Browns, and Charlie Weis accepted the job as head coach at Notre Dame. The Super Bowl championship was the final game together for three coaches who had built a remarkable bond.

"I think the world of those two guys," Belichick said after the game. "They've done a tremendous job. I don't know what the future holds for Romeo,

Rodney Harrison (37) celebrates with Asante Samuel (22) and Mike Vrabel (50) after Harrison's interception with 10 seconds left in the game sealed the victory for New England in Super Bowl XXXIX. *Brian Bahr/Getty Images*

but I'm sure, in my opinion, he certainly deserves an opportunity to be a head coach in this league, or wherever he wants to do it. And Charlie has done a tremendous job, especially the last few weeks, especially with his responsibilities. I was thrilled to be able—for the three of us to be able to hug each other. We've been together a long time, all the way back to the Giants. It was a good feeling."

After accepting the Lombardi Trophy for the third time in four years, Kraft took to the podium and delivered a fitting postscript for a collection of players who had carved out the NFL's first real dynasty of the salary-cap era.

"Fans of New England—the best fans that any team could wish for. This is your third Super Bowl in four years. This great accomplishment happened because we are blessed to have smart and talented players, a brilliant and tireless coach in Coach Belichick and his entire staff, and a great personnel department led by Scott Pioli. The NFL is the great leveler of all sports. And the Super Bowl is the highest form of competition. Competition is the foundation of what made this country great. And I am proud that we were able to win this Super Bowl stressing team, and not individual accomplishment. We're honored to be here."

That cool February night in Jacksonville marked the end of one of the most remarkable runs in NFL history. Over the next few years, the Patriots would lose key coaches, players, and personnel men, and they would be forced to reinvent themselves. For Belichick and Brady, their greatest challenge still lay ahead.

GLORY DAYS

2006–2009

The games are sold out. The players are constantly in demand for personal appearances and endorsements. National media flock to Foxborough on a regular basis. Businessmen and titans of industry look upon the team as a model for how to build a brand. And professional sports executives marvel at New England's management style, using it as a blueprint for their own approaches to success.

These modern Patriots resemble their forebears in name only. Instead of traveling to practice by car, they have a state-of-the-art practice facility directly behind the stadium. Instead of a cramped locker room, they have one of the most spacious in the league. Instead of woeful and sorry management, they have a front office and ownership group that are recognized as among the finest in professional sports. And even with this seemingly well-oiled machine, there's no shortage of drama surrounding the Patriots.

"The Patriots are like a soap opera," linebacker Rosevelt Colvin once said.

NEW FACES, NEW CHALLENGES

To that end, the Patriots' 2006 season opened with a contract dispute. Wide receiver Deion Branch was upset about his status. Since the turn of the century, the Patriots organization had been highly effective in preaching the team concept above all else, but that team-first approach also meant they couldn't shell out money for individual contracts like other clubs did. So, while the Patriots were able to win games, contracts were a lingering problem in New England—even if the team was successful at keeping a lid on those problems. The occasional crack in the armor did emerge, however. In the spring of 2004, veteran Ty Law, angry when negotiations for an extension didn't go his way, ripped Bill Belichick and the Patriots. Claiming he was lied to, Law told the *Boston Globe* that he "no longer want[ed] to be a Patriot. I can't even see myself putting on that uniform again, that's how bad I feel about playing here." (Law would play one more season with New

The New England Patriots have fostered a deep winning tradition at Gillette Stadium. *Kirby Lee/NFL/ Getty Images*

England before being released.) Later that summer, first-round pick Benjamin Watson held out for roughly three months before signing his rookie contract. And Richard Seymour was a brief holdout the following year but relented and came into training camp after the sides reached a contract agreement.

The contract dispute between the team and Branch simmered from the end of the 2005 season until the start of the following season. Even though they exchanged offers, the two sides remained apart through the spring and into the summer, and Branch broke off negotiations in June. The holdout lasted throughout training camp and into the preseason, and in late August, the team took the unprecedented step of allowing Branch to negotiate a deal with another team. Branch and his representation were unable to reach a deal with another team, and on September 11, 2006, New England traded Branch to Seattle for a first-round pick in the 2007 draft.

The move was surprising on a number of levels. Under Belichick, the Patriots had never had a player engage in such an extended holdout. In addition, they had never caved in to a player's demands in such a fashion before, allowing him to dictate the terms. The Belichick/Pioli Patriots certainly had never allowed a player to negotiate with other teams. While the trade wasn't as shocking as the release of Lawyer Milloy before the start of the 2003 season had been, the move was a stunner for many in the locker room.

With Deion Branch holding out and David Givens signed by Tennessee as a free agent, the Patriots opened training camp in 2006 with a bunch of newcomers at wide receiver. Among those shown here, only Reche Caldwell (87) made the team; he went on to lead New England with 61 catches. *Stephan Savoia/ AP Images*

"When you look at Deion Branch, he embodies everything we want in a football player," said Seymour, one of the few players who spoke to the media the day of the trade. "Everything we talk about, the kind of guy we want on this football team, he did as good a job as anybody of embodying that. It's a tough day for a lot of guys on this football team, especially guys like myself who came in with Deion Branch. . . . To not have number eighty-three in a Patriots uniform definitely hurts."

Brady had now seen the occasionally gruesome reality of personnel decisions in the NFL on two occasions. First, his good friend Milloy was shown the gate in 2003. Now, it was Branch. He had grown close to the wide receiver, doing his part to raise Branch's profile whenever he could, including inviting him along as part of a *60 Minutes* piece on the quarterback.

"I think everybody would have wanted Deion here. Certainly myself, knowing what kind of person and player he is. But as coach kind of said to us, it didn't work out," said Brady after the trade was made. "I speak for myself when I say that I'm a very emotional person, and over the last four or five months it's been draining. So in a sense I learned a valuable lesson last week that when something is really out of your control, you can't let it drain you. At least I feel like now I can move on. I know he's moved on, and I wish him luck. This team now has to really look forward and, with the guys we have, go out and do the best we can."

Brady went on to talk about the close relationships players develop with one another, noting that coaches don't have the same kind of relationships with players and management doesn't know the individuals as well. "In that sense," Brady added, "it's probably tougher for players to see players go because we hang out. We're buddies. It goes far beyond the football field. . . . We hate to see players like Deion go. We hate to see Willie [McGinest] go and Adam [Vinatieri]. The list goes on for the last three or four years. But . . . I have to focus on playing quarterback now and that just means I have to play that much better and I'm fully prepared to do that. I'm going to do my best to help this team win, and I support our team and our organization just as I support players

and their decisions." Taking an almost philosophical approach, Brady added that players coming and going is part of this process. "I've learned to kind of expect the unexpected."

Seymour's words proved prescient: not having No. 83 in a Patriots uniform that season definitely hurt. Without Branch and the usually reliable David Givens, who had left for Tennessee as a free agent, the Patriots opened the 2006 season a little thin at the receiver position. Instead of the 137 combined receptions the Branch-Givens tandem brought to the offense the season before, New England had veteran free agent Reche Caldwell move into the number-one receiver position. Veteran Troy Brown was still around, but there were fewer and fewer familiar faces for Brady to throw to. Instead of old favorites, such as Branch and Givens, there were players like Doug Gabriel and Chad Jackson, two newcomers who struggled at times to pick up the offense. In addition, after two seasons in which he totaled nearly 600 carries, running back Corey Dillon was starting to break down and could no longer be the consistent presence in the running game he had been in 2004 and 2005.

While the Patriots were no longer the unstoppable force that had rolled through the league in 2003 and 2004, they were still head and shoulders above most of the rest of the NFL. They had Brady, who was doing wonders with what, in retrospect, was a slapped-together offensive unit. And the defense was as potent as ever. Led by veterans Richard Seymour, Rodney Harrison, Mike Vrabel, Tedy Bruschi, and Vince Wilfork, New England played "bend-but-don't-break defense"—opposing offenses moved the ball up and down the field, but failed to break the goal line on a consistent basis—allowing the Patriots to more than make up for any sort of offensive deficiencies. Early on, although blowouts were few and far between, New England won six of its first seven before dropping back-to-back home games for the first time since 2002, losing to Peyton Manning and the Colts, 27–20, and suffering a stunner at the hands of Eric Mangini and the Jets, 17–14.

The loss to Mangini, New England's former defensive coordinator, was particularly galling for the Patriots. Mangini, who just a year earlier was

MIKE VRABEL

Mike Vrabel was contemplating law school before he got a call in 2001 from Bill Belichick.

The undersized defensive lineman out of Ohio State who was taken in the third round by the Steelers in 1997 was a sack machine in college—he had 36 over the course of his college career with the Buckeyes—but was sitting behind a collection of great linebackers in Pittsburgh. In addition, he was considered too small to play defensive end in the pros and too big and slow to play the role of traditional linebacker in the NFL. His one brief, shining moment came during the 1997 playoffs, when he delivered a late sack of Patriots quarterback Drew Bledsoe to cement a postseason victory over New England.

Steelers coach Bill Cowher had told him that while it was unlikely he would start for the Steelers, he would almost certainly play somewhere in the NFL—he was too good and too smart not to find a job somewhere. (Vrabel later credited Cowher for his decision not to retire.) And so, in the spring of 2001, when Vrabel was cut loose by Pittsburgh, the Patriots were one of the first teams that came calling. Belichick needed fast, strong, and smart former defensive linemen to be plugged in as linebackers in his 3–4 defense in New England. He had two guys like that in Willie McGinest and Tedy Bruschi, and he believed Vrabel could be another one. He convinced Vrabel to sign as a free agent in the spring of 2001.

Vrabel exceeded all expectations, slipping right into the New England defense. He quickly became a stalwart at the linebacker spot for the Patriots, and he started 110 games between 2001 and 2008. (He also checked in occasionally as a pass-catching tight end, most notably in goal-line situations in big games.) When it came to versatility and flexibility, no defensive player was perhaps more identifiable as the face of the Patriots than Vrabel, who was ultimately dealt to Kansas City following the 2008 season.

"When Mike arrived in 2001, we knew we were adding a solid outside linebacker," said Belichick in a statement the day the trade was made. "But where Mike took it from there exceeded our highest hopes. Mike Vrabel epitomizes everything a coach could seek in a professional football player: toughness, intelligence, playmaking, leadership, versatility, and consistency at the highest level. Behind the scenes, Mike's wit and personality [are] things we have all enjoyed about coming to work every day.

"The toughest aspect of my job is the day I stop coaching people like Mike, who did everything in his power to contribute to team success. Of all the players I have coached in my career, there is nobody I enjoyed working with more than Mike. In the same way people recognize guys like Troy Brown, we appreciate and thank Mike Vrabel. He is one of the very special Patriots champions."

Showing his versatility, tight end Vrabel hauls in a touchdown reception against the Eagles during Super Bowl XXXIX. *Julie Jacobson/AP Images*

Mike Vrabel, 2003. *Ronald Martinez/ Getty Images*

Defensive end Ty Warren was part of a formidable defensive line in 2006. Here he brings down Buffalo quarterback J. P. Losman for a game-winning safety in the fourth quarter of the season opener in Foxborough. *Michael Valeri/ NFL/Getty Images*

celebrated as the next great young defensive mind to come out of Foxborough, was now Public Enemy No. 1 around Gillette Stadium, not only for taking a job with a hated division rival, but also for raiding the Patriots coaching staff and personnel department on the way out the door. (One defensive player derisively called Mangini "Fredo," in reference to the brother from the *Godfather* movies who eventually went against the family.)

But the Patriots would right the ship. Brady and his new receivers managed to make things work, and New England suffered just one more

regular-season loss the rest of the way before sailing into the playoffs as division champs with a 12–4 mark. They got a measure of revenge against Mangini and the Jets, knocking them out of the playoffs with a 37–16 win at Gillette Stadium. That set the stage for a battle with the San Diego Chargers, which many believed to be the team with the most pure talent in the league.

The division-round matchup in San Diego started as a bitter, physical game—and went downhill from there. The young Chargers had done their share of boasting in the days leading up to the

ERIC MANGINI

Say the words "Eric Mangini" around Foxborough these days, and you are most likely met with a dismissive wave of the hand. Some members of the organization openly mock him as a turncoat, a traitor. One player has gone so far as to refer to him as "Fredo," after the weak and traitorous son from *The Godfather*.

But back in the early days of the twenty-first century, Mangini's name was spoken of in reverential tones. He was going to be the next great defensive mind to spring from the Belichick/Parcells coaching tree, a talented young man who had worked his way up from a job as a PR intern and ball boy—thanks in large part to his association with Belichick—with the Browns to spend a year as New England's defensive coordinator in 2005.

However, it all started to go sour for Mangini when he took the head coaching job with the Jets in 2006. Mangini, who became the youngest head coach in the league at age 35 when he took over in New York, had somehow alienated Belichick by deciding to jump ship to the Jets. Whether it was the fact that Belichick believed he wasn't ready for the job, the fact that he poached many coaches on his way out the door, or the fact that he ended up going to a team that had openly feuded with Belichick in the past, no one is sure. But the relationship between Belichick and Mangini went from warm and friendly to frosty in a matter of weeks.

Mangini did have a strong first year, leading the Jets to a 10–6 mark and a playoff berth. In the season opener against the

Patriots in 2007, he was seen as the one who blew the whistle on New England's videotaping, leading to the "Spygate" scandal and further tarnishing his image. Mangini was fired at the end of the 2008 season by the Jets, and he has struggled since then, having his troubles in 2009 with the woeful Cleveland Browns.

Defensive coordinator Eric Mangini confers with linebacker Tedy Bruschi during a game against the Buffalo Bills in Foxborough in October 2005. Mangini departed to became head coach of the Jets following the season. *Robert E. Klein/AP Images*

contest. They had every reason to feel good about their chances—they had talented young quarterback Philip Rivers, all-world running back LaDainian Tomlinson, and linebacker Shawne Merriman, who led the league with 17 sacks despite sitting out four games for violating the NFL's steroid policy.

The Chargers took control early, taking an eight-point lead into the final quarter as the San Diego fans went crazy. Trailing 21–13 in the fourth, Brady was intercepted by safety Marlon McCree. Rather than going down, McCree tried to return the interception, and as he had been so many times before, Troy Brown

was in the right place at the right time. Brown hit McCree, causing him to fumble, and receiver Reche Caldwell recovered. The Chargers challenged, but the play was upheld, and the Patriots had the ball at the Chargers' 32. Five plays later, Brady hit Caldwell, a former Charger, for a touchdown, and New England added the two-point conversion on a direct snap to running back Kevin Faulk, tying the score. Then with 1:10 left in the game, Stephen Gostkowski kicked a field goal to give the Patriots a 24–21 lead; Chargers kicker Nate Kaeding missed a 54-yard attempt to tie in the final seconds.

Reche Caldwell is about to haul in a pass from Tom Brady in the fourth quarter of the AFC Divisional Playoff Game against San Diego. The 49-yard reception set up the winning field goal for New England. *Mark J. Terrill/ AP Images*

At the end of the game, the Patriots celebrated with their own version of Merriman's spasmodic "Lights Out" sack dance, drawing the ire of the San Diego players. Rivers started screaming at New England cornerback Ellis Hobbs, and Tomlinson—who had to be restrained from going after some of the Patriots players on the field after the game—lashed out in his postgame press conference. "I would never react in that way. I was very upset," Tomlinson said. "When you go to the middle of our field and start doing the dance Shawne Merriman is known for, that is disrespectful. They showed no class and maybe that comes from the head coach."

Brady, who shook off a poor first half to finish 27-for-51 for 280 yards and two touchdowns, did his part to show some class in his postgame remarks.

"That was a tougher game than I could ever remember playing," the quarterback said. "It was just a great team we played, so we knew it was going to be sixty minutes that we had to do it, and it was just great to come out of here with a win."

And so, with a motley collection of receivers and an inconsistent running game, the Patriots were headed to their fourth AFC Championship Game in six years, this time in Indianapolis to take on Peyton Manning and the Colts. To almost everyone's surprise, New England took control early, building an 18-point lead midway through the second quarter, thanks in large part to a 39-yard interception return for a touchdown by cornerback Asante Samuel. Indianapolis' only first-half scores came on field goals by an old Patriots hero, Adam Vinatieri.

This game, however, did not follow the same trends as previous Patriots–Colts playoff matchups. Indianapolis came marching back, tying the game at 21 midway through the third quarter and setting off a memorable game of can-you-top-this between the two best quarterbacks of their generation.

Manning ultimately got the better of his rival when, trailing 34–31, he led the Colts on a late touchdown drive to take a four-point lead. Brady and the Patriots got the ball back in the final minute with a chance to win, but the quarterback threw an interception to defensive back Marlin Jackson, ending the game and allowing the Colts to finally get that long-desired win postseason over New England.

"It was a very tough football game against a good team—you've got to give the Colts credit; they made more plays than we did, and they deserved to win," Belichick said after the game. "It was about as competitive a game as you can get."

"We just let too many opportunities get away," Brady said. "We had the ball in good field position at certain times. We should have got the ball in the end zone. We look at this one [as a game] against a good team that plays well at home."

It was New England's first loss in the championship game in six appearances, and the Patriots saw their hopes of winning four Super Bowls in six years—à la the Steelers of the late 1970s—derailed. But that postseason loss to Manning and Company brought about a new mantra for Belichick and the Patriots: 60 minutes. It would be an approach that in many ways defined their attitude for the 2007 season.

Asante Samuel, who led the league with 10 interceptions during the season, picks off a Peyton Manning pass and runs it back for a touchdown in the second quarter of the AFC Championship Game against the Colts. *Jed Jacobsohn/Getty Images*

After years of scorching the Patriots as a member of the Dolphins, Wes Welker became an integral part of New England's offense. He led the league with 112 catches in 2007. *Scott Boehm/Getty Images*

SETTING THE STAGE FOR PERFECTION

One of the most memorable offseasons in NFL history began less than two months after the defeat to Indianapolis in the RCA Dome. The Patriots were hell-bent on making sure they didn't go into the regular-season with a second-rate collection of pass-catchers again, so they went out and acquired slot receiver Wes Welker from the Dolphins for a pair of draft picks. During his time in Miami, the undersized receiver had been an eternal nemesis for Belichick and the Patriots—Welker was often the very best thing about a bad Dolphins team.

"He killed us in Miami. I remember it. We had someone double [him] down there, when he was playing in the slot in Miami, and we still couldn't cover him," Belichick later recalled, referencing a 2006 game in which Welker had nine catches for 77 yards as well as 103 yards in kick returns. "He killed us. The next time we played him, we doubled him, but we still had trouble with him."

"If you can't beat him, join him. If you can't stop him, then try to get him on your team. That's basically the philosophy."

Then, on draft weekend, New England acquired mercurial wide receiver Randy Moss. After several successful but tumultuous years in Minnesota, Moss initially welcomed a new start with the Raiders, but he soured on the experience when he realized that the franchise was in a state of disarray. The Patriots were able to acquire Moss for a fourth-round draft pick, an extraordinary gamble for a franchise that—with a few notable exceptions—had always prided itself on selecting players of high character first and foremost. Moss' checkered reputation was a concern for some, who believed he would poison the New England locker room. He reportedly had a "one-strike" policy when he arrived with the Patriots, and he was determined to make that chance count.

"I don't think you all understand how excited I am to really be a part of this organization," Moss said on his introductory conference call. "I think [the Patriots'] record and what they're about speaks massive volumes, and I'm just very happy to find some happiness and get back to what I love to do, which is play football and go out there and compete."

When asked about a report that Belichick had seen Moss run a 4.29 40-yard dash, Moss dropped a classic soundbyte that left the rest of the NFL shuddering.

"Let's put it this way—the Moss of old is back," he said. "We'll leave it at that."

But after a preseason in which Moss struggled to get on the field, the reference to the "Moss of old" brought back negative connotations. Then came the season opener, where Moss announced his presence with authority against the Jets, putting up 183 receiving yards and a touchdown in a rout at the Meadowlands. Everything worked that afternoon for the Patriots. The combination of Moss and Brady was a marvel. Welker caught virtually everything that was thrown in his direction. Ellis Hobbs returned a kickoff 108 yards. And the defense bottled up the New York passing attack along the way to a 38–14 win that wasn't even as close as the score suggests.

"I think there were a lot of positives," Brady said after the game. "Anytime you get a win on the road in this division, it's a tough way to start. I am really proud of the way the team prepared."

The day eventually would be remembered for much more than the final score, however. On a tip from the Jets, NFL security confiscated cameras from the New England sideline that showed the Patriots videotaping New York's defensive signals. A flagrant breach of league rules, the Patriots were slapped with a $500,000 fine (Belichick himself was hit with an additional $250,000 fine) and the loss of a first-round draft pick. The incident, which came to be known as "Spygate," would dominate NFL headlines for the rest of the season. Setting aside the fact that most teams have been known to engage in similar chicanery—and the fact that most teams knew the Patriots had been engaging in the act for years—the league predictably cried "foul!" as New England's three Super Bowl titles were called into question.

After the league instituted the stiff penalties on the organization, the team circled the wagons, and the incident proved to be a rallying cry on the field for the Patriots, who used a "shock and awe" offense to dominate the rest of the league. In a Sunday night game against the Chargers the following weekend,

Always explosive—with both his play and his actions—Randy Moss made his presence felt immediately upon joining the Patriots. His nine catches for 183 yards, including a 51-yard touchdown play, helped New England kick off 2007 with a 38–14 win over the Jets. *Scott Boehm/Getty Images*

with the whole country watching, New England served notice that it wasn't about to back down. In a rematch of their bitterly contested playoff game from the year before, the Patriots throttled San Diego, 38–14. All of New England's options were on display on both sides of the ball. Brady tossed three touchdown passes; Moss had 105 yards on eight receptions with two touchdown catches; new linebacker Adalius Thomas had a pick-six, taking the ball back 65 yards on an interception; and veteran linebacker Rosevelt Colvin had two sacks and an interception of his own. It was a truly awesome display of football, leaving a stunned Chargers team looking for the license plate of the truck that had just run them over.

"They just jumped on us like a spider monkey," said Chargers fullback Lorenzo Neal.

After the game, Belichick was surrounded by his players, who embraced him. In his postgame press conference, Brady left no doubt as to where he stood in the wake of the scandal.

"We still have a lot of fun coming in and playing for Coach Belichick who—I've said this so many times—I think we're all lucky to play for him, because he's the best. There's no question," Brady said. "I haven't played for a lot of other head coaches, but I couldn't imagine anyone else being as disciplined as he is in getting us prepared to play. I hope our fans realize how lucky they have it, because there's not a lot of teams in the NFL that are like this.

"We're all lucky to play for him. He's the best coach probably in the history of the NFL."

There was no middle ground about the man at the center of the scandal. In New England, Belichick was cast as a hero, someone unfairly put upon by the national press and enemy fans.

"In New England, the Patriots' videotape scandal has yielded an unlikely outcome: Belichick as victim," wrote Judy Battista in *The New York Times*. "As the final seconds ticked off the clock Sunday night, several Patriots, including Tedy Bruschi and Brady, embraced him. When Belichick walked toward the tunnel, the crowd cheered loudly, eliciting so many waves of acknowledgment from Belichick that it appeared as if he were running for office. In the locker room, Bruschi emotionally defended Belichick, the

Rosevelt Colvin is about to wrap up San Diego quarterback Philip Rivers for one of his two sacks during New England's 38–14 win over the Chargers on September 16, 2007. *David Drapkin/Getty Images*

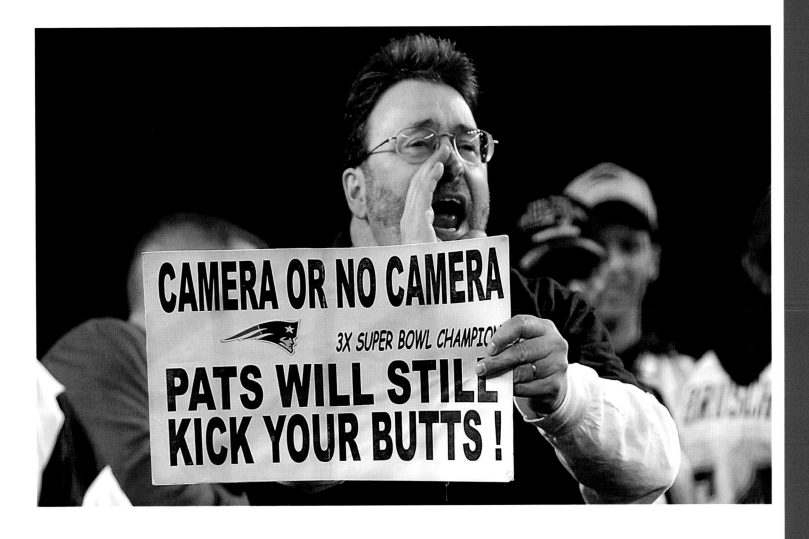

Patriots, and the owner Robert K. Kraft—who was not happy with the embarrassment Belichick's ploys brought to the franchise—and handed Belichick the game ball."

"He's always had our backs; now, we have his," said running back Laurence Maroney, one of several players who embraced Belichick on the field after the game. "He's like our brother. He's family. We look after family around here."

Belichick himself weighed in that Monday. "The team was very supportive, the entire organization, starting with Mr. Kraft going all the way down to the players and everybody else," the coach said. "I appreciate it. It was a nice gesture. The most important thing is for us right now to put all of that behind us. As good of a win as San Diego was, it's time to move on to Buffalo."

A REMARKABLE RUN

On to Buffalo they went, continuing what turned out to be one of the most memorable regular seasons in NFL history. The New England offense shattered records and steamrolled opponents. Brady passed for a league-record 50 touchdowns and 4,806 yards, while Moss shattered the NFL mark for TD catches in a year with 23. The receiver actually led the team in scoring, a rare feat for a non-kicker, with 138 points; kicker Stephen Gostkowski had 137. But it wasn't just the dynamic pairing of Brady and Moss that other teams had to contend with. Wes Welker, freed from football purgatory in South Florida, led the team with 112 receptions, while third receivers Donte Stallworth and Jabar Gaffney chipped in with a combined 82 catches. Maroney was a revelation at running back, finishing with 835 rushing yards and a 4.5-yards-per-carry average.

Fans and players alike rallied behind the team in the wake of the "Spygate" scandal. *Rhons Wise/ Bloomberg/Getty Images*

Complementing the Patriots' record-breaking passing attack in 2007 was the running game of Laurence Maroney. The second-year player tallied 156 rushing yards against Miami in Week 15. *Jim Rogash/Getty Images*

Opposing defenses either had to focus all their attention on stopping Moss or look in another direction. Either way, it was a dicey proposition.

"You've got to pick your poison," Cleveland coach Romeo Crennel said after a game in which the Browns focused on Moss, only to get lit up by tight end Benjamin Watson and running back Sammy Morris in a 34–17 Patriots victory. "Randy Moss has been killing people. We didn't want him to kill us.

"So we died by the hands of somebody else."

Game after game, opponents and records continued to fall. In Week 6, the Patriots carried their 5–0 mark to Dallas to take on the Cowboys. Billed as a showdown of two dangerous receivers, Moss outplayed Dallas' Terrell Owens, and the Patriots crushed the Cowboys, 48–27. Two weeks after that, New England flexed so much offensive muscle in 52–7 slaughter of the Redskins that Washington veterans were left shaking their heads in amazement and left the Redskins franchise with its worst loss in 46 years.

"I don't know of a weakness that they have," said Redskins coach Joe Gibbs.

New England went into the bye week at 9–0, buoyed by a dramatic 24–20 win over the Colts in Indianapolis where the Patriots had to overcome a halftime deficit for the first time all season. A huge effort from Moss in the second half—including a ridiculous one-handed catch in the third quarter and a 55-yard reception in the fourth quarter—allowed New England to get back into the game. But it wasn't over until veteran running back Kevin Faulk extended his arms into the end zone on a 13-yard Tom Brady pass with 3:15 remaining, giving the Patriots a 24–20 lead, their first edge all day.

In the second half of the season, the games started getting tighter. There were three-point wins over the Eagles and Ravens, the latter one a dramatic affair that saw the Patriots score the go-ahead touchdown with less than a minute to go and then hold on for the win when a last-second Hail Mary fell just short of the end zone.

As the victories kept coming, the country continued to splinter into two different sects—those who appreciated the greatness of the 2007 Patriots and those who wanted them to lose, and lose badly.

Moss' amazing one-handed grab helped the Patriots rally back from a second-half deficit against the Colts in early November. *Bob Rosato/Sports Illustrated/ Getty Images*

Kevin Faulk's lunge for the end zone sealed New England's 24–20 win over Indianapolis. *Al Tielemans/Sports Illustrated/Getty Images*

Randy Moss lets Pittsburgh safety Anthony Smith know that his pregame prediction of a Steelers victory over the Patriots on December 9, 2007, had fallen short. *David Drapkin/Getty Images*

One group saw them as an unstoppable football machine, while the other saw them as a bunch of cheating bullies who would stop at nothing to win. And then, there were the veterans of the 1972 Miami Dolphins team, who were in danger of seeing their legacy as the only team to finish an NFL season with a perfect mark in jeopardy. Several of the players were unabashed in their dislike of New England, none more vocal than former Miami running back Mercury Morris. Asked about the Patriots' run at perfection after the 7–0 start, Morris said, "They're comparing them [the Patriots] to a 17–0 team [the 1972 Dolphins]? If they were 17–0, but I think they are like ten games short right now, right? They got ten more icebergs to go through in this *Titanic* trip that they're talking about. So far nobody's made it across there except us! So we're docked over here waiting on ya! . . . Don't call me when you're in my town. Call me when you're on my block and I see ya next door when you're moving your furniture in. That's when I know you're going to the championship to play. And if you win it, I'll be dressed up in a tuxedo waiting on my bride."

And the Patriots kept on plowing through those icebergs, piling victory on top of victory and drawing closer to perfection. The contest against Pittsburgh on December 9 was highlighted by a pregame guarantee of victory by Steelers' defensive back Anthony Smith—only to have the Patriots turn him into a punch line with not one but two touchdowns coming at his expense in a 34–13 pasting. There was a 20–10 win over the Jets on a nasty December day that wasn't as close as the score would indicate. A 28–7 win over the Dolphins at home two days before Christmas put New England at 15–0 heading into the regular-season finale against the exceptionally physical Giants in the Meadowlands.

Even though the Giants were locked into a playoff position and, theoretically, had nothing to play for, New York coach Tom Coughlin played his starters for all four quarters. The Patriots were gunning for history—trying to become the first team in NFL history to go 16–0 through the regular season—and the Giants wouldn't lie down for them. New York dominated in much of the early going and built a 12-point lead in the third quarter behind quarterback Eli Manning, who finished with four touchdown passes. But New England responded with a pair of second-half rushing touchdowns by Maroney and a beautifully executed 65-yard touchdown pass from Brady to Moss that gave the Patriots the lead for good. The scoring strike was the fiftieth of the season for Brady, breaking the NFL record for TD passes in a season held by Peyton Manning. It was also Moss' twenty-third touchdown catch, breaking another league record set by Jerry Rice. New England went on to win, 38–35, and complete a 16–0 regular season.

"That was some way to finish the season today," exclaimed Belichick. "It is really exciting to be a part of this football team and what these guys did today— all the credit goes to the players. They stepped up and made a lot of outstanding plays at critical times in the game, especially there in the second half and in the fourth quarter. They came through like they have all year.

"It's a great feeling and now is the time to take a day or two and appreciate what this team has done, but at the same time we have our biggest game of the year coming up and we are going to have to be ready for that."

As time ticked down, the Patriots allowed themselves to start celebrating, if only for a little bit.

"You work all year to try and win every game," Belichick said, "and to win them all is great. I'm very happy about it."

The Patriots stood on the cusp of history—if they won all three playoff games, they would accomplish just the second perfect season in league history, and they would be the first team in league history to run the table and go 19–0. (Miami's 17–0 season had come at a time when the NFL had a 14-game regular-season schedule.)

New England downed the Jaguars 31–20 in the divisional playoff game at Gillette Stadium, and Brady was almost perfect, going 26-for-28 with three touchdowns. The Patriots beat the Chargers, 21–12, in another bitterly contested game between the two teams, to stand at 18–0 heading into Super Bowl XLII. It looked like history was going to be made, especially when it was revealed that the Giants would be their opponents in the title

In a familiar pose, Tom Brady celebrates throwing a record-tying 49th touchdown of the season during the second quarter against the Giants on December 29, 2007. He would break the record with number 50 in the fourth quarter of the 38–35 win. *Al Bello/Getty Images*

game—the same New York team they had beaten in the regular-season finale. Morris, who remained the most outspoken advocate in support of the legacy of the 1972 Dolphins, seemed almost resigned to the fact that Miami would finally have some company in the undefeated club.

"It has been thirty-five years. This record is old enough to be president," Morris said. "These guys are the first guys who have actually come close. I take my hat off to them."

In the days after the AFC Championship, however, things started to slowly unravel. The quarterback clearly had not been at his best against the Chargers, throwing three interceptions and getting knocked around pretty good by the San Diego defense. He appeared to walk gingerly from the podium in the postgame press conference, and he was caught by the paparazzi a day or two later hobbling down a New York City street with a supportive boot over his right foot, sparking an uproar in the media about his medical condition. The quarterback told WEEI later that week it was nothing. "There are always kind of bumps and bruises," he said. "I'll be ready for the Super Bowl. I'm not missing this one.

16–0

Date	Opponent	Score	Record
September 9	@ New York Jets	38–14	1–0
September 16	San Diego Chargers	38–14	2–0
September 23	Buffalo Bills	38–7	3–0
October 1	@ Cincinnati Bengals	34–13	4–0
October 7	Cleveland Browns	34–17	5–0
October 14	@ Dallas Cowboys	48–27	6–0
October 21	@ Miami Dolphins	49–28	7–0
October 28	Washington Redskins	52–7	8–0
November 4	@ Indianapolis Colts	24–20	9–0
November 18	@ Buffalo Bills	56–10	10–0
November 25	Philadelphia Eagles	31–28	11–0
December 3	@ Baltimore Ravens	27–24	12–0
December 9	Pittsburgh Steelers	34–13	13–0
December 16	New York Jets	20–10	14–0
December 23	Miami Dolphins	28–7	15–0
December 29	@ New York Giants	38–35	16–0

I'd have to be on a stretcher to miss this one. There will just be some treatment this week and like I said, games like this you get a little nicked up."

A SUPER FALL

When the Giants showed up at the Super Bowl in Arizona, they were wearing black—ostensibly, to go to a "funeral," said wide receiver Plaxico Burress. It was a gimmicky thing to do, but it got the attention of the media. The media was further taken with Burress when he predicted that New York would win, 23–17. Brady snickered. "We're only going to score seventeen

points?" he said before chuckling about it. "OK. Is Plax playing defense? I wish he had said 45–42 and gave us a little credit for scoring more points."

But that night in the Arizona desert, the Giants showed they were made of sterner stuff. From the start, the heavy underdogs got to the hobbled Brady, knocking him off his spot and slowing the mighty New England offense. On the evening, the Giants sacked Brady five times, a season high for the quarterback. It was a very physical game on both sides that ended up taking its toll on several players, many of whom were injured over the course of the contest.

Wes Welker charges into the end zone with a fourth-quarter touchdown to cinch New England's victory over San Diego in the AFC Championship Game on January 20, 2008. *Jim Rogash/Getty Images*

Heading into Super Bowl XLII, the one obstacle left for the Patriots in their quest for a perfect 19–0 season was a New York Giants team that they had defeated six weeks earlier. *Rob Tringali/Sportschrome/ Getty Images*

The Patriots slugged their way to a 7–3 lead at halftime, but the offensive production that had helped New England outscore opponents all season was nowhere to be seen, lost in the face of a furious New York pass rush. For many, the game bore eerie similarities to the Patriots' upset of the Rams in Super Bowl XXXVI: one high-powered offense stuck in neutral against a sizable underdog. The Giants took a 10–7 lead late in the second half before the New England offense really got going. A gutty drive engineered by Brady ended with him hitting Moss on a 6-yard scoring pattern to make it 14–10 Patriots with just over three minutes left. But the Giants responded with a wild drive, a series in which Manning nearly turned the ball over three times but still found a way to keep the drive alive. The series was highlighted by a ridiculous Eli Manning–to–David

Tyree pass play that started with Manning almost being sacked twice and ended with the quarterback somehow slipping free and finding little-used Tyree for a 32-yard catch that Tyree secured by pinning the ball to the side of his helmet as he fell to the ground.

Buoyed by the amazing sequence, the Giants got new life. When Manning found Burress in the corner of the end zone on a 13-yard pass play with 39 seconds remaining in regulation, New York found itself holding a 17–14 lead. It was a stunning turn of events, and New England was unable to answer. On their final shot, a pair of Brady-to-Moss deep pass attempts were off the mark, and Belichick left the field as time ran out. The perfect season was over.

Eighteen and one. It was a stunning way to end the season, a strange and surreal turn of events that left New York fans delirious with glee and Patriots fans pondering a missed opportunity at perfection. For many New York sports fans who had lost the opportunity to chant "1918" at Boston baseball fans after the Red Sox won the 2004 World Series, "18 and 1" had a fresh ring to it, and many gleefully repeated the sing-song on their way out of the stadium that night.

"We wanted to win the game as bad as the Giants did," said Brady, who was 29-for-48 passing, but mainly unimpressive—completing no pass longer than 19 yards and throwing just one touchdown. "This team worked extremely hard for six months, throughout camp and the season. It was good enough for eighteen wins. It's just the most important one we ended up losing.

"I wish we would have played a little better," the quarterback added. "We played them five weeks ago, and it was a three-point game. Our team is extremely disappointed. Coach Belichick is extremely disappointed. We left it all out there. Guys are spent. Guys played hard and played hurt. I'm sure it will be hard to swallow."

"The players did a great job all year long," Belichick said in a conference call two days after the game. "We played a lot of good football, but we're certainly disappointed about the way it ended. We came so close, but it just didn't work out. It takes a lot to get to this point, but we're starting all over into the '08 season. It's already time to move on. We're into the offseason, and that's just the way it is. So we'll start moving toward next year."

LIFE WITHOUT BRADY

In 2008, the Patriots were expected to get their revenge. The entire cast of characters returned from the 2007 squad, and there was no reason to think that New England wouldn't be able to take the league by storm again. Brady, Moss, and Welker all returned on offense, and the defense, led by veterans like Mike Vrabel, Rodney Harrison, Richard Seymour, Vince Wilfork, and Tedy Bruschi, had a new key component—first-round pick Jerod Mayo, a preternatural linebacker who certainly didn't play like a rookie when he first arrived in Foxborough. All the pieces were in place.

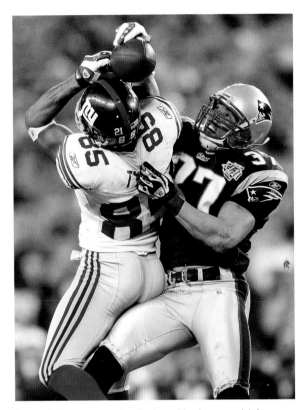

Even tight coverage by Rodney Harrison couldn't prevent New York's David Tyree from making one of the most remarkable catches in football history during Super Bowl XLII. *Andy Lyons/Getty Images*

A disappointed Coach Belichick walks off the field as time runs out on the Patriots' dream season. *Ben Liebenberg/NFL Photos/Getty Images*

But less than a full quarter into the season opener, Chiefs safety Bernard Pollard came up the middle on a blitz. He was met and flattened by New England running back Sammy Morris, but he was able to get up and take one last dive at Brady. As Pollard lunged, Brady was stepping forward to throw a pass to Moss when he was hit in the left knee and fell to the ground, screaming. Just like that, the course of the 2008 season had changed. The Patriots won the game 17–10, but the extent of the injury wasn't known until later in the week— he suffered a torn anterior cruciate ligament and a torn medial collateral ligament in his left knee. Surgery would put him out for the year. It felt like the season had come careening to a halt before it even got started.

The hit drew the ire of Patriots players. "I don't really want to get into it, but for me personally, I think it was dirty," Moss said. "I've never been a dirty player. I honestly don't even know how to play dirty. I just play the game. Any time you see something like that that looks foul, that looks dirty, it opens your eyes. So for me personally, it looked dirty."

The hit was later ruled clean by the league. ("It is not a foul because the defensive player was coming off and affected by a block by the offense," NFL spokesman Greg Aiello told reporters.) Pollard apologized, saying, "It was really an accident. I can't change what happened. I can't do anything but pray for him and hope he has a speedy recovery."

The job now belonged to Matt Cassel, a career backup who last started a game in high school. Cassel

JEROD MAYO

He is the latest star, the unquestioned leader of a new generation of Patriots defenders. Jerod Mayo is the fastest, strongest, and best young linebacker to be drafted by Bill Belichick since he took over the Patriots in 2000 and the finest young linebacker selected since a three-year period in the mid-1990s when the franchise selected Willie McGinest (1994), Ted Johnson (1995), and Tedy Bruschi (1996) in consecutive drafts.

Taken in the first round of the 2008 draft out of Tennessee, Mayo stepped right into the heart of the New England defense, playing almost every snap as a rookie and turning the age-old myth that rookies can't play linebacker in a Bill Belichick–coached defense on its ear.

Of course, he's proven to be much more than just another young linebacker. Mayo finished his rookie season with 128 total tackles (100 solo, 28 assists) and a forced fumble. As a result, he was named the Associated Press Defensive Rookie of the Year for 2008 in a near-unanimous vote: Mayo received 49 of 50 votes cast, with Cincinnati Bengals linebacker Keith Rivers receiving the other vote.

"Jerod has done a lot for us. We have asked a lot of him," Belichick said of Mayo at the end of his rookie season. "From day one, he has been a well-prepared, very mature player who can do a lot of things: play in the running game, play in the

passing game, blitz, help us in the kicking game. He's a good football player [who] has good versatility. He's smart, makes a lot of defensive adjustments and calls for us. He runs well. He is tough. He is a good all-around football player. He is very mature. He is very professional. For a rookie, he is probably as professional as anybody I've coached."

Jerod Mayo quickly asserted himself in the Patriots defense, leading the team in tackles in each of his first two seasons.
Tom Hauck/Getty Images

Tom Brady's 2008 season came to an early—and painful—end when Kansas City's Bernard Pollard hit him in the left leg in the opener, tearing Brady's ACL and MCL and sidelining him for the year. *Paul Jasienski/ Getty Images*

The 49ers defense gave Matt Cassell a rough welcome in the young quarterback's third NFL start, on October 5, 2008. Despite being sacked five times and throwing a pair of interceptions, Cassell led New England to a 30–21 win. *Jed Jacobsohn/ Getty Images*

had played in all four games in the preseason, and his performance had been distinctly underwhelming, sparking some speculation that the Patriots might cut him before the start of the season. He rebounded nicely to help New England win the opener against the Chiefs, but it was clear the Patriots had entered a brave new world with Cassel at the helm of the offense.

"This is something I've been preparing for a long time," Cassel said after the season opener, the first meaningful regular-season action of his career. "It's not something that we expected to come up on the opening day. I went out there, I got a lot of reps during preseason, and that ended up being pretty fortunate for me because I got a lot of looks and everything like that. Obviously, there's an adrenaline pump that went on immediately, and then you just come back and focus on the job at hand and what needed to get done."

Cassel and the Patriots started 3–2, with the two defeats (one to Miami and another to San Diego) by a combined 45 points. But Cassel and the offense started to rally. They didn't come close to the numbers the 2007 team posted, but the young quarterback was able to lead several impressive performances, including four different games in which the offense topped 40 points. In the wake of one of those occasions—a 41–7 victory over Denver— Cassel was named AFC Offensive Player of the Week for his 18-for-24, 185-yard, three-touchdown, zero-turnover performance. Cassel had a career-high passer rating of 136.3, the fifth-highest passer rating in franchise history.

Perhaps Cassel's finest performance of the year came in defeat. On November 13, Brett Favre and the Jets came into Gillette Stadium tied with the Patriots at 6–3 for first place in the division, and New York took a 24–6 lead in the game. But Cassel evoked images of Brady throughout the second half and coolly led New England back into the contest. The comparisons to Brady really took hold in the fourth quarter, when the Patriots took over with 1:04 left, no timeouts, the ball on their own 38-yard line, and trailing by seven. Cassel guided the team downfield, hitting Moss with a dart from 16 yards out with one second on the clock to tie the game. The Jets won in overtime, but Cassel's performance

did not go unnoticed—he completed 30 of 51 passes for 400 yards, all career highs, and three touchdowns. He ran eight times for 62 yards, sixth-most in team history by a quarterback and the most since Steve Grogan ran for 65 in consecutive games in 1978. Cassel became the first Patriot to throw for 300 yards and rush for 50 yards in the same game, and he was the first player since at least the AFL-NFL merger to have 400 passing yards and 60 rushing yards in the same game.

"It's not enough," Cassel said glumly after the game.

A week later, Cassel went 30-for-43 for 415 yards and threw three touchdowns to Randy Moss in a 49–28 blowout of the Dolphins in Miami. The performance made Cassel the first quarterback in franchise history—and only the fifth quarterback in NFL history—to have consecutive games with 400-plus yards passing. His efforts earned a second AFC Offensive Player of the Week honor. It was sweet vindication for Cassel, who wasn't Tom Brady, but he wasn't that bad, either.

"I don't read the papers or anything like that. Once preseason was over, I knew the feedback that I was getting from the coaches, which was all positive. And a lot of people with an outsider's perspective had a different opinion," Cassel said. "It's funny to me that a lot of people casted me out and said, 'This guy's not even going to make the team.' But that's part of sports and that's part of football and overcoming adversities and doing these kinds of things. . . . That's what sports is all about."

Randy Moss' diving catch in the end zone brought New England even, 31–31, against the Jets late in the fourth quarter, after the Patriots trailed by as much as 18 points in the game at home on November 13, 2008. *Jim Rogash/ Getty Images*

Assuming a Brady-esque pose, Matt Cassell signals a touchdown at a snowy Gillette Stadium in late December 2008. Cassell passed for 345 yards and three touchdowns in the 47–7 win over Arizona. *Jim Rogash/Getty Images*

Despite winning four straight and five of their last six games—including an awesome 47–7 win over the eventual NFC champion Cardinals on a snowy December day in Foxborough—the 11–5 Patriots missed the playoffs by a single game. In the meantime, Cassel won himself a fat new contract, as well as the starter's job with the Kansas City Chiefs when the Patriots dealt him away in the offseason along with linebacker Mike Vrabel for a second-round draft pick.

"It is very easy to root for guys like Matt Cassel, who do everything the right way and flourish as a result," Belichick said. "As much as we would have loved to continue working with Matt, we wish him nothing but the best as he takes this next step forward in his career."

THE NEXT GENERATION

At the end of the 2008 season, the Patriots continued to suffer losses. In addition to trading away Vrabel and Cassel, the team lost its offensive coordinator, Josh McDaniels, who was plucked away to become the new head coach in Denver. Perhaps the biggest subtraction was in the front office, where Scott Pioli, who for so many years had been the yin to Belichick's yang, left the Patriots to take the general manager job in Kansas City.

"To sum up in words everything Scott Pioli has meant to this organization and to me personally would be difficult, if not impossible," said Belichick. "From the day I met him, he has demonstrated a passion for football and respect for the game that is second to none."

Nick Caserio does more than just sit behind a desk in his role as director of player personnel. Here he works out with wide receiver Julian Edelman during training camp in August 2009. *Robert E. Klein/AP Images*

The move forced the Patriots to shuffle their front office. They effectively split Pioli's duties between senior football advisor Floyd Reese and director of player personnel Nick Caserio, with Caserio immediately tagged with the mantle of the next great football mind to come out of Foxborough. The move was hailed around the league.

"Nick is a fantastic evaluator. He's a very organized guy," said Atlanta GM Thomas Dimitroff, who worked alongside Caserio in New England before taking the job with the Falcons. "I don't think there are many people in this league that work harder than him. I think he's going to fit in very well with Coach Belichick. He's been around him on the coaching staff on the scouting side. He's very accomplished, and I think he'll be a [very good fit] in this league."

As more and more assistant coaches and executives left Foxborough, it became clear that New England didn't have the trademark on the "Patriot Way" anymore. Instead, their brand was being exported throughout the National Football League. Pioli said as much shortly after taking the job in Kansas City; when he was asked what sort of player he was looking for with the Chiefs, his answer came right out of the Patriots' mission statement: "The same kind of player we're looking for with the 34th pick, that we'll look for in the third round, the fourth round—big, strong, tough, smart, disciplined football players," he proclaimed. "That's the kind of team we're going to build. Every program that I've been in that has been successful, we've gone out and found football players. The best moves we made

Back to his old form, Tom Brady led the Patriots to a 59–0 thrashing of the Titans on October 18, 2009. Brady threw six touchdowns in the snowy conditions at Gillette Stadium, while Wes Welker (83) pulled in 150 receiving yards and two touchdowns. *Winslow Townson/AP Images*

player-personnel-wise is players who can play football—not necessarily guys who tested best or had the higher test scores. It's a mosaic of all this information that you piece together."

While the front office and coaching staff went through a kind of transitional phase, the Patriots and their fans looked forward to 2009 with great anticipation. The return of Brady from the season-ending injury suffered the year before, combined with the continued excellence of receiving stars Moss and Welker, had many fans believing that New England would be able to finish off the unfinished business that had haunted the franchise from 2007.

But it was also clear that this would be a different season for the Patriots. In the offseason, longtime defensive stalwarts Harrison and Bruschi retired, and Vrabel and Seymour were traded away before the start of the season. In their absence, the defense lacked leadership. The defensive unit struggled with inconsistency throughout the season and appeared overwhelmed at times against superior offenses, such as the eventual Super Bowl champion New Orleans Saints, who beat New England 38–17 in late November.

Meanwhile, Brady and the offense also struggled to achieve consistency. Moss was accused of dogging it by opposing defensive backs, including Darrelle Revis of the Jets and Chris Gamble of Carolina. (It was later revealed that Moss was suffering from a shoulder injury for much of the season.) Veteran pickup Joey Galloway proved to be ineffective in the Patriots' system at wide receiver, and the running

game failed to deliver on a number of occasions during the year, gaining fewer than 100 yards six times.

All that being said, the Patriots were still able to win the AFC East for the seventh time in nine years. A late-season knee injury to Welker hampered the offense even more, and when New England suffered a 33–14 loss at home in a wild-card playoff game against the Ravens, no one was particularly surprised.

"Whether it's the first round or whether it's the divisional round, whether it's in the championship game or whether it's in the Super Bowl," Belichick said the day after the loss to Baltimore, "if you don't win at any one of those . . . , the treadmill stops, and you don't take another step. It doesn't go, and you fall off it. The other teams keep playing.

"No matter when that feeling comes, it's a pretty disappointing feeling."

At the dawn of a new decade, the Patriots franchise remains at the top of its game, both on and off the field. This is one of the most valuable franchises in all of professional sports, and the Patriots have achieved a near-perfect balance of power among the ownership, the front office, and the coaching staff. Their team-building technique remains the gold standard. They are grudgingly admired by rivals, are studied by other professional teams around the globe, and have become a desired landing spot for available players. A half-century after their creation, the New England Patriots stand tall as one of the NFL's supreme powerhouses, a franchise at the height of its power.

With three championship banners hanging at Gillette Stadium and millions of loyal fans throughout New England and the world, the Patriots stand tall as an elite sports franchise of the twenty-first century.
Al Messerschmidt/ Getty Images

NEW ENGLAND PATRIOTS ALL-TIME RECORD BOOK

THROUGH THE 2009 SEASON

NEW ENGLAND PATRIOTS YEAR-BY-YEAR

Year	W–L–T	Postseason	Points Scored	Points Allowed	Head Coach
1960	5–9		286	349	Lou Saban
1961	9–4–1		413	313	Lou Saban, Mike Holovak
1962	9–4–1		346	295	Mike Holovak
1963	7–6–1*	1–1; lost AFL championship	327	257	Mike Holovak
1964	10–3–1		365	297	Mike Holovak
1965	4–8–2		244	302	Mike Holovak
1966	8–4–2		315	283	Mike Holovak
1967	3–10–1		280	389	Mike Holovak
1968	4–10		229	406	Mike Holovak
1969	4–10		266	316	Clive Rush
1970	2–12		149	361	Clive Rush, John Mazur
1971	6–8		238	325	John Mazur
1972	3–11		192	446	John Mazur, Phil Bengtson
1973	5–9		258	300	Chuck Fairbanks
1974	7–7		348	289	Chuck Fairbanks
1975	3–11		258	358	Chuck Fairbanks
1976	11–3^	0–1; lost divisional round	376	236	Chuck Fairbanks
1977	9–5		278	217	Chuck Fairbanks
1978	11–5*	0–1; lost divisional round	358	286	Chuck Fairbanks, Hank Bullough, Ron Erhardt
1979	9–7		411	326	Ron Erhardt
1980	10–6		441	325	Ron Erhardt
1981	2–14		322	370	Ron Erhardt
1982	5–4	0–1; lost wild card game	143	157	Ron Meyer
1983	8–8		274	289	Ron Meyer
1984	9–7		362	352	Ron Meyer, Raymond Berry

Year	Record	Playoffs	PF	PA	Coach
1985	11–5	3–1; lost Super Bowl	362	290	Raymond Berry
1986	11–5*	0–1; lost divisional round	412	307	Raymond Berry
1987	8–7		320	293	Raymond Berry
1988	9–7		250	284	Raymond Berry
1989	5–11		297	391	Raymond Berry
1990	1–15		181	446	Rod Rust
1991	6–10		211	305	Dick MacPherson
1992	2–14		205	363	Dick MacPherson
1993	5–11		238	286	Bill Parcells
1994	10–6^	0–1; lost wild card game	351	312	Bill Parcells
1995	6–10		294	377	Bill Parcells
1996	11–5*	2–1; lost Super Bowl	418	313	Bill Parcells
1997	10–6*	1–1; lost divisional round	369	289	Pete Carroll
1998	9–7	0–1; lost wild card game	337	329	Pete Carroll
1999	8–8		299	284	Pete Carroll
2000	5–11		276	338	Bill Belichick
2001	11–5*	3–0; won Super Bowl	371	272	Bill Belichick
2002	9–7^		381	346	Bill Belichick
2003	14–2*	3–0; won Super Bowl	348	238	Bill Belichick
2004	14–2*	3–0; won Super Bowl	437	260	Bill Belichick
2005	10–6*	1–1; lost divisional round	379	338	Bill Belichick
2006	12–4*	2–1; lost AFC championship	385	237	Bill Belichick
2007	16–0*	2–1; lost Super Bowl	589	274	Bill Belichick
2008	11–5^		410	309	Bill Belichick
2009	10–6*	0–1; lost wild card game	427	285	Bill Belichick

* = won division title
^ = tied for best record in division, but lost tiebreaker

INDIVIDUAL HONORS

NEW ENGLAND PATRIOTS HALL OF FAME

Name (uniform no.)	Position	Years with Patriots	Induction Year
John Hannah* (73)	G	1973–1985	1991
Nick Buoniconti* (85)	LB	1962–1968	1992
Gino Cappelletti (20)	WR/K/DB	1960–1970	1992
Bob Dee (89)	DE	1960–1967	1993
Jim Lee Hunt (79)	DT	1960–1971	1993
Steve Nelson (57)	LB	1974–1987	1993
Babe Parilli (15)	QB	1961–1967	1993
Mike Haynes* (40)	CB	1976–1982	1994
Steve Grogan (14)	QB	1975–1990	1995
Andre Tippett* (56)	LB	1982–1993	1999
Bruce Armstrong (78)	T	1987–2000	2001
Stanley Morgan (86)	WR	1977–1989	2007
Ben Coates (87)	TE	1991–1999	2008
Jim Nance (35)	RB	1965–1971	2009
Billy Sullivan Jr.	team executive	1960–1988	2009

* Also a member of the Pro Football Hall of Fame

FIRST-TEAM ALL-PROS

Name	Position	Years
John Hannah	G	7 (1976, 1978–1981, 1983, 1985)
Nick Buoniconti	LB	4 (1964–1967)
Larry Eisenhauer	DE	3 (1962–1964)
Richard Seymour	DE/DT	3 (2003–2005)
Jim Nance	RB	2 (1966, 1967)
Andre Tippett	LB	2 (1985, 1987)
Ben Coates	TE	2 (1994, 1995)
Ty Law	DB	2 (1998, 2003)
Adam Vinatieri	K	2 (2002, 2004)
Tom Addison	LB	1 (1961)
Houston Antwine	DT/DE	1 (1963)
Ron Hall	DB	1 (1964)
Billy Neighbors	G	1 (1964)
Babe Parilli	QB	1 (1964)
Jon Morris	C	1 (1966)
Jim Whalen	TE	1 (1968)
Leon Gray	T/G	1 (1978)
Marv Cook	TE	1 (1991)
Lawyer Milloy	DB	1 (1999)
Rodney Harrison	DB	1 (2003)
Tom Brady	QB	1 (2007)
Matt Light	T	1 (2007)
Randy Moss	WR	1 (2007)
Asante Samuel	DB	1 (2007)
Mike Vrabel	LB	1 (2007)
Stephen Gostkowski	K	1 (2008)
Wes Welker	WR	1 (2009)

PRO BOWLERS

Players with five or more Pro Bowl selections

Name	Position	Years
John Hannah	G	9 (1976, 1978–1985)
Jon Morris	C	7 (1964–1970)
Houston Antwine	DT/DE	6 (1963–1968)
Bruce Armstrong	T/G	6 (1990, 1991, 1994–1997)
Mike Haynes	DB	6 (1976–1980, 1982)
Tom Brady	QB	5 (2001, 2004, 2005, 2007, 2009)
Nick Buoniconti	LB	5 (1963–1967)
Gino Cappelletti	WR/K/DB	5 (1961, 1963–1966)
Ben Coates	TE	5 (1994–1998)
Richard Seymour	DE/DT	5 (2002–2006)
Andre Tippett	LB	5 (1984–1988)

PATRIOTS ANNIVERSARY & ALL-DECADE TEAMS

As selected by the Patriots Hall of Fame nomination committee

50TH ANNIVERSARY TEAM

HEAD COACH	Bill Belichick	

OFFENSE

OT	Bruce Armstrong
OT	Matt Light
G	John Hannah
G	Logan Mankins
C	Jon Morris
TE	Ben Coates
WR	Stanley Morgan
WR	Troy Brown
WR	Irving Fryar
QB	Tom Brady
RB	Jim Nance
RB	Sam Cunningham

DEFENSE

DE	Julius Adams
DE	Richard Seymour
DT	Houston Antwine
DT	Vince Wilfork
OLB	Andre Tippett
OLB	Mike Vrabel
ILB	Steve Nelson
ILB	Nick Buoniconti
CB	Mike Haynes
CB	Ty Law
S	Fred Marion
S	Rodney Harrison

SPECIALISTS

K	Adam Vinatieri
P	Rich Camarillo
Spec.T	Mosi Tatupu
KR/PR	Kevin Faulk

CAPTAINS

Offense	Gino Cappelletti (WR/K)
Defense	Tedy Bruschi (LB)

1960s ALL-DECADE TEAM

HEAD COACH	Mike Holovak	

OFFENSE

OT	Charlie Long
OT	Tom Neville
G	Billy Neighbors
G	Lennie St. Jean
C	Jon Morris
TE	Jim Whalen
WR	Jim Colclough
WR	Art Graham
QB	Vito Babe Parilli
RB	Larry Garron
RB	Jim Nance

DEFENSE

DE	Bob Dee
DE	Larry Eisenhauer
DT	Houston Antwine
DT	Jim Lee Hunt
OLB	Tom Addison
OLB	Ed Philpott
MLB	Nick Buoniconti
CB	Chuck Shonta
CB	Daryl Johnson
S	Don Webb
S	Ron Hall

SPECIALISTS

K	Gino Cappelletti
P	Tom Yewcic
Ret.	Larry Garron
Spec.T	Don Webb

1970s ALL-DECADE TEAM

HEAD COACH	Chuck Fairbanks	

OFFENSE

OT	Leon Gray
OT	Tom Neville
G	John Hannah
G	Sam Adams
C	Bill Lenkaitis
TE	Russ Francis
WR	Stanley Morgan
WR	Randy Vataha
QB	Steve Grogan
RB	Sam Cunningham
RB	Andy Johnson

DEFENSE

DE	Julius Adams
DE	Tony McGee
NT	Ray Hamilton
OLB	Steve Zabel
OLB	Steve King
ILB	Steve Nelson
ILB	Sam Hunt
CB	Raymond Clayborn
CB	Mike Haynes
S	Tim Fox
S	Prentice McCray

SPECIALISTS

K	John Smith
P	Mike Patrick
Ret.	Mack Herron
Spec.T	Mosi Tatupu

1980s ALL-DECADE TEAM

HEAD COACH	Raymond Berry	

OFFENSE

OT	Bruce Armstrong
OT	Brian Holloway
G	John Hannah
G	Ron Wooten
C	Pete Brock
TE	Lin Dawson
WR	Irving Fryar
WR	Stanley Morgan
QB	Steve Grogan
RB	Tony Collins
RB	Craig James

DEFENSE

DE	Julius Adams
DE	Garin Veris
NT	Richard Bishop
OLB	Andre Tippett

OLB	Don Blackmon
ILB	Steve Nelson
ILB	Johnny Rembert
CB	Raymond Clayborn
CB	Ronnie Lippett
S	Roland James
S	Fred Marion
SPECIALISTS	
K	Tony Franklin
P	Rich Camarillo
Ret.	Irving Fryar
Spec.T	Mosi Tatupu

1990s ALL-DECADE TEAM

HEAD COACH	Bill Parcells
OFFENSE	
OT	Bruce Armstrong
OT	Pat Harlow
G	Todd Rucci
G	Max Lane
C	Dave Wohlabaugh
TE	Ben Coates
WR	Terry Glenn
WR	Shawn Jefferson
QB	Drew Bledsoe
RB	Curtis Martin
RB	Leonard Russell
DEFENSE	
DE	Willie McGinest
DE	Brent Williams
NT	Tim Goad
OLB	Andre Tippett
OLB	Chris Slade
ILB	Vincent Brown
ILB	Ted Johnson
CB	Maurice Hurst
CB	Ty Law
S	Willie Clay
S	Lawyer Milloy
SPECIALISTS	
K	Adam Vinatieri
P	Tom Tupa
Ret.	Dave Meggett
Spec.T	Larry Whigham

2000s ALL-DECADE TEAM

HEAD COACH	Bill Belichick
OFFENSE	
OT	Nick Kaczur
OT	Matt Light
G	Joe Andruzzi
G	Logan Mankins
C	Dan Koppen
TE	Daniel Graham
WR	Troy Brown
WR	Randy Moss
WR	Wes Welker
QB	Tom Brady
RB	Corey Dillon
DEFENSE	
DE	Richard Seymour
DE	Ty Warren
NT	Vince Wilfork

OLB	Willie McGinest
OLB	Mike Vrabel
ILB	Tedy Bruschi
ILB	Roman Phifer
CB	Ty Law
CB	Asante Samuel
S	Rodney Harrison
S	Lawyer Milloy
SPECIALISTS	
K	Adam Vinatieri
P	Josh Miller
Ret.	Kevin Faulk
Spec.T	Larry Izzo

PLAYER RECORDS

SERVICE

Most Seasons

16	Steve Grogan, 1975–1990
16	Julius Adams, 1971–1985, 1987
15	Troy Brown, 1993–2007
14	Steve Nelson, 1974–1987
14	Bruce Armstrong, 1987–2000

Most Games Played

212	Bruce Armstrong, 1987–2000
206	Julius Adams, 1971–1987
194	Mosi Tatupu, 1978–1990
192	Troy Brown, 1993–2007
191	Raymond Clayborn, 1977–1989

Most Games Started

212	Bruce Armstrong, 1987–2000
183	John Hannah, 1973–1985
173	Steve Nelson, 1974–1987
165	Raymond Clayborn, 1977–1989
165	Stanley Morgan, 1977–1989

OFFENSE

SCORING RECORDS

Most Points Scored

Career

1,158	Adam Vinatieri, K, 1996–2005
1,130	Gino Cappelletti, WR/K, 1960–1970
692	John Smith, K, 1974–1983
513	Stephen Gostkowski, K, 2006–2009
442	Tony Franklin, K, 1984–1987

Season

155	Gino Cappelletti, WR/K, 1964
148	Stephen Gostkowski, K, 2008
147	Gino Cappelletti, WR/K, 1961
141	Adam Vinatieri, K, 2004
140	Tony Franklin, K, 1986

Game

28	Gino Cappelletti, WR/K, vs. Houston, 12/18/1965 (2 TD, 4 PAT, 4 FG)

Touchdowns Scored

Career

68	Stanley Morgan, WR, 1977–1989 (67 rec., 1 ret.)
50	Ben Coates, TE, 1991–1999 (50 rec.)
49	Sam Cunningham, RB, 1973–1982 (43 rush., 6 rec.)
47	Randy Moss, WR, 2007–2009 (47 rec.)
46	Jim Nance, RB, 1965–1971 (45 rush, 1 rec.)

Season

23	Randy Moss, WR, 2007 (23 rec.)
17	Curtis Martin, RB, 1996 (14 rush., 3 rec.)
15	Curtis Martin, RB, 1995 (14 rush., 1 rec.)
13	Accomplished 8 times

Game

4	Randy Moss, WR, @ Buffalo, 11/18/2007 (4 rec.)

PASSING RECORDS

Quarterback Wins

Career

97	Tom Brady, 2000–2009
75	Steve Grogan, 1975–1990
63	Drew Bledsoe, 1993–2001
44	Babe Parilli, 1961–1967
28	Tony Eason, 1983–1989

Season

16	Tom Brady, 2007
14	Tom Brady, 2003
14	Tom Brady, 2004
12	Tom Brady, 2006
11	Accomplished 4 times

Pass Attempts

Career

4,518	Drew Bledsoe, 1993–2001
4,218	Tom Brady, 2000–2009
3,593	Steve Grogan, 1975–1990
2,413	Babe Parilli, 1961–1967
1,503	Jim Plunkett, 1971–1975

Season

691	Drew Bledsoe, 1994
636	Drew Bledsoe, 1995
623	Drew Bledsoe, 1996
601	Tom Brady, 2002
578	Tom Brady, 2007

Game

70	Drew Bledsoe, vs. Minnesota, 11/13/1994*

* NFL record

Pass Completions

Career

2,672	Tom Brady, 2000–2009
2,544	Drew Bledsoe, 1993–2001
1,879	Steve Grogan, 1975–1990
1,140	Babe Parilli, 1961–1967
876	Tony Eason, 1983–1989

Season

400	Drew Bledsoe, 1994
398	Tom Brady, 2007
373	Drew Bledsoe, 1996
373	Tom Brady, 2002
371	Tom Brady, 2009

Game

45	Drew Bledsoe, vs. Minnesota, 11/13/1994*

* NFL record

Completion Percentage

Career (min. 250 attempts)

63.3%	Tom Brady, 2000–2009 (2,672–4,218)
62.9%	Matt Cassell, 2005–2008 (349–555)
60.5%	Hugh Millen, 1991–1992 (370–612)
58.4%	Tony Eason, 1983–1989 (876–1,500)
56.3%	Drew Bledsoe, 1993–2001 (2,544–4,518)

Season (min. 100 attempts)

68.9%	Tom Brady, 2007 (398–578)
65.7%	Tom Brady, 2009 (371–565)
63.9%	Tom Brady, 2001 (264–413)
63.4%	Matt Cassell, 2008 (327–516)
63.0%	Tom Brady, 2005 (334–530)

Game (min. 20 attempts)

88.5%	Tom Brady, vs. Jacksonville, 12/27/2009 (23–26)

Passing Yards

Career

30,844	Tom Brady, 2000–2009
29,657	Drew Bledsoe, 1993–2001
26,886	Steve Grogan, 1975–1990
16,747	Babe Parilli, 1961–1967
10,732	Tony Eason, 1983–1989

Season

4,806	Tom Brady, 2007
4,555	Drew Bledsoe, 1994
4,398	Tom Brady, 2009
4,110	Tom Brady, 2005
4,086	Drew Bledsoe, 1996

Game

426	Drew Bledsoe, vs. Minnesota, 11/13/1994

Longest Pass Play from Scrimmage

91 yards Tom Brady to David Patten, @ Indianapolis, 10/21/2001

Most Yards per Game

Career (min. 50 games)

239.2	Drew Bledsoe, 1993–2001 (29,657–124)
239.1	Tom Brady, 2000–2009 (30,844–129)
180.4	Steve Grogan, 1975–1990 (26,884–149)
178.2	Babe Parilli, 1961–1967 (16,747–94)
162.8	Jim Plunkett, 1971–1975 (9,932–61)

Season (min. 10 games)

300.4	Tom Brady, 2007 (4,806–16)
284.7	Drew Bledsoe, 1994 (4,555–16)
274.9	Tom Brady, 2009 (4,398–16)
259.5	Drew Bledsoe, 1998 (3,633–14)
256.9	Tom Brady, 2005 (4,110–16)

Most Yards per Attempt

Career (min. 200 attempts)

7.84	Matt Cavanaugh, 1979–1982 (3,018–385)
7.48	Steve Grogan, 1975–1990 (26,886–3,593)
7.31	Tom Brady, 2000–2009 (30,844–4,218)
7.15	Tony Eason, 1983–1989 (10,732–1,500)
7.11	Matt Cassell, 2005–2008 (3,946–555)

Season (min. 50 attempts)

9.57	Steve Grogan, 1986 (976–102)
8.61	Steve Grogan, 1981 (1,859–216)
8.43	Matt Cavanaugh, 1980 (885–105)
8.40	Steve Grogan, 1985 (1,311–156)
8.31	Tom Brady, 2007 (4,806–578)

Touchdown Passes

Career

225	Tom Brady, 2000–2009
182	Steve Grogan, 1975–1990
166	Drew Bledsoe, 1993–2001
132	Babe Parilli, 1961–1967
62	Jim Plunkett, 1971–1975

Season

50	Tom Brady, 2007
31	Babe Parilli, 1964
28	Steve Grogan, 1979
28	Drew Bledsoe, 1997
28	Tom Brady, 2002
28	Tom Brady, 2004
28	Tom Brady, 2009

Game

6	Tom Brady, @ Miami, 10/21/2007
6	Tom Brady, vs. Tennessee, 10/18/2009

Consecutive Games with a Touchdown Pass

16	Tom Brady, 12/17/2006–12/9/2007

Most Interceptions Thrown

Career

208	Steve Grogan, 1975–1990
138	Babe Parilli, 1961–1967
138	Drew Bledsoe, 1993–2001
99	Tom Brady, 2000–2009
87	Jim Plunkett, 1971–1975

Season

27	Babe Parilli, 1964
27	Drew Bledsoe, 1994
26	Babe Parilli, 1965
25	Jim Plunkett, 1972
24	Babe Parilli, 1963
24	Babe Parilli, 1967

Game

6	Babe Parilli, vs. Denver, 9/3/1967
6	Steve Grogan, vs. San Francisco, 11/30/1980

Fewest Interceptions per Attempt

Career Percentage (min. 200 attempts)

2.34%	Matt Cassell, 2005–2008 (13–555)
2.35%	Tom Brady, 2000–2009 (99–4,218)
2.87%	Scott Zolak, 1992–1998 (7–244)
3.05%	Drew Bledsoe, 1993–2001 (138–4,518)
3.20%	Tony Eason, 1983–1989 (48–1,500)

Season Percentage (min. 50 attempts)

1.38%	Tom Brady, 2007 (8–578)
1.85%	Brian Dowling, 1972 (1–54)
1.86%	Tony Eason, 1984 (8–431)
1.96%	Steve Grogan, 1986 (2–102)
2.13%	Matt Cassell, 2008 (11–516)

Most Pass Attempts Without an Interception, Game

70	Drew Bledsoe, vs. Minnesota, 11/13/1994*

* NFL record

Quarterback Rating

Career (min. 200 attempts)

93.3	Tom Brady, 2000–2009
88.2	Matt Cassell, 2005–2008
80.6	Tony Eason, 1983–1989
75.9	Drew Bledsoe, 1993–2001
71.8	Hugh Millen, 1991–1992

Season (min. 50 attempts)

117.2	Tom Brady, 2007
113.8	Steve Grogan, 1986
96.2	Tom Brady, 2009
95.9	Matt Cavanaugh, 1980
93.4	Tony Eason, 1984

RUSHING RECORDS

Attempts

Career

1,385	Sam Cunningham, 1973–1982
1,323	Jim Nance, 1965–1971
1,191	Tony Collins, 1981–1987
958	Curtis Martin, 1995–1997
891	John Stephens, 1988–1992

Season

368	Curtis Martin, 1995
345	Corey Dillon, 2004
316	Curtis Martin, 1996
300	Leonard Russell, 1993
299	Jim Nance, 1966

Game

40	Curtis Martin, vs. NY Jets, 9/14/1997

Yards

Career

5,453	Sam Cunningham, 1973–1982
5,323	Jim Nance, 1965–1971
4,647	Tony Collins, 1981–1987
3,799	Curtis Martin, 1995–1997
3,505	Kevin Faulk, 1999–2009

Season

1,635	Corey Dillon, 2004
1,487	Curtis Martin, 1995
1,458	Jim Nance, 1966
1,227	Craig James, 1985
1,216	Jim Nance, 1967

Game

212	Tony Collins, vs. NY Jets, 9/18/1983

Longest Run from Scrimmage

85 yards   Larry Garron, vs. Buffalo, 10/22/1961

Rushing Yards per Carry

Career (min. 250 carries)

4.89	Steve Grogan, 1975–1990 (2,176–445)
4.55	Sammy Morris, 2007–2009 (1,430–314)
4.22	Corey Dillon, 2004–2006 (3,180–753)
4.22	Craig James, 1984–1988 (2,469–585)
4.18	Kevin Faulk, 1999–2009 (3,505–839)

Season (min. 100 carries)

5.59	Don Calhoun, 1976 (721–129)
5.45	Mosi Tatupu, 1983 (578–106)
5.04	Carl Garrett, 1969 (691–137)
4.94	Craig James, 1984 (790–160)
4.91	Horace Ivory, 1978 (693–141)

Game (min. 10 carries)

11.6	Larry Garron, vs. Buffalo, 10/22/1961 (116–10)

Rushing Touchdowns

Career

45	Jim Nance, 1965–1971
43	Sam Cunningham, 1973–1982
37	Corey Dillon, 2004–2006
35	Steve Grogan, 1975–1990
32	Tony Collins, 1981–1987
32	Curtis Martin, 1995–1997

Season

14	Curtis Martin, 1995
14	Curtis Martin, 1996
13	Corey Dillon, 2006
12	Steve Grogan, 1976
12	Antowain Smith, 2001
12	Corey Dillon, 2004
12	Corey Dillon, 2005

Game

3	Accomplished 5 times

RECEIVING RECORDS

Receptions

Career

557	Troy Brown, 1993–2006
534	Stanley Morgan, 1977–1989
490	Ben Coates, 1991–1999
418	Kevin Faulk, 1999–2009
363	Irving Fryar, 1984–1992

Season

123	Wes Welker, 2009
112	Wes Welker, 2007
111	Wes Welker, 2008
101	Troy Brown, 2001
98	Randy Moss, 2007

Game

16	Troy Brown, vs. Kansas City, 9/22/2002

Receiving Yards

Career

10,352	Stanley Morgan, 1977–1989
6,366	Troy Brown, 1993–2006
5,726	Irving Fryar, 1984–1992
5,471	Ben Coates, 1991–1999
5,001	Jim Colclough, 1960–1968

Season

1,493	Randy Moss, 2007
1,491	Stanley Morgan, 1986
1,348	Wes Welker, 2009
1,264	Randy Moss, 2009
1,199	Troy Brown, 2001

Game

214	Terry Glenn, @ Cleveland, 10/3/1999

Yards per Reception

Career (min. 100 receptions)

20.3	Harold Jackson, 1978–1981 (3,162–156)
19.4	Stanley Morgan, 1977–1989 (10,352–534)
17.7	Jim Colclough, 1960–1968 (5,001–283)
17.3	Shawn Jefferson, 1996–1999 (3,081–178)
17.2	Randy Vataha, 1971–1976 (3,055–178)

Season (min. 25 receptions)

26.1	Ron Sellers, 1969 (705–27)
24.1	Stanley Morgan, 1978 (820–34)
23.4	Stanley Morgan, 1981 (1,029–44)
22.8	Stanley Morgan, 1979 (1,002–44)
22.7	Shawn Jefferson, 1998 (771–34)

Game (min. 5 receptions)

36.4	Stanley Morgan, 11/8/1981 (182–5)

Touchdown Receptions

Career

67	Stanley Morgan, 1977–1989
50	Ben Coates, 1991–1999
47	Randy Moss, 2007–2009
42	Gino Cappelletti, 1960–1969
39	Jim Colclough, 1960–1968

Season

23	Randy Moss, 2007
13	Randy Moss, 2009
12	Stanley Morgan, 1979
11	Randy Moss, 2008
10	Stanley Morgan, 1986
10	Jim Colclough, 1962

Game

4	Randy Moss, @ Buffalo, 11/18/2007

SPECIAL TEAMS

KICKOFF RETURNS

Most Kickoff Returns

Career

181	Kevin Faulk, 1999–2009
107	Stephen Starring, 1984–1987
105	Dave Meggett, 1995–1997
105	Ellis Hobbs, 2005–2008
101	Bethel Johnson, 2003–2005

Season

48	Stephen Starring, 1985
45	Derrick Cullors, 1998
45	Ellis Hobbs, 2008
42	Ricky Smith, 1983
41	Mack Herron, 1973
41	Bethel Johnson, 2004

Game

8	Willie Porter, vs. NY Jets, 11/22/1968

Kickoff Return Yardage

Career

4,098	Kevin Faulk, 1999–2009
2,913	Ellis Hobbs, 2005–2008
2,561	Dave Meggett, 1995–1997
2,557	Bethel Johnson, 2003–2005
2,299	Larry Garron, 1960–1967

Season

1,281	Ellis Hobbs, 2008
1,092	Mack Herron, 1973
1,085	Derrick Cullors, 1998
1,016	Bethel Johnson, 2004
1,012	Stephen Starring, 1985

Game

237	Ellis Hobbs, vs. Miami, 9/21/2008

Longest Return

108 yards Ellis Hobbs, @ NY Jets, 9/9/2007*
* NFL record

Yards per Kickoff Return

Career (min. 25 returns)

27.7	Ellis Hobbs, 2005–2008 (2,913–105)
27.2	Allen Carter, 1975–1976 (898–33)
27.0	Raymond Clayborn, 1977–1979 (1,538–57)
26.5	Horace Ivory, 1978–1981 (1,191–45)
25.9	Laurence Maroney, 2006–2009 (1,062–41)

Season (min. 15 returns)

31.0	Raymond Clayborn, 1977 (869–28)
28.6	Larry Garron, 1962 (686–24)
28.5	Ellis Hobbs, 2008 (1,281–45)
28.3	Carl Garrett, 1969 (792–28)
28.2	Bethel Johnson, 2003 (847–30)

Game (min. 3 returns)

52.0	Ellis Hobbs, @ NY Jets, 9/9/2007 (156–3)

Kickoffs Returned for Touchdown

Career
3	Raymond Clayborn, 1977–1979
3	Ellis Hobbs, 2005–2008
2	Larry Garron, 1960–1967
2	Jon Vaughn 1991–1992
2	Kevin Faulk, 1999–2009
2	Bethel Johnson, 2003–2005

Season
3	Raymond Clayborn, 1977
2	Kevin Faulk, 2002
1	Accomplished 17 times

Game
1	Accomplished 22 times (last: Ellis Hobbs, @ Oakland, 12/14/2008)

PUNT RETURNS

Most Punt Returns

Career
252	Troy Brown, 1993–2007
206	Irving Fryar, 1984–1991
142	Dave Meggett, 1995–1997
111	Mike Haynes, 1976–1981
99	Kevin Faulk, 1999–2009

Season
52	Dave Meggett, 1996
45	Mike Haynes, 1976
45	Dave Meggett, 1995
45	Dave Meggett, 1997
39	Troy Brown, 2000

Game
10	Ronnie Harris, @ Pittsburgh, 12/5/1993

Punt Return Yardage

Career
2,625	Troy Brown, 1993–2007
2,055	Irving Fryar, 1984–1991
1,443	Dave Meggett, 1995–1997
1,159	Mike Haynes, 1976–1981
960	Stanley Morgan, 1977–1989

Season
608	Mike Haynes, 1976
588	Dave Meggett, 1996
520	Irving Fryar, 1985
517	Mack Herron, 1974
504	Troy Brown, 2000

Game
156	Mike Haynes, vs. Buffalo, 11/7/1976

Longest Return
89	Mike Haynes, vs. Buffalo, 11/7/1976

Yards per Punt Return

Career (min. 20 returns)
12.0	Mack Herron, 1973–1975 (888–74)
11.33	Carl Garrett, 1969–1972 (487–43)
10.44	Mike Haynes, 1976–1981 (1,159–111)
10.43	Stanley Morgan, 1977–1989 (960–92)
10.42	Troy Brown, 1993–2007 (2,625–252)

Season (min. 10 returns)
14.8	Mack Herron, 1974 (517–35)
14.2	Troy Brown, 2001 (413–29)
14.1	Irving Fryar, 1985 (520–37)
13.8	Stanley Morgan, 1977 (220–16)
13.5	Mike Haynes, 1976 (608–45)

Game (min. 3 returns)
39.0	Mike Haynes, vs. Buffalo, 11/7/1976 (156–4)

Punts Returned for Touchdown

Career
3	Irving Fryar, 1984–1991
3	Troy Brown, 1993–2007
2	Mike Haynes, 1976–1981
1	Stanley Morgan, 1977–1989
1	Roland James, 1980–1985
1	Dave Meggett, 1995–1997

Season
2	Mike Haynes, 1976
2	Irving Fryar, 1985
2	Troy Brown, 2001
1	Stanley Morgan, 1979
1	Roland James, 1980
1	Irving Fryar, 1986
1	Dave Meggett, 1996
1	Troy Brown, 2000

Game
1	Accomplished 11 times (last: Troy Brown, @ Carolina, 1/6/2002)

KICKING

PAT Attempts

Career
374	Adam Vinatieri, 1996–2005
353	Gino Cappelletti, 1960–1970
323	John Smith, 1974–1983
205	Stephen Gostkowski, 2006–2009
166	Tony Franklin, 1984–1987

Season
74	Stephen Gostkowski, 2007
51	John Smith, 1980
50	Gino Cappelletti, 1961
49	John Smith, 1979
48	Adam Vinatieri, 2004

Game
8	Stephen Gostkowski, vs. Tennessee, 10/18/2009

PATs Made

Career
367	Adam Vinatieri, 1996–2005
342	Gino Cappelletti, 1960–1970
308	John Smith, 1974–1983
204	Stephen Gostkowski, 2006–2009
163	Tony Franklin, 1984–1987

Season
74	Stephen Gostkowski, 2007
51	John Smith, 1980
48	Gino Cappelletti, 1961
48	Adam Vinatieri, 2004
47	Stephen Gostkowski, 2009

Game
8	Stephen Gostkowski, vs. Tennessee, 10/18/2009

PAT Percentage

Career (min. 30 attempts)
100%	Charlie Gogolak, 1970–1972 (42–42)
100%	Matt Bahr, 1993–1995 (73–73)
99.5%	Stephen Gostkowski, 2006–2009 (204–205)
98.2%	Tony Franklin, 1984–1987 (163–166)
98.1%	Adam Vinatieri, 1996–2005 (367–374)

Most PATs Without a Miss

Season
74	Stephen Gostkowski, 2007
51	John Smith, 1980
48	Adam Vinatieri, 2004
47	Stephen Gostkowski, 2009
42	Tony Franklin, 1984

Field Goal Attempts

Career
333	Gino Cappelletti, 1960–1970
321	Adam Vinatieri, 1996–2005
191	John Smith, 1974–1983
125	Tony Franklin, 1984–1987
121	Stephen Gostkowski, 2006–2009

Season
41	Tony Franklin, 1986
40	Stephen Gostkowski, 2008
39	Gino Cappelletti, 1964
39	Adam Vinatieri, 1998
38	Gino Cappelletti, 1963

Game
7	Gino Cappelletti, @ San Diego, 9/20/1964
7	Gino Cappelletti, @ Buffalo, 9/24/1967
7	Gino Cappelletti, @ Cincinnati, 11/16/1969
7	Jason Staurovsky, vs. Indianapolis, 12/3/1989

Field Goals Made

Career
263	Adam Vinatieri, 1996–2005
176	Gino Cappelletti, 1960–1970
128	John Smith, 1974–1983
103	Stephen Gostkowski, 2006–2009
93	Tony Franklin, 1984–1987

Season
36	Stephen Gostkowski, 2008
32	Tony Franklin, 1986
31	Adam Vinatieri, 1998
31	Adam Vinatieri, 2004

Game
6   Gino Cappelletti, @ Denver, 10/4/1964

Most Field Goals of 50+ Yards, Career
8   Adam Vinatieri, 1996–2005

Longest Field Goal Made
57 yards Adam Vinatieri, @ Chicago, 11/10/2002

Field Goal Percentage

Career (min. 20 attempts)
85.1%   Stephen Gostkowski, 2006–2009 (103–121)
81.9%   Adam Vinatieri, 1996–2005 (263–321)
76.4%   Matt Bahr, 1993–1995 (55–72)
74.4%   Tony Franklin, 1984–1987 (93–125)
72.5%   Jason Staurovsky, 1988–1991 (50–69)

Season (min. 10 attempts)
93.9%   Adam Vinatieri, 2004 (31–33)
90.0%   Stephen Gostkowski, 2008 (36–40)
90.0%   Adam Vinatieri, 2002 (27–30)
87.5%   Stephen Gostkowski, 2007 (21–24)
86.2%   Adam Vinatieri, 1997 (25–29)

PUNTING

Most Punts

Career
468   Rich Camarillo, 1981–1987
377   Tom Yewcic, 1961–1966
243   Tom Janik, 1969–1971
222   Mike Patrick, 1975–1978
215   Tom Tupa, 1996–1998

Season
103   Shawn McCarthy, 1992
92   Rich Camarillo, 1985
91   Jeff Feagles, 1988
90   Brian Hansen, 1990
90   Lee Johnson, 1999

Game
11   Accomplished 4 times

Total Yardage

Career
19,922   Rich Camarillo, 1981–1987
14,553   Tom Yewcic, 1961–1966
9,602   Tom Tupa, 1996–1998
9,516   Tom Janik, 1969–1971
8,578   Lee Johnson, 1999–2001

Season
4,227   Shawn McCarthy, 1992
3,953   Rich Camarillo, 1985
3,798   Lee Johnson, 1999
3,752   Brian Hansen, 1990
3,746   Rich Camarillo, 1986

Game
514   Rich Camarillo, @ Chicago, 9/15/1985 (11 punts)

Longest Punt
93 yards Shawn McCarthy, @ Buffalo, 11/3/1991

Yards per Punt

Career (min. 100 punts)
44.7   Tom Tupa, 1996–1998 (9,602–215)
43.6   Josh Miller, 2004–2006 (7,629–175)
42.6   Rich Camarillo, 1981–1987 (19,922–468)
42.3   Lee Johnson, 1999–2001 (8,578–203)
41.5   Chris Hanson, 2007–2009 (6,185–149)

Season (min. 40 punts)
45.8   Tom Tupa, 1997 (3,569–78)
45.1   Josh Miller, 2005 (3,431–76)
44.6   Rich Camarillo, 1983 (3,615–81)
44.5   Tom Tupa, 1998 (3,294–74)
43.7   Chris Hanson, 2008 (2,143–49)

Game (min. 4 punts)
55.6   Tom Tupa, @ Indianapolis, 9/7/1997 (278–5)

DEFENSE

INTERCEPTIONS

Most Interceptions

Career
36   Raymond Clayborn, 1977–1989
36   Ty Law, 1995–2004
29   Ron Hall, 1961–1967
29   Roland James, 1980–1989
29   Fred Marion, 1982–1991

Season
11   Ron Hall, 1964
10   Asante Samuel, 2006
9   Ty Law, 1998
8   Bob Suci, 1963
8   Mike Haynes, 1976
8   Ronnie Lippett, 1986

Game
3   Accomplished 9 times (last: Leigh Bodden, vs. NY Jets, 11/22/2009)

Interception Return Yardage

Career
583   Ty Law, 1995–2004
555   Raymond Clayborn, 1977–1989
476   Ron Hall, 1961–1967
457   Fred Marion, 1982–1991
420   Ronnie Lippett, 1984–1991

Season
277   Bob Suci, 1963
189   Fred Marion, 1985
182   Prentice McCray, 1976
181   Otis Smith, 2001
159   Ron Hall, 1966

Game
118 yards Prentice McCray, @ NY Jets, 11/21/1976 (2 int.)

Longest Return
100 yards Jimmy Hitchcock, vs. Miami, 11/23/1977

Most Interceptions Returned for Touchdown

Career
6   Ty Law, 1995–2004
4   Tedy Bruschi, 1996–2008
3   Asante Samuel, 2003–2007
2   Held by 7 players

Season
2   Don Webb, 1961
2   Bob Suci, 1963
2   Prentice McCray, 1976
2   Ronnie Lippett, 1987
2   Ty Law, 2001
2   Otis Smith, 2001
2   Tedy Bruschi, 2002
2   Tedy Bruschi, 2003

Game
2   Prentice McCray, @ NY Jets, 11/21/1976

SACKS

Most Sacks

Career
100.0   Andre Tippett, 1982–1993
79.5   Julius Adams, 1971–1987
78.0   Willie McGinest, 1994–2005
72.5   Tony McGee, 1974–1981
54.0   Ray Hamilton, 1973–1981

Season
18.5   Andre Tippett, 1984
16.5   Andre Tippett, 1985
12.5   Andre Tippett, 1987
12.5   Mike Vrabel, 2007
12.0   Tony McGee, 1978
12.0   Tony McGee, 1979

Game
4   Julius Adams, @ Atlanta, 12/4/1977
4   Tony McGee, @ Baltimore, 11/16/1978
4   Mike Hawkins, vs. NY Jets, 9/9/1979

FUMBLE RETURNS

Most Fumble Returns for Touchdown

Career
2   Andre Tippett, 1982–1993
2   Johnny Rembert, 1983–1992
2   Cedric Jones, 1984–1989
2   Brent Williams, 1986–1993
2   Willie McGinest, 1994–2005
2   Randall Gay, 2004–2007

TEAM RECORDS

Super Bowl Wins   3 (2001, 2003, 2004)
Conference Championships
  6 (1985, 1996, 2001, 2003, 2004, 2007)
Playoff Berths   17 (1963, 1976, 1978, 1982, 1985,
  1986, 1994, 1996–1998, 2001, 2003–2007, 2009)
Winning Seasons   29
Most Wins, Regular Season   16 (2007)
Most Consecutive Wins, Regular Season
  21 (12/17/2006–9/14/2008)
Most Consecutive Wins, All Games
  21 (10/5/2003–10/24/2004)
Most Losses, Season   15 (1990)
Most Consecutive Losses   14 (1990)

SCORING AND TOTAL OFFENSE

Most Points, Season   589 (2007)
Most Points, Game   59
  (vs. Tennessee, 10/18/2009)
Most Points, Half
  45 (first half, vs. Tennessee, 10/18/2009)
Most Points, Quarter
  35 (second quarter, vs. Tennessee, 10/18/2009)
Largest Point Differential, Season
  315 (2007, 589–274)
Largest Margin of Victory, Game
  59 (59–0, vs. Tennessee, 10/18/2009)
Fewest Points Scored per Game, Season
  10.6 (1970, 149 points/14 games)
Fewest Points Scored, Game
  0 (accomplished 20 times)
Largest Margin of Defeat
  53 (56–3, vs. NY Jets, 9/9/1979)
Most Touchdowns, Season   75 (2007)
Most Touchdowns, Game
  8 (accomplished 4 times)
Most PATs, Season   74 (2007)
Most PATs, Game   8 (vs. NY Jets, 9/9/1979; @
  Buffalo, 11/18/2007; vs. Tennessee, 10/18/2009)
Most Field Goals Made, Season   36 (2008)
Most Field Goals Made, Game
  6 (@ Denver, 10/4/1964)
Most Yards Total Offense, Season   6,580 (2007)
Most Yards Total Offense, Game
  619 (vs. Tennessee, 10/18/2009)
Fewest Yards Total Offense, Season   2,626 (1970)
Fewest Yards Total Offense, Game
  57 (@ NY Jets, 9/19/1982)
Most First Downs, Season   393 (2009)
Most First Downs, Game
  34 (vs. Washington, 10/28/2007)

PASSING

Most Pass Attempts, Season   699 (1994)
Most Pass Attempts, Game
  70 (vs. Minnesota, 11/13/1994)
Most Pass Completions, Season   405 (1994)
Most Pass Completions, Game
  45 (vs. Minnesota, 11/13/1994)
Most Yards Passing, Season   4,859 (2007)
Most Yards Passing, Game
  426 (vs. Minnesota, 11/13/1994; vs. Tennessee,
  10/18/2009)
Fewest Pass Attempts per Game, Season
  20.8 (1982, 187 attempts/9 games)
Fewest Pass Attempts, Game
  5 (vs. Miami, 12/12/1982)
Fewest Pass Completions per Game, Season
  10.3 (1982, 93 completions/9 games)
Fewest Pass Completions, Game
  2 (vs. Miami, 11/9/1969; vs. Miami, 12/12/1982)
Fewest Yards Passing per Game, Season
  113.3 (1970, 1,586 yards/14 games)
Fewest Yards Passing, Game
  4 (@ NY Jets, 9/19/1982)
Most Touchdown Passes, Season   50 (2007)
Fewest Touchdown Passes, Season   7 (1970)
Most Interceptions Thrown, Season   34 (1981)
Fewest Interceptions Thrown, Season
  11 (2008, 16 games); 9 (1982, 9 games)

RUSHING

Most Rushing Attempts, Season   671 (1978)
Most Rushing Attempts, Game
  62 (vs. Denver, 11/28/1976)
Most Rushing Yards, Season   3,165 (1978)
Most Rushing Yards, Game
  332 (vs. Denver, 11/28/1976)
Fewest Rushing Attempts per Game, Season
  23.9 (1970, 334 attempts/14 games)
Fewest Rushing Attempts, Game
  6 (@Pittsburgh, 10/31/2004)
Fewest Rushing Yards, Season   1,040 (1970)
Fewest Rushing Yards, Game
  2 (@ New Orleans, 11/30/1986)
Most Rushing Touchdowns, Season   30 (1978)
Most Rushing Touchdowns, Game
  4 (accomplished 6 times)
Fewest Rushing Touchdowns, Season
  3 (1982, 9 games); 4 (1990, 16 games)

SPECIAL TEAMS

Most Punts, Season   103 (1992)
Most Punts, Game   11 (accomplished 5 times)
Most Punting Yards, Season   4,212 (1992)
Most Punting Yards, Game
  514 (@ Chicago, 9/15/1985)
Most Yards per Punt, Season   45.2 (1997)
Fewest Punts, Season   44 (2007)
Fewest Punts, Game   0 (accomplished 3 times)
Fewest Punting Yards, Season   1,821 (2007)
Fewest Punting Yards, Game
  0 (accomplished 3 times)
Fewest Yards per Punt, Season   34.6 (1977)
Most Punt Returns, Season   60 (1980)
Most Punt Returns, Game
  10 (@ Pittsburgh, 12/5/1993)
Most Punt Return Yards, Season   628 (1976)
Most Punt Return Yards, Game
  167 (vs. Buffalo, 11/7/1976)
Most Yards per Punt Return, Season
  13.3 (1974, 2001)
Most Punt Return Touchdowns, Season
  2 (1976, 1985, 2001)
Fewest Punt Returns, Season
  16 (1982, 9 games); 17 (1972, 14 games)
Fewest Punt Return Yards, Season   37 (1972)
Fewest Yards per Punt Return, Season   2.2 (1972)
Most Kickoff Returns, Season   77 (1990)
Most Kickoff Returns, Game
  10 (vs. Buffalo, 12/9/1967)
Most Kickoff Return Yards, Season   1,771 (2002)
Most Kickoff Return Yards, Game
  248 (vs. Miami, 9/21/2008)
Most Yards per Kickoff Return, Season   26.9 (1977)
Most Kickoff Return Touchdowns, Season
  3 (1977)
Fewest Kickoff Returns, Season
  28 (1982, 9 games); 39 (1977, 14 games)
Fewest Kickoff Returns, Game
  0 (accomplished 5 times)
Fewest Kickoff Return Yards, Season
  646 (1982, 9 games); 819 (1993, 16 games)
Fewest Kickoff Return Yards, Game
  0 (accomplished 5 times)
Fewest Yards per Kickoff Return, Season 17.4 (1993)

DEFENSE

Fewest Points Allowed per Game, Season
    14.8 (2006, 237 points/16 games)
Fewest Points Allowed, Game
    0 (accomplished 24 times)
Most Points Allowed, Season   446 (1972, 1990)
Most Points Allowed, Game
    52 (@ Miami, 11/12/1972)
Fewest Total Yards Allowed per Game, Season
    273.9 (1963, 3,834 yards/14 games)
Fewest Total Yards Allowed, Game
    65 (vs. Seattle, 12/4/1988)
Fewest Pass Completions Allowed, Season
    134 (1973)
Fewest Pass Completions Allowed, Game
    1 (vs. NY Jets, 10/14/1973)
Fewest Passing Yards Allowed, Season
    1,338 (1973)
Fewest Passing Yards Allowed, Game
    0 (vs. NY Jets, 10/14/1973)
Fewest Passing Touchdowns Allowed, Season
    9 (1982, 9 games); 10 (2006, 16 games)
Fewest Rushing Yards Allowed, Season
    1,041 (1961)
Fewest Rushing Yards Allowed, Game
    6 (vs. NY Jets, 10/27/1968)
Fewest Rushing Touchdowns Allowed, Season
    5 (1991)
Fewest First Downs Allowed, Season
    185 (1982, 9 games); 215 (1973, 1977, 16 games)
Fewest First Downs Allowed, Game
    2 (vs. Seattle, 12/4/1988)
Most Interceptions Made, Season   31 (1964)
Most Interceptions Made, Game
    7 (@ NY Jets, 11/21/1976)
Most Yards on Interception Returns, Season
    645 (1963)
Most Yards on Interception Returns, Game
    204 (vs. Houston, 11/1/1963)
Most Interception Return Touchdowns, Season
    5 (2001, 2003)
Most Interception Return Touchdowns, Game
    2 (accomplished 6 times)
Most Sacks, Season   58 (1977)
Most Sacks, Game   10 (@ Oakland, 9/22/1963)

TURNOVERS AND PENALTIES

Most Fumbles, Season   51 (1973)
Most Fumbles, Game   8 (vs. Baltimore, 10/7/1973)
Fewest Fumbles, Season   14 (2007)
Most Opponents' Fumbles Recovered, Season
    27 (1976)
Most Opponents' Fumbles Recovered, Game
    6 (@ Pittsburgh, 9/26/1976; @ LA Rams,
    12/11/1983)
Most Penalties, Season   114 (1985)
Most Penalties, Game
    15 (@ Indianapolis, 12/15/1999)
Fewest Penalties, Season   50 (1973)
Fewest Penalties, Game   0 (vs. St. Louis,
    10/26/2008)
Most Yards Penalized, Season   1,051 (1992)
Most Yards Penalized, Game   146 (@ Indianapolis,
    12/15/1999)
Fewest Yards Penalized, Season   412 (1982, 9
    games); 456 (1962, 14 games); 501 (2008, 16
    games)

INDEX